The Christian Woman's
Guide to Sexuality

ALSO BY DEBRA EVANS

The Complete Book on Childbirth

The Mystery of Womanhood

Heart & Home

Fragrant Offerings

Beauty for Ashes

Without Moral Limits

Blessed Events

Preparing for Childbirth

*The Woman's Complete Guide
to Personal Health Care*

Beauty and the Best

*Christian Parenting Answers
(General Editor)*

Women of Character

Kindred Hearts

Ready or Not, You're a Grandparent

The Christian Woman's Guide to Sexuality

DEBRA EVANS

CROSSWAY BOOKS • WHEATON, ILLINOIS
A DIVISION OF GOOD NEWS PUBLISHERS

DEDICATION

To my husband, DAVID:

Grow old along with me!
The best is yet to be,
The last of life,
for which the first was made.
Our times are in his hand. . . .

ROBERT BROWNING

CONTENTS

$\mathcal{L}$IST OF FIGURES

$\mathscr{A}$CKNOWLEDGMENTS

For the Lord is good and his love endures forever;
his faithfulness continues through all generations.

PSALM 100:5

While writing this book, I often thought about the women who have influenced my life and work:

My mother, Nancy, taught me the joy of being able to appreciate the unspoken things in life. She helped guide me to Christ through her prayers and continuing reliance upon God's strength. There is no greater gift a mother can give her daughter.

My daughters, Joanna and Katherine, introduced me to the joys of mothering. They are teaching me anew as they creatively learn how to express their individuality as adults while using their unique, God-given gifts. I cherish their presence in my life.

My sisters, Kerry and Nancy, know how to make me laugh and how to comfort me when I cry. Through them I have received the joy of being a big sister—a wonderful and unique bond that immutably joins the three of us together in spite of our divergent lives.

My paternal grandmother, Marie, taught me the joy of cooking through her willingness to let me help her make pies when I was barely out of toddlerhood. My mom's mother, Helen, shared her joy of new life, encouraging me by her example to have two of my children at home. Since Grandma had done the same thing and it had worked, I knew that it could work for me too.

My piano teacher Laura Marr provided her patient guidance through six years of lessons, during which the joy of music arrived. The joy of writing came when I was a pupil in Nova Runyon's Honors English class in ninth grade. The joy of teaching appeared when Peg Beals, a seasoned childbirth educator, skillfully showed her students how to follow her suggestions. Cheryl Bauman and Rea Siffring brought encouragement, by example, regarding the joys of breastfeeding. With Anne Marie Mitchell, now a certified nurse-midwife, the joy of supporting laboring women during birth blossomed. Through Tryn Clark's open acceptance and unwavering friendship, I saw the joy of spiritual mothering.

I thank God for the joys He has imparted to me through each of these women to whom I owe a debt of love and my lasting appreciation. Most important, I want to acknowledge my husband David's continuing contribution to my life and ministry—especially his generosity, wisdom, and vision. David, your companionship has brought me indescribable joy. Thank you, dear husband, for your love these past twenty-eight years: I cherish you and deeply value your presence in my life.

$\mathscr{P}$REFACE

to the Revised Edition

Our earthly song is bound to God's revealing Word
in Jesus Christ. It is the simple song of the children of this earth
who have been called to be God's children . . . not enraptured,
but sober, grateful, reverent, addressed steadily
to God's revealed Word.[1]

DIETRICH BONHOEFFER

When I wrote *The Mystery of Womanhood*, the first edition of the book you are now holding, I approached my task with the zeal and enthusiasm typical for a woman of my age (thirty-four years old), personal experience (married for seventeen years; mother of four children), professional position (part-time sexuality educator at a secular university), and spiritual background (evangelical Christian).

But over the past ten years, I have learned to be kinder and gentler. I have gained some wisdom that I did not have a decade ago. And I am not nearly so busy. I am able to spend longer periods in prayer without regularly recurring interruptions. I have learned to trust God in ways that I didn't even know existed when I became a follower of Christ in the early seventies.

In learning to let go of the desire to competently control my world, I can see more clearly the painful and difficult aspects of living in relationship with my loved ones being transformed by God's tenacious grace. I expect imperfection in myself and others; then I wait to see how God will bring His healing help. My ideals have found a way to mesh with what is real. *The Christian Woman's Guide to Sexuality* reflects these changes.

More than ever, I believe the Bible is true, that it can be applied to all of life as it is actually lived, moment by moment, before the wondrous reality of Christ's love. No matter where we have been, we can walk with Jesus in newness of life, set free from the strongholds of the past and supernaturally strengthened by the Holy Spirit for the work "God prepared in advance for us to do" (Ephesians 2:10).

Within this context, marriage requires our strenuous commitment—a continuing, conscious effort to remain open and obedient to God's transforming work in our lives—over a period, in many cases, of hundreds of months and thousands of days. A successive series of seasons *will* bring changes, some welcome and some not, to the cherished bond we share with our husbands. Adapting across a span of years takes us deep into the hidden places of our hearts.

Sexuality was never intended to be simple or superficial. Making love to a man within the bond of marriage isn't based on a shallow success formula. It springs from our sincere desire to love, forgive, and accept our husbands through the relationship we share in the Lord.

Jesus is actively at work at the center of our marriages. His plans and purposes for us are for our good. And if we are sincerely willing to learn from our Good Shepherd, choosing to believe and obey His precepts, commandments, and instructions, we will find His burden light and His yoke easy. Resting upon the firm foundation of His love, we will find healing, peace, and joy in His quieting, majestic presence.

$\mathcal{I}$NTRODUCTION

It is ten at night. Your husband arrived a few moments ago, looking energized and eager to talk. As you yearn for a little peace and quiet, you wonder how you will find the energy to invest in the next half hour.

Suddenly skimming your list of options, you think: *What are my choices? I could say that I prefer being alone for a while, but he might feel rejected. A nice warm bath would be wonderful, but I can't picture him sitting on a stool next to the tub scrubbing my back after the day he has had. Maybe if we got ready for bed and simply made love, he would be satisfied. And I would finally get some sleep.*

Pressures. Expectations. Roles. Do you ever have moments when none of your choices appear appealing?

We receive multiple messages from our churches and our culture, family and friends, ministers and the media. We are influenced by the times we live in as well as by the Christ-centered values we have adopted. We have never had so many choices, such diversity of information, and as great a selection of role models to choose from. Balancing everyday responsibilities with family, marital, and personal needs often can be exhausting. On some days, it seems possible to accomplish everything God wants of us. But on other days the tasks before us may seem overwhelming.

Where do we find the balance between pleasing God and pleasing others? Whom are we modeling our lives after? What are our responsibilities to our husbands? Ourselves? The Lord? Where can we even find the *time* to sort out all of these things?

I believe that it *is* possible to find the answers to these questions. Walking with the Lord isn't intended to be constantly wearying or unbearably burdensome. Even on difficult days, we can know and experience the truth of what it means to be surrounded by God's grace, forgiveness, and love. Like clay in the hands of a master potter, our Creator is molding and shaping us moment by moment—and His Word promises that He will faithfully complete the work He has begun in us. Each day we encounter brings us closer to that longed-for instant when we will see Jesus face to face as we join Him in eternity.

Until then, living with the daily realities of womanhood requires that we understand the distinctiveness with which we were created. We live with a cyclical nature substantially different in form and function from that of our husbands. We need to learn to understand and appreciate these differences—and, if and when the time comes, to teach our daughters to do the same. To this end, *The Christian Woman's Guide to Sexuality* offers practical information about women's sexuality within marriage from a Christ-centered perspective.

As you read these pages, my prayer is that you will gain a great appreciation for the body, spirit, heart, and mind the Lord has given to you. I encourage you to take time out after reading each section to reflect upon the wonder of your unique design and your God-given ability to be your husband's life partner. At the end of each chapter, I have included unfinished statements and Bible passages for your study and reflection. Keep a journal of your thoughts and reactions to what you read and discover. Be absolutely honest, and you will have a lasting record to refer to in the future. May you find continuing contentment and refreshing joy in Jesus' presence in the days and years ahead. . . .

May God himself, the God of peace, sanctify you through and through. May your whole spirit, soul and body be kept blameless at the coming of our Lord Jesus Christ. The one who calls you is faithful and he will do it.

1 THESSALONIANS 5:23

$\mathcal{A}$ GOOD BEGINNING

Ask the beauty of the earth, the beauty of the sky.

Question the order of the stars, the sun whose brightness lights

the day, the moon whose splendor softens the gloom of night.

Ask of the living creatures that move in the waves, that roam

the earth, that fly in the heavens. Question all these and

they will answer, "Yes, we are beautiful." Their very loveliness

is their confession of God: for who made these things, but

he who is himself unchangeable beauty?[1]

AUGUSTINE

The origin of human sexuality is recorded in simple language in the second chapter of Genesis—words that can either be a troublesome stumbling block or a cause for joyous celebration, depending on one's viewpoint. Regardless of how the words are interpreted, they shape our sexuality in manifold ways. These powerful statements have survived into our age beyond the downfall of civilizations and the passing of many generations since ancient times: "The man said, 'This is now bone of my bones, and flesh of my flesh; she shall be called "woman," for she was taken out of man.' For this reason a man will leave his father and mother and be united to his wife, and they will become one flesh" (Genesis 2:23).

These words were carefully recorded. Though we may try, we cannot avoid them or explain them away. But why do so many women recoil at them? Has the meaning of creation changed, or have we? Are we becoming all that we are created to be? What is our outlook on sexuality—and where did we get it?

In the past thirty years, we have witnessed tremendous shifts in attitudes, behaviors, lifestyles, and values concerning women's sexuality. A revolution has taken place in our culture. Ever since the 1960s, we have been experiencing its wide-ranging effects. Yet one thing that has not changed is the condition of the human heart. In spite of countless new therapies and self-help movements, sexual unhappiness still exists.

A CLOSER LOOK

C. S. Lewis was fond of referring to human beings as "sons of Adam and daughters of Eve" to remind us of our spiritual legacy: God's glorious design for the first man and woman; humanity's transformation after the Fall; Christ's conquest of evil via the Cross on our behalf. Our identity continues to be directly influenced by Eden's—and Calvary's—earth-shaking events. Thus, we benefit from thinking, studying, talking, and praying about what the Genesis account of our beginnings says.

But we must be careful to avoid reading into the text things that are not there. For example, some have interpreted the idea that the Lord "made a woman from the rib he had taken out of the man" to suggest that females must become the sexual property of their husbands, thus denying that the woman's identity is as equally unique as the man's. Upon closer inspection, though, the text concerning humanity's creation says absolutely nothing about the woman's sexual position in relationship to the man's, except that they were made by God to become one flesh.

Living in bondage to one's mate does not fulfill the purpose for which woman was created. It debases the value of our being made in the image of God and undermines our human identity—who we were created to be. Yet for many centuries throughout the world, women have been considered a form of property belonging to their husbands, with few, if any, rights of their own. And in some places, it is still this way.

The idea of sexual enslavement within marriage comes from looking at the words of the Bible without understanding what they mean in the light of Christ's life-changing truth. Where sexual oppression exists, it stands in clear opposition to Jesus' teachings. Just as Christ refuses to enslave us, a loving husband does not seek or demand from his wife something different from what the Lord asks her to give to her husband. When the Genesis account of creation tells us that God created a partner for the man who would share a common identity and yet be a separate and unique individual, there is no statement implying subjection, domination, oppression, or ownership: "So the man gave names to all the livestock, the birds of the air and all the beasts of the field. But for Adam no suitable helper was found. So the Lord God caused the man to fall into a deep sleep; and while he was sleeping, he took one of the man's ribs and closed up the place with flesh. Then the Lord God made a woman from the rib he had taken out of the man, and he brought her to the man" (Genesis 2:20-22).

This event, we are told, took place in response to the Lord's decision that it was "not good for the man to be alone." Interestingly, the Hebrew word for "help" used in this passage means "to surround, protect, or aid."

The first chapter of Genesis also gives a summary of the events as the Lord created the world and everything in it. Of all that God created, it could be said of our kind only: "So God created man in his own image, in the image of God he created him; male and female he created them" (Genesis 1:27).

When God declared that man's isolation from the other living things was "not good," woman was the Lord's idea of how to perfectly complete His design. Eve was the final missing piece of the interwoven ecology that formed the basis of life on earth. The Lord did not declare that all He had made was good until after the woman was created. She was the counterpart of the man. Together they stood apart from the rest of creation. The union of the man and the woman resulted from the common bond of their shared humanity as well as from the physical joining of their separate, complementary identities as one flesh through sexual intercourse. *Sexuality was the expression of the reunion through which the man and the woman became physically joined together once again.*

"The male and the female know themselves only in relation to each other because they are made for each other," observes Dr. Lewis Smedes in *Sex for Christians*. "This is the deep origin of the powerful drive between the sexes to come together. It arises from the body-life we share, with a difference. Male and female are driven towards each other until they become 'one flesh' in intimate body-union." He adds: "God did not wince when Adam, in seeing Eve, was moved to get close to her. Male and female were created sexual to be sexual together."[2]

The Lord could have formed the woman in the exact manner that He had formed the man—by putting dust together and breathing His life into it. But that was not His choice. Perhaps this was because these two "living beings" would have remained isolated in their separateness. Any joining would have to be conceptual rather than actual; the mystery of what it means to become one flesh would have been an ideal rather than a reality.

Tragically, the man and the woman were not content to remain in this state of marital bliss. Instead, we are told they believed the serpent's lie, freely choosing to disobey God. Covering their nakedness, they hid themselves from their Creator and from each other. In this way, the position of all human beings before God was altered. Toiling for food became a daily experience; childbirth became markedly more laborious; Adam, Eve, and all of their children eventually faced death.

We can be thankful indeed that Jesus Christ was sent to earth to reconcile us to God. "God's salvation restores men and women to the true image of God, the original," proclaims Dick Keyes in *Beyond Identity*. "The Christian is a reconciled child, welcomed into God's family by the love of the Father, the sacrificial death of the Son, and the work of the Holy Spirit within him."[3]

Isn't this amazing? Through our Savior's death, we have been given the joy of experiencing new life in Christ—not just in the hereafter, but in the here-and-now of our everyday existence. Though God's creation still awaits its final, complete liberation from the effects of the Fall (Romans 8:19-23), we can live in confidence and hope, trusting that our Maker is with us, knowing "that in all things God works for the good of those who love him, who have been called according to his purpose" (Romans 8:28).

But growing in the image of God requires our steady cooperation with the Spirit's work within us. As Dr. Keyes wisely reminds us, "We must grow out of many things that we put in God's place. . . . We cannot simply *put on* the image of God without first taking a great deal *off*. Our lives are a process of taking off and putting on, reorganizing and consolidating. Whatever stands in the way of the image of God must be put off—whether it be a habit, an attitude, an idea. . . . To grow as a Christian we must be weaned from the things which are less than God which have come to take the place of God for us."[4]

IS FREE EXPRESSION *REALLY* FREE?

Another common stumbling block to understanding the beauty of what the Bible says about marriage and human sexuality arises from the belief that our sex drive is a built-in irresistible force that is the primary factor motivating human behavior. This way of thinking claims that if we do not express our sexuality openly and give it a "healthy" outlet, it will become a destructive force internally within the individual and/or externally within society.

Hedonism incorporates this view. The hedonist denies that there is anything awaiting her in the hereafter. Or perhaps she thinks an awesome white light exists, waiting to absorb her spirit as a benign conclusion to a life spent in pursuit of pleasure. "It feels right to me," she says, "so how can what I'm doing be wrong? I need to be true to myself."

There are no moral absolutes guiding the hedonist; self-gratification is all-important. Abstinence outside marriage is viewed as an outdated, unhealthy concept. Often both the immediate and long-term consequences of one's lifestyle choices are largely ignored.

But isn't it predominantly women—not men—who most often end up the victims of hedonism, displayed in full color in the pages of men's magazines? Or kept in a penthouse to serve as an afternoon respite from a high-pressure job? Or traded in for a second or third spouse who is much younger and more impressionable? No matter how it may look on the surface, hedonism does not serve women's (or men's) best interests in the long run. The irony is that this lifestyle is often portrayed as bringing more satisfaction into women's lives than the way of life Christ offers us—the liberating, joyful, tender experience of being cared for by a Lover who gently safeguards us as we entrust our hearts to His keeping.

"Christ is the way out, and the way in: the way from slavery, conscious or unconscious, into liberty; the way from the unhomeliness of things to the home we desire but do not know; the way from the stormy skirts of the Father's garments to the peace of His bosom," George MacDonald explained.[5] Realizing that many of the voices we hear around us advocate lifestyles that will draw us away from the Lord's design for us, we must learn to ignore those who have not yet heard the Father's homeward call. Though we no longer live in Eden, loving sexual expression between a man and a woman within marriage is still part of what it means to be under the Lord's protection.

Does the Bible recommend sexual abstinence outside of marriage because God likes rules but dislikes sex, as some hedonists claim? Or is it because the Lord's laws reflect His profound love for us? Ultimately, every time we break God's rules, we find ourselves farther and farther from home. If we act in a manner that cannot fulfill the needs we were created with, we will end up hurt, with an empty ache inside. It may take years for one to recognize this emptiness, or it can drive someone toward suicide at an early age. It is not a feeling that has been induced by "religion." It is a very real part of our inner nature.

When we violate the Lord's design for our lives, we are not behaving in accord with the reality of our physical, emotional, and spiritual makeup. It is like pouring ice-cold water into a glass that has just been removed from a steaming hot dishwasher. The glass *must* crack. It cannot do anything else because of its molecular structure. That structure must conform to the physical laws of nature.

Intimate sexual experience exposes the deepest part of oneself to one's partner. Two people united by sexual intercourse become one flesh whether this occurs within a lifelong, loving relationship or is simply the result of a one-night stand. That is the reality of how we are structured physically, emotionally, and spiritually.

When two people who have been sexually joined together walk away from one another, a kind of inner shattering takes place, even if they vehemently deny the feeling exists. Some people become so splintered through repeated episodes of this kind that real loving becomes seemingly impossible; it hurts far too much. In attempts to put the pieces together, sexually broken people harden their hearts with self-made patches that become solid as cement. They may even become numb. Instead of having hearts that are soft and pliable, tender and transparent, their hearts turn into stone.

Only the powerful love of Christ can heal such hearts, mending them so that they are capable of truly loving another person and of loving God. Thank God that He is able to mend our broken hearts so they are better than new. He can heal sexually shattered lives and transform us with the fire of His incredible love.

THE TRUTH THAT SETS US FREE

Over the twenty years I spent teaching childbirth and human sexuality classes, I found that only a few of my students had ever received Christ-centered instruction about their sexuality. Let's face it: the majority of us were given a short list of do's and don'ts without an adequate framework with which to interpret and make sense out of what our parents expected of us regarding our sexual behavior.

Think back for a moment, and try to remember how you learned about how babies are conceived. Who told you? Did you feel surprised? Ashamed? Curious? Delighted? Horrified? How did you verify what you had heard? Did you talk to your mom about your reaction? Did she act embarrassed, or was she prepared to respond to your questions? Did she give you the impression that she was comfortable with her own sexuality or repelled by it?

Was the atmosphere in your home conducive to talking about sexuality, or did you find that you had to rely on other sources? Were you expected to remain a virgin until after marriage without being told why sex outside of marriage is emotionally hurtful? Who became your authority on sexual values?

For most of us, our self-taught methods of sex education—most of it conducted informally in conjunction with our friends and siblings—rarely considered the tenderness of God's love for us in His design for sex. With nothing but a confusing road map and a set of conflicting instructions to follow, many of us wound up lost in our contemporary culture's sexual wilderness.

Without a steadying understanding of God's compassionate design for our lives, it can be incredibly easy to justify engaging in a wide range of sexual activities, "as long as no one gets hurt." By discounting the emotional wounds suffered as a result of multiple sexual relationships, many of us learned too late what we could have known earlier.

Surrounded by contradictory messages that undermine our ability to understand our sexuality, we have been pulled in two opposing directions over the years: between attitudes from the present that promote open sexual expression in a variety of different forms, and attitudes from the past that create shame by implying that the enjoyment of sexual pleasure is not part of God's design for "good" women. Add to this the day-to-day temptations, urges, and struggles men and women face regarding sex, romance, and relationships—and what do we get? A combustible mixture of ideas, attitudes, and feelings with the potential to wreck our lives.

Is it any wonder many of us are more than a little confused? *The good news is that it doesn't have to be this way. Sexual sanity is possible. And it is a goal worth reaching for.*

You will probably be uncomfortable with this book if you think that the Genesis story is an irrelevant fairy tale with no bearing on people's lives. But I invite you to keep reading. At the very least, you will become more familiar with a point of view that is not encountered in the media or through university classes much these days. It is my hope that you will be encouraged by the following chapters to faithfully love your husband with understanding and compassion, realizing with greater clarity what it means to express your love toward him, through Christ, in a world of confusing, competing voices.

> What can be more foolish than to think that all this rare fabric of heaven and earth could come by chance, when all the skill of science is not able to make an oyster.
>
> JEREMY TAYLOR

Chapter Review

Personal Reflections

1. After reading the passages from Genesis, I thought about:

2. In the past, I found myself becoming skeptical about the goodness of God's design for my sexuality when:

3. Talking with my mother about sexuality taught me:

4. My greatest stumbling block to sexual sanity at this point in my life seems to be:

5. The best arguments in favor of my honoring and keeping sexual relations an exclusive activity between myself and my husband are:

6. If I could ask God three questions about His design for human sexuality, they would be:

Related Bible Passages for Further Study

- Psalm 139:13-16
- Psalm 145:1-18
- Proverbs 3:3-8
- John 8:1-12
- 1 Corinthians 6:12-20
- Ephesians 2:1-10

$\mathscr{C}$HOICES AND CHALLENGES

*Christianity does not exist in an external conformity
to practices which, though right in themselves, may be adopted
from human motives and to answer secular purposes. It is
not a religion of forms, modes, and decencies. It is being transformed into the image of God. It is being like-minded
with Christ. It is considering Him as our sanctification as well
as our redemption. It is endeavoring to live to Him here, that
we might live with Him hereafter. It is desiring earnestly
to surrender our will to His, our heart to the conduct of His
Spirit, our life to the guidance of His Word.*[1]

HANNAH MORE

$\mathscr{A}$llen Wheelis made a profound statement when he wrote, "Values determine goals, and goals define identity. The problem of identity, therefore, is secondary to some basic trouble about value."[2]
Knowing we are created in the image of God enables us to resolve the
questions we have about our identity. Believing what His Word says
about who we are will provide the values and goals that guide our lives.

Our sexual identity is a part of our identity as a whole, shaped by our
families, our culture, our environment, and our physical, emotional, and
spiritual makeup. The way we express our sexuality is determined by our
values and beliefs about what it means to be a woman—the conclusions
we have reached about who we are. *Our sexual behavior is a reflection of our
sexual identity.*

Separating our identities from cultural norms concerning female sexuality isn't easy when that pattern predominates all around us on billboards, movie screens, and magazine covers. Yet in his letter to the Romans, the apostle Paul wrote, "Don't let the world around you squeeze you into its own mold, but let God re-make you so that your whole attitude of mind is changed. Thus you will prove in practice that the will of God is good, acceptable to him and perfect" (Romans 12:2 PHILLIPS).

In this passage, the phrase "squeeze you into its own mold" is based upon a Greek word that means "to fashion ourselves according to the same pattern." As followers of Christ, we become new creations. We are called by God to base our identity upon the Bible, not on current cultural beliefs. Our identity is derived from what the Lord says about who we are rather than from our own efforts to create it. When our sexual identity does not conform to the Lord's pattern for our lives, it becomes confused.

Becoming a "new creation" is like being told that we are not who we thought we were. Give your imagination free rein for a moment. Suppose someone had been raised as an English citizen named Claire Brett. Then this woman is approached by a policeman, a government official, the American ambassador, and an FBI agent, who inform her that she had been kidnapped as a young child. She learns that members of the English crime syndicate took her from her parents when she was two years old—that she is really an American citizen named Sally Young. The fact that she *believes* she is Claire Brett does not change the fact of who she really is. But she would most likely feel shock and disbelief at the news of her real identity. She would probably need some kind of reassurance, some proof, that she is Sally Young. In order to be able to take up this new identity, she would want to see a birth certificate or pictures of herself with her real family. Without such proof, she would have difficulty grasping the truth and would always wonder who she really was.

Her ability to conform to her true identity would not develop overnight. Day by day, she would need to learn about her real family, about the circumstances that surrounded the kidnapping, about her heritage as a member of the Young family. And she would have to *want* to believe it.

OUR IDENTITY IN CHRIST

When we open our hearts to receive Christ, we obtain a new identity. Our former selves actually pass away, and we become new creations. Here is Peter's way of expressing what we have gained in this respect through Jesus:

> *All honor to the God and Father of our Lord Jesus Christ, for it is by his boundless mercy that God has given us the privilege of being born again. Now we live with a wonderful expectation because Jesus Christ rose again from the dead. For God has reserved a priceless inheritance for his children. It is kept in heaven for you, pure and undefiled, beyond the reach of change and decay. And God, in his mighty power, will protect you until you receive this salvation, because you are trusting him. It will be revealed on the last day for all to see. So be truly glad! There is wonderful joy ahead, even though it is necessary for you to endure many trials for a while.*
>
> 1 PETER 1:3-6 NLT

Each of us who believes in Christ will receive the inheritance that Peter and the apostles wrote about, and we are to rejoice greatly in this regardless of what we encounter in our earthly lives. We choose to accept our new identity based on the faith that comes from hearing God's Word, not on what can be proven via a county clerk's birth certificate. We are heading home, our inheritance is assured, and we are shielded by God's power as we await His coming. We have cause to celebrate! We can *know* who we are, in Christ, in spite of what our upbringing has taught us. We are *His*. God is our true Father, and our homeland is not of this world.

If we fail to grasp the amazing truth of what our redemption means, we will feel torn between two worlds that are in opposition to one another. We cannot both believe *and* doubt and fully understand our relationship with our real Father. Belonging to the Lord means also deriving our identity from Him.

Establishing our true identity is quite challenging at this time and place in history. We live in a culture that has come to value *androgynous* sex roles. Androgynous is a botanical term for plants that have both anthers (pollen-producing organs) and ovaries (seed-producing organs). An androgynous

person is one who has both male and female qualities, seeming to be neither one or the other in a "traditional" sense. This glamorization of androgynous sex roles erases our sexual distinctiveness, not respecting the
biological, emotional, and spiritual realities of maleness and femaleness.

The fallacy here is that human beings were not created to be asexual
or bisexual or homosexual; we were created to be sexually distinct, het-
erosexual men and women. The Lord created us to be male *or* female, to
have testicles *or* ovaries, so that males and females complement one
another sexually, not become the same as one another. God did not make
people to be both female and male, as He did certain plants and animals.

Within the last fifteen years, sex roles in our culture have changed
tremendously. For those of us who have become followers of Christ during this era, it is sometimes difficult to know how we are to live out the
truth of our natural sexual design.

Feminism has had a far-reaching impact for better and for worse on
the hearts and minds of women born after World War II. Classic Christian
values now are seen by many women as oppressive, outmoded, and
archaic. But in the long run, basing our sexual identity exclusively on culturally based sexual norms brings confusion about the beauty and wonder of God's design for our sexuality. Thus, when we pray for wisdom,
we must ask and not doubt, even when we initially may have a hard time
accepting what the Lord reveals to us.

The Bible instructs us that "the way of the Lord is a refuge for the
righteous" (Proverbs 10:29). We can choose to walk in that way as followers of Christ, or head in a different direction. We cannot walk along
two paths at once, each aimed at different destinations, and expect to discover the freedom and fullness associated with our God-given identity.

Our identity will set our goals; our identity will determine which
road we travel. Once we see this truth, we welcome the opportunity to
walk in the way of the Lord with our whole hearts.

THE WAY OF THE LORD

We can thank God that He has given His timeless Word to us to guide us
throughout our lives. When we study the Scriptures, we find that even
though some of the specifics might be different, little has changed regarding the human heart.

When we are born again, the way we look at things changes. Paul wrote, "And God has actually given us his Spirit (not the world's spirit) so we can know the wonderful things God has given us. . . . But people who aren't Christians can't understand these truths from God's Spirit. It all sounds foolish to them because only those who have the Spirit can understand what the Spirit means" (1 Corinthians 2:12, 14 NLT).

Paul went on to say: "If any one of you thinks he is wise by the standards of this age, he should become a 'fool' so that he may become wise. For the wisdom of this world is foolishness in God's sight. As it is written: 'He catches the wise in their craftiness'; and again, 'The Lord knows that the thoughts of the wise are futile'" (1 Corinthians 3:18-20).

These words apply to us today as much as they fit Paul's time. God alone remains our safe fortress, our protective shield, and our mighty deliverer. He protects, guides, and gives us the things we need so that we will know how we are to live in this present age. And He supplies the necessary spiritual strength and power for us to accomplish all that He asks us to do. As John's first letter tells us: "You belong to God, my dear children. You have already won your fight with these false prophets, because the Spirit who lives in you is greater than the spirit who lives in the world" (1 John 4:4 NLT).

Praying for the wisdom, we need to discern what is going on around us. We need the compassion that enables us to express Christ's redemptive love to those who are perishing. If we are to be the "salt of the earth," we need a clear understanding of the meaning and implications of our sexuality.

What is at stake if we become obedient to God? Our pride? Our vanity? Our selfishness? Yes. In exchange for surrendering our hearts to Jesus, consider what He has promised to give us: peace . . . joy . . . love . . . and everlasting life. We can't have it both ways. Walking in the Lord's way requires that we turn away from the spirit of this world and base our identity on a brand-new foundation.

A GENTLE AND HUMBLE HEART

"Because they have been created by God with equal dignity, men and women must respect, love, serve, and not despise one another,"[3] John Stott wrote. An imbalance occurs when women give, submit, follow, and surrender to their husbands' wishes, and their husbands do not accept God's call to lovingly and compassionately consider, respect, understand, and meet the needs of their wives.

The Bible teaches us—as Christians and as couples—to practice this principle in our relationships: "Submit to one another out of reverence for Christ" (Ephesians 5:21). Another translation of the same verse puts it this way: "And 'fit in with' each other, because of your common reverence for Christ" (PHILLIPS).

I like J. B. Phillips's simple way of summarizing this key statement, don't you? We are to be a blessing to our husbands, as they are to be to us. We fit in with each other as we become "as one" within the ongoing context of our everyday existence—spiritual, social, legal, financial, vocational, intellectual, emotional, and sexual life partners.

For followers of Jesus, obedience to God's will where we live is central to living out our calling as believers. Our victory in Christ comes by lifting up the Lord in love and humility instead of exalting ourselves. Jesus told us that the "least among you all—he is the greatest,"(Luke 9:48), and "the greatest among you will be your servant" (Matthew 23:11). "Let me teach you," He calls to us today, "because I am humble and gentle, and you will find rest for your souls" (Matthew 11:29 NLT).

We have been sold a false bill of goods by our culture. But the Word has a way of turning everything that is upside down right-side-up. *God's way of loving is costly*, but as we identify with our crucified Lord—apparently powerless when He humbly poured himself out as a gentle servant for us all—we also experience the breaking forth of hope at His resurrection and celebrate His triumph on our behalf.

From the world's viewpoint, it makes no sense to be humble. But from the perspective of the New Testament, humility takes on a new meaning within marriage. As the Cross enters our relationships, we are released from our pride and the need to be Number One; as the redemptive power of the Resurrection breaks forth upon our lifetime covenant to love and cherish one another, we are renewed and restored by God's life-changing love.

The attraction of a woman who seeks to love others as Christ loves her is part of a circular process that spirals heavenward as a "fragrant offering" to the Lord. When we love our husbands wisely, their love for us is nurtured, and they are encouraged to love us in return.

The apostle Paul explained, "The love a man gives his wife is the extending of his love for himself to enfold her" (Ephesians 5:29 PHILLIPS). Isn't this a lovely way of expressing it? The growth of love continues as our husbands' love draws us even closer to their hearts, influencing our responses. This process, as it goes back and forth, is intended to deepen the bond we share with our husbands, strengthening our attachment to one another and reinforcing our commitment over a lifetime.

The principle of mutual submission in the Bible is not a face-in-the-dust experience of humiliation. It is an act of our wills as we respond to the Holy Spirit's help and are conformed to the example of our Lord and Savior. As we base our lives upon the enduring truth of Scripture and the transforming power of Christ's love within us, we learn to love our husbands with greater insight, wisdom, and patience.

I bring up the issue of submission here because it can be a stumbling block to women. Though some people may ridicule us for following Christ's example, cautioning us to assert ourselves against the "tyranny" of our husbands, it is likely that they do so because they are not yet acquainted with the virtues of gentleness and humility. There were also many who jeered at Christ for His apparent powerlessness on the Cross, history's most perfect symbol of love and submission. But God is not a tyrant, our husbands are not dictators, and we are not slaves. *Constrained and guided by love, we have the freedom to choose how to live out our calling as Christ's gentle and humble followers in obedience to God's will.*

LIVING LIFE CREATIVELY

Learning to be comfortable with the bodies and roles God has given to us is a different process than exploring one's sexuality from a perspective of self-gratification. It means that we are to take a radical departure from the spirit of this age, delve into the Word of God, and be transformed by the renewing of our minds. It means that we are to tune out culturally based voices and images of sexuality that beckon to us to put ourselves first; we can choose instead to value sexual relations within marriage as the way God created a man and a woman to share their bodies with one another. It means that the "fruit of the womb" and the "blessings of the breast" can bring satisfying fulfillment to women as the Lord establishes our families and brings new life into His creation. It means being able to discern the will of God in our lives and being unashamed of proclaiming His truth to a dying world, not as arrogant know-it-alls, but as Jesus' humble servants.

Within this framework, the Lord grants us great flexibility to express who we are as individuals. As Dick Keyes explained:

> God's commitment to marriage extends beyond creating it. He has also given us a way of life within the institution he made. His form of marriage allows great freedom. Elaborate rules, roles and job descriptions for husband and wife are conspicuously absent from the New Testament itself. The Bible says nothing of who should earn the most money, cook the most meals, balance the checkbook, or change the most diapers. The form that God has given is flexible enough for Christians in many different times and cultures to be imaginative in the way they build relationships.[4]

Even though we each have our own opinions about how to live out our roles within marriage, the way of life God has provided for us is based upon mutual love, respect, honor, and understanding; upon the solid truths of Scripture that guard our hearts and minds from harm; and upon the grand reality of our new identity in Christ as we walk with Him, step by step, toward eternity.

"What we love we shall grow to resemble," wrote Saint Bernard in the twelfth century. That principle still applies today. *Values influence identity.* As we focus our attention on loving and serving Christ, everything else will follow.

> What are we supposed to believe and do? We are to believe that the Bible is *true*. Then we are to come into God's family and sit in the light all the time. That is, when we are reborn into God's family by believing what He tells us in the Bible about Himself, and by accepting what Jesus came to do for us, we are children of light. We are supposed to get our ideas and our understanding from Him so we will not have fuzzy, dark, foggy ideas, but *truth*.[5]

EDITH SCHAEFFER

Chapter Review

Personal Reflections

1. I believe that "becoming a new creation" means that I:

2. Humility of heart is a key to understanding:

3. As a woman, I feel God has created me to express my sexuality by:

4. My identity as a woman has been most influenced by:

5. Submission to one's husband may best be defined as:

6. As I walked with the Lord today, He seems to be telling me to:

Related Bible Passages for Further Study

- Psalm 37:5-9
- Proverbs 2:1-11
- Isaiah 43:18-21
- John 10:14-16, 27-30
- Romans 8:1-16
- Galatians 5:15-25
- Ephesians 5:15-33

$\mathcal{M}$AKING PEACE WITH OUR BODIES

God be in my head, and in my understanding;

God be in my eyes, and in my looking;

God be in my mouth, and in my speaking;

God be in my heart, and in my thinking.

ANONYMOUS

May the eternal God bless and keep us, guard our bodies,

save our souls, direct our thoughts, and bring us safe to the

heavenly country, our eternal home, where Father, Son and

Holy Spirit ever reign, one God forever and ever.[1]

It is an inescapable fact—our culture idolizes physical attractiveness. Images of 85 percent fat-free physiques and media-magnified sex appeal seem to be everywhere, from the magazine covers lining the racks at the grocery store to the strategically placed highway billboards. Most popular models and actresses are thinner than 95 percent of the female population in the United States—where 60 percent of us wear a size twelve or larger.[2] Though the average American woman weighs 146 pounds, this is considered too fat in an era where the average model or actress weighs 23 percent below this amount.[3]

Is it any wonder that most of us today—Christians and non-Christians alike—experience a lingering dissatisfaction with our physical appearance?[4] As a result, women collectively pay millions of dollars to have wrinkles removed, faces lifted, noses trimmed, hips and thighs suctioned, breasts enlarged, and tummies tucked. Many of us have had first-hand experience with chronic dieting, compulsive eating, bulimia, exercise addiction, or anorexia. We know the way we look as women significantly influences whom we marry, how much money we earn, and whether people will, at least initially, accept or reject us.

But what is really important is what *we* see when we look in the mirror. Our attitudes about the way our bodies look have a powerful impact on the way we think and feel about our self-worth and our sexuality.

It is time we gave ourselves a break! Our spiritual value does not reside in our bodies, which the apostle Paul aptly called "jars of clay" (2 Corinthians 4:7). It lies in the glorious treasure God has placed inside these earthly vessels. *Our bodies deserve our tender loving care rather than our constant criticism and contempt.*

Scripture teaches us that our bodies are temples of God—the place where the Holy Spirit resides (1 Corinthians 6:19-20). The Bible also clearly emphasizes that the human body is a temporary tent that we will cast off at the point of physical death (2 Corinthians 5:1-5). Someday we will receive a brand-new shape and form, "raised imperishable . . . raised in glory . . . raised in power . . . raised a spiritual body" (1 Corinthians 15:42-44). Until then, it is our responsibility to honor what Paul aptly described as our "perishable," "weak," "natural" bodies by viewing them from a balanced biblical perspective rather than from the narrow-minded approach of our culture.

Something beautiful happens when a woman lets go of the fear, shame, and anxiety she feels about the way she looks and accepts her body, rich with imperfection, as a gift of God. When she stops despising certain aspects of her appearance—her wide hips, pesky cellulite, double chin, droopy abdomen, small breasts, or bony backside—and smiles at the imperfect reflection in the mirror. When she learns to appreciate her body with the humor and grace God alone can give. When she warmly welcomes her husband with her body.

If we are to be on comfortable terms with our sexuality, we need to make peace with our bodies, including the way they look. Achieving a delicate balance in the way we view our physical form and appearance requires a certain measure of self-acceptance. And as we learn to appreciate our God-given uniqueness with genuine joy and humility, we find a measure of peace about ourselves that the world cannot give us. How we look is no longer a ruling factor of our identity. Who we are in Christ matters to us much more.

PONDERING OUR DIFFERENCES

"In the absence of any other proof, the thumb alone would convince me of God's existence," noted Isaac Newton.[5] Have you, like this famous physicist, ever stopped to ponder how the complexity and wisdom of God are reflected in your wondrous design? Do you accept your physical beauty and praise God for the wonder of your body's intricate structure, head to toe, inside and outside, seen and unseen?

The Bible invites us to think about our own bodies with the same dignity and joy that are evident in the Genesis account of the first woman's creation. When we contemplate what this means to us, we have ample cause to appreciate our uniqueness:

> *For you created my inmost being; you knit me together in my mother's womb. I praise you because I am fearfully and wonderfully made; your works are wonderful, I know that full well. My frame was not hidden from you when I was made in the secret place. When I was woven together in the depths of the earth, your eyes saw my unformed body. All the days ordained for me were written in your book before one of them came to be.*
>
> PSALM 139:13-16

When I read this passage, it is as if I hear the Lord saying: *You are a living example of My handiwork. There is no one else like you in My creation. You are a precious, one-of-a-kind woman with personal worth—unique in the universe, complete in Christ, headed for heaven. I have always known and loved you. Nothing can separate you from My love.*

I have never been able to remain quiet about my amazement at God's handiwork, the human body. I am continually fascinated (and sometimes frustrated!) by its complex intricacies, need for ongoing balance, and ability to carry out so many different functions, regardless of my level of conscious cooperation. Whenever I witness a newborn infant taking a first breath of air, I still can hardly believe that the baby I am looking at began just nine short months ago as two microscopic cells inside a woman's womb.

Each of us enters life in this almost miraculous way. Ever since that time, our growth and development have proceeded along a highly complicated, well-organized pathway resulting in our becoming who we are today. We are rather complex individuals, you and me, with a unique set of physical, emotional, and intellectual capabilities and characteristics. As a result, many factors influence how we experience and express our sexuality (see Figure 3-1).

How We Experience Our Sexuality
Figure 3-1

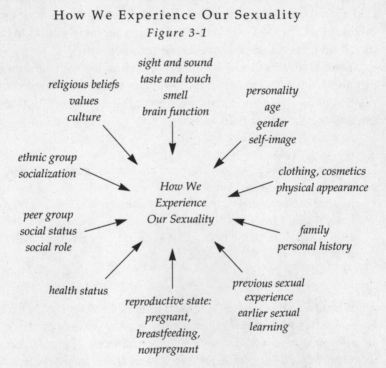

As we learn about our bodies, we are more likely to take good care of them. We may even become better stewards of what the Lord has given to us. When we take the time to discover how our bodies work, we are also better able to talk about the sexual sensations and experiences we have. Through understanding what is happening inside our bodies, communicating with our spouses takes on greater importance. We are more likely to place a higher value on talking about the things that please, bother, surprise, irritate, and excite us.

ENLARGING OUR VIEW

The qualities that distinguish women from men are closely tied to the design of our bodies. Our sexual differences as women enhance our ability to be wives and mothers. Our ability to be intuitive, nurturing, and receptive is closely tied to our physical, emotional, and spiritual inheritance.

I am well aware of what some people would say about this statement. But I am not going to apologize for it or pretend there are no basic sexual differences between men and women. And I appreciate the strengths associated with my womanly nature. Being a wife and a mother has brought me a profound, lasting sense of satisfaction unmatched by any other life experiences I have had.

What do you think? Is it possible for a woman to base her identity on a genitally oriented view of sexuality, as our culture does, and be fulfilled and satisfied? Do you think your most valuable assets reside in your bust, waist, and hip measurements—or in your level of sexual performance in the bedroom? Or do you believe your best sexual qualities are related to something quite different?

When we are honest with ourselves about our sexual makeup, it becomes evident that we experience our sexuality in a strikingly different manner than our husbands. This knowledge can enhance our ability to accept our bodies and to make decisions regarding our sexuality based on a coherent biblical perspective. *By exchanging a socially restrictive view about women's sexuality for a larger multidimensional outlook, we increase our understanding of the amazing qualities the Lord has given to us as women.*

From the first moment of our existence, we were females. The Lord created us with real differences from males. I, for one, am thoroughly convinced that God designed our sexual differences for a magnificent purpose. When we ignore our sexual design and live according to culturally based norms, our marital and family roles are altered in a number of notable ways.

As you consider the following chart, I invite you to spend time reflecting on what the sexual differences between you and your husband mean to you (Fig. 3-2). You may also want to make a list of ways the culture specifically diminishes or erases aspects of women's sexual design.

Summary of Reproductive Roles
of Males and Females
Figure 3-2

MALES:

Spermatogenesis—the production of male sex cells, or sperm, within the testes.

Ejaculation—the release of semen through the male reproductive tract that accompanies the orgasmic phase of sexual response. During intercourse, sperm are deposited at the base of the cervix within the woman's vagina.

FEMALES:

Ovulation—the release of a female sex cell, or ovum, from an ovary.

Menstruation—the monthly shedding of the superficial lining of the uterus.

Sexual response during intercourse—the immersion of the cervix in the seminal pool that follows uterine contractions and facilitates conception after lovemaking.

Gestation—an approximately 266-day period following the fertilization of an ovum during which an unborn child is nurtured within the uterus and develops the capacity for independent survival outside the mother's body.

Parturition—the process of human labor and birth involving contractions of the uterus that move the baby through the mother's pelvis and out into the world.

Lactation—the production of human milk by the mammary glands in response to the suckling of an infant at the breast.

In summary, a healthy woman's body is capable of performing six separate yet interrelated sexual functions, while a man's is capable of two. The sexual strengths we bring into our marital relationships are precious, rich, and diverse. Our bodies' changing cycles of quiet inactivity and intense activity are entirely different from our husbands' bodies. We make love through the same passageway where we give birth. Our breasts provide pleasure for us and our mates, yet they were also designed to nurture our infants. (Please know that as I write this, I am also thinking of women who have experienced the grief of infertility, child-birth loss, or difficulties with lactation. The point I am making is not intended in any way to imply that you are not a whole sexual person. *You are*. These generalized statements are not intended to suggest that sexual wholeness is based on reproductive function, but to refute popular cultural views that sexualize women's breasts and wombs.)

As we embrace our husbands with our bodies, we invite them to experience our femininity through their masculine touch. The diverse capabilities of our sexuality as women is often discounted by our society through its "genital orientation" to human sexuality. Many men and women value a hedonistic view of female sexuality that emphasizes one aspect of our reproductive capabilities—genital pleasure—over all the others. But our sexual design was created to have a far greater impact upon marriage and family life than what this reduced version of human sexuality provides.

REAL SATISFACTION

It takes time and energy to foster a compassionate atmosphere in which we can discuss with our spouses our thoughts, feelings, and reactions to our sexual differences. We are called to pay close attention to the sexual aspect of our marriages and to focus upon meeting one another's needs (1 Corinthians 7:5). Within marriage, both husbands and wives are called to compassionately consider one another's strengths and weaknesses. In addition, God's Word makes it clear that we are not obligated to take part in any out-of-bounds sexual activity (Ephesians 5:3; 1 Thessalonians 4:3-6; Hebrews 13:4). Ongoing communication is necessary if we are to understand our spouse's sexual desires, differences, and struggles.

Hurrying through lovemaking just to get it over with may mean we are avoiding an honest discussion about why we are uncomfortable with lovemaking—or simply need a break from it. Ignoring our cyclical nature or our emotional and physical responses to our husbands may prevent us from enjoying sex or may keep us from facing what is really going on in our minds and hearts. So the next time your back hurts or you are too exhausted to make love or you feel emotionally unable to participate in lovemaking or your spouse wants to try something new that you are uncomfortable with, tell your husband how you are really feeling.

When it comes to this area of our lives, we are vulnerable to our husbands' complaints and criticisms, as they are to ours. This is one reason why talking about sexual issues can be more difficult than quietly covering up what we are sensing and feeling. But, in the long run, our marriages can be hurt when we hide the real reasons for our reluctance. As Jean Banyolak and Ingrid Trobisch remind us:

> To prepare for the act of love both the husband and wife must know what the other partner needs and desires. If either is full of fear, unresolved conflict or feelings of hurt or inadequacy, then he or she will draw back and not find the joy which is rightfully theirs in the act of love. The secret then is to be able to talk to each other and to share that which hurts. To keep silent is harmful to both.[6]

Our needs, opinions, preferences, attitudes, insights, and beliefs are not to be discounted. *Our concerns about sexuality will not simply disappear. Therefore, it is essential to learn how to talk about sexual issues with our husbands and not be afraid to ask for what we need from them. When a husband consistently refuses to acknowledge or accommodate his wife's concerns, she should prayerfully consider seeking pastoral or professional marriage guidance.*

Remember, open discussion is not the same thing as a one-sided demand. A sincere request or concern, spoken because we value ourselves and our partners, fosters our ability to love our husbands and their ability to love us. With self-acceptance, good communication, and genuine willingness to understand one another in love, the marriage bed can be a warm and welcome meeting place for wedded lovers.

> Our natural life is a fury of desire for the things we can see. That is the meaning of lust—I must have it at once, a fury of desire without

any regard for the consequences. I have to be detached from the things I can see and be brought into a living relationship with the Creator of those things. If I am taken up with the created things and forget Jesus Christ, I shall find that things disappoint and I get disillusioned. If my body is "bossed" by personal self-realization, I am defiling the temple of the Holy Ghost: I may be moral and upright, but I have become ruler of my own life. "Give your right to yourself to me," says Jesus. "Let me realize myself in you."[7]

OSWALD CHAMBERS

Chapter Review

Personal Reflections

1. When I look in the mirror at my face and body, I see:

2. The greatest sources of pressure concerning my physical appearance are:

3. In the past I have dealt with my desire to change my appearance and/or reshape my body by:

4. I find it easier to accept the varied facets of my sexuality if I:

5. Talking to my husband about my sexual needs and limits is/isn't always comfortable, mostly because:

6. If I asked God for His perspective on my body's sexual design, I think He would tell me:

Related Bible Passages for Further Study

- Psalm 100
- Isaiah 45:9-12; 64:8
- Jeremiah 18:1-6
- Ecclesiastes 3:11-14; 11:5
- Matthew 6:25-33
- Romans 12:1-3

4

𝒰NDERSTANDING OUR CYCLICAL NATURE

One reason why Christian women have such a hard time
accepting themselves, including their bodies, is because the idea
still prevails that the spiritual and mental areas of our lives are
somehow closer to God, more pleasing to him and more "Christian"
than the physical realm. The Bible, which calls the body the
"temple of the Holy Spirit," says the contrary: the more authentic
our faith is, the more we are able to live at peace with our bodies. The
more I succeed in accepting myself as a physical creature, the more
I am able to live in harmony and peace with myself.[1]

INGRID TROBISCH

In the healthy female body, six reproductive functions may take place
once puberty has ushered in its changes. Each function is accompanied
by its own set of physiological events. Only two of these functions
involve the sexuality of our husbands in a direct, physical way.

Menstruation, the monthly shedding of the lining of the uterus, is the
first function to become evident. About half of all American girls are
thought to begin menstruating between the ages of twelve and a half and
fourteen and a half. The onset of the menses follows approximately two
years of breast development and other physical changes. This process
continues until menopause, which usually takes place between the ages
of forty-seven and fifty.

The second function, ovulation, involves the release of a mature egg,
or ovum, from an ovary and does not usually begin until about one year
after a girl's periods start. As a female moves into adolescence, genital

changes prepare her to participate in the third function, sexual inter-course, when the mons pubis (the fleshy area covering the pubic bones) becomes more prominent and the labia majora (major lips) develop and become fuller, covering the rest of the external genitalia that are normally visible throughout childhood. Also, the labia minora (inner lips) develop and grow, and the Bartholin's glands on each side of the vaginal opening become capable of releasing fluid to lubricate the vagina during sexual arousal. The clitoris, a small sensitive organ that is mainly composed of erectile nerve tissue, develops an extensive system of blood vessels at this time, and the vagina changes in color to a deeper red. The mucous lining of the vagina becomes thicker and remains so except during lactation and after menopause, when it becomes considerably thinner and drier. Even the secretions of the cervix change, becoming more acidic than in the past.

Sometime between the ages of ten and twelve, the uterus begins to grow fairly rapidly, until it doubles in size, usually between the ages of sixteen and eighteen. Once it has reached its mature size, the fourth func-tion—gestation or pregnancy—may safely take place. Pregnancy in turn prepares the maternal body for the fifth function—parturition, or child-birth. After giving birth, a woman's body triggers the onset of lactation. Through the amazing process of breastfeeding, a baby can be completely nourished by the mother's body after she gives birth until sometime around the middle of the first year of life.

These functions comprise the range of women's reproductive activi-ties. All six functions normally appear in the developmental sequence I have briefly described. When any of these sexual functions become dis-rupted by illness, stress, malnutrition, or chronic disease, medical assis-tance is needed to diagnose and treat the difficulty.

Our reproductive activities are dependent upon the secretion of chemical substances called hormones, which are produced within the body and carried in the bloodstream to the specific sites they are designed to stimulate. Hormones act as messages to cells as a means of increasing their activity.

The primary "sex hormones" secreted by the female body are estro-gen and progesterone. Both are produced by the ovaries. The principal sex hormone for males, referred to as an androgen, produces masculine characteristics and is called testosterone. Sex hormones are responsible for a wide range of reproductive functions and for our "secondary sexual characteristics," which we closely associate with our ideas of femininity and masculinity—the amount and location of body hair, breast development, sex drive, location of body fat deposits, deepening of the voice, development of muscle tissue, and changes in external genitalia.

AN INSIDE VIEW OF THE MENSTRUAL CYCLE

At a very early stage during our prenatal development, a group of cells organized in response to hormonal stimulation to become our ovaries. Also referred to as gonads, ovaries are the sex glands that secrete estrogen and progesterone. Male gonads are called testes, which begin to secrete testosterone by the seventh or eighth week after conception.

In the developing female, the gonads begin to change into ovaries by the tenth or eleventh week of gestation, developing high in the abdomen near the kidneys. They descend downwards and outwards before birth and end up being located closer to the brim of the pelvis.

Each ovary is approximately one inch wide, one and a half inches long, and one quarter of an inch thick, resembling an almond in shape and appearance. In younger women, the ovaries are smooth and pink; in older women, the ovaries are shrunken, pitted, and gray. This change is the result of repeated discharges of "eggs," or ova, through the surface of the ovaries, causing them to become wrinkled up and puckered-looking as scars form.

The ovaries have two responsibilities: the production of ova and the secretion of female sex hormones. At birth, each ovary contains about 250,000 small saclike structures called primary follicles. Within these follicles lie immature ova. By puberty, all but approximately 10,000 of these primary follicles degenerate. During our reproductive lives, about 375 of these follicles expel ova. By the age of fifty, most of the remaining follicles have disappeared.

Around eight years of age, girls begin to secrete a "hormonal messenger" from the pituitary gland that signals the ovaries to prepare their bodies for other reproductive functions. The pituitary gland steps up its secretion of hormones between the ages of eleven and fourteen, and these hormones bring about puberty. During puberty, the ovaries begin to release estrogen into the bloodstream in response to the stimulation from the pituitary glands (Fig. 4-1).

Female Hormones
Figure 4-1

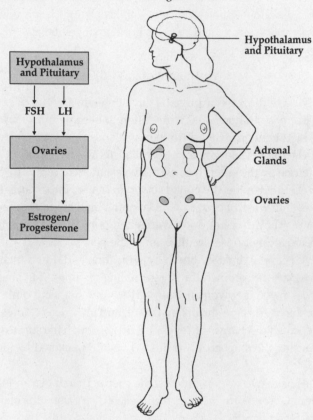

Estrogen is the key hormone responsible for further developments in the female reproductive system. It stimulates the oviducts (Fallopian tubes), uterus, and vagina to mature, increasing their size and ability to function.

The secondary sexual characteristics produced by estrogens include:

- the broadening of the pelvis so that its outlet changes from a narrow, funnel-shaped opening to a broad oval outlet.

- the development of smooth, soft skin.

- the formation of an elaborate duct system in the breasts.

- the deposition of fat in the breasts, buttocks, and thighs.

- the growth of pubic hair that has a flat upper border.

- the early uniting of the growing end of long bones within the bone shaft to limit height.

The primary follicles in the ovaries are stimulated to develop and mature by two hormones released from the pituitary gland: follicle stimulating hormone (FSH) and luteinizing hormone (LH). Ovulation may not take place when the release of these hormones is inhibited by disease or the use of oral contraceptives.

FSH is responsible for the early growth of immature ova and the enlargement of the primary follicle. This process of enlargement is due to an accumulation of fluids in the follicle similar to the formation of a skin blister. Fifteen to twenty immature follicles are stimulated to grow every month. Of these, only one bulges outward—like a balloon in the wall of the ovary—developing to full maturity. This mature follicle is called a graafian follicle. The other budding follicles simply degenerate (Fig. 4-2).

Ovarian Changes During the Menstrual Cycle
Figure 4-2

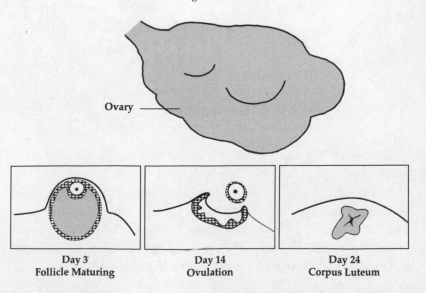

Ovary

Day 3	Day 14	Day 24
Follicle Maturing	Ovulation	Corpus Luteum

In the surface of the graafian follicle is a small, nipplelike protrusion called a stigma. As the stigma develops, the pituitary gland ups its output of LH. As the level of LH rises, the stigma disintegrates and causes the graafian follicle to burst (Fig. 4-3). Some women feel this happen—it is called *mittelschmerz* after a German term that means "pain in the middle." It is a sharp sensation felt in the mid-abdomen towards either the right or left side, depending on which ovary has released an ovum through the graafian follicle.

Insider's View: The Follicle Bursts
Figure 4-3

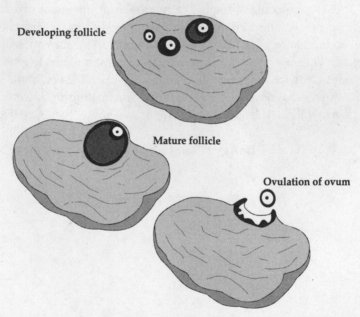

Developing follicle

Mature follicle

Ovulation of ovum

The ovum that escapes from the follicle is very fragile and requires nourishment and protection as it travels down the oviduct. It can be fertilized for only twelve to twenty-four hours after ovulation. The cells remaining in the graafian follicle that has just released the ovum are then stimulated by LH to become a temporary gland called the corpus luteum (yellow body). The corpus luteum then secretes two important hormones that prepare the oviducts and the uterus to receive the ovum.

The oviducts are trumpet-shaped structures, three to five inches long, that lie close to the ovaries and extend to the upper corners of the top of the uterus. It is thought that at the time of ovulation the muscles within the walls of the oviduct begin to contract and create suction to draw the ovum into the tube. The ligaments that support the oviducts from the uterus draw the fingerlike ends of the tube, called fimbria, toward the ovary as a means of directing the ovum into the oviduct (Fig. 4-4).

Oviducts, Fimbria, and Ligaments
Figure 4-4

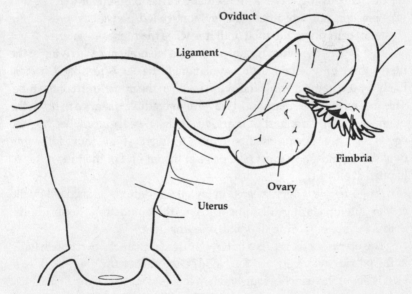

The inside walls of the oviduct are covered with tiny hairlike projections called cilia that create a constant current by beating in a direction that encourages the egg to move toward the uterus. The ova from the right ovary normally enter the right oviduct, and those released from the left side are directed into the left tube. Cases have been recorded that show it is also possible for a crossover to occur, with the oviduct of the right side, for example, moving over to the left ovary to "pick up" an egg.

When the graafian follicle ruptures, a discharge is released with the ova that contain "nurse cells," called cumulus cells. A cumulus is a cloud that is especially billowy looking, with heaped-up masses. That is exactly how these cells look as they surround the egg, helping to sustain it during its journey to the uterus. As the ova passes through the oviduct, the ever-beating cilia partially separate the cumulus from the ovum as the mass passes through the tube.

DOWN TO THE UTERUS

Upon entering the tube, the ovum, with its nurse cells, is moved through the duct by pulsing wavelike muscular contractions similar to those that take place in our intestines. This motion, called peristalsis, presses the cluster of cells down the tube until it reaches the uterus.

In this way, the ovum is transported at a leisurely pace, arriving at the uterus three to seven days after ovulation. If the egg is fertilized, it most likely would happen while the ovum is still in the upper third of the tube. This means that the sperm must travel an incredible distance to reach the ovum—only the strongest can survive the distance required. Because the egg is fertilized during the first twelve to twenty-four hours following ovulation, conception must take place at the far end of the tube if it is to happen at all.

Progesterone, which means "in favor of gestation," is secreted by the corpus luteum during this time, causing the glands that lie inside the oviduct to secrete a fluid that nourishes the ovum.

The uterus, or womb, is a hollow, muscular pear-shaped pouch lying in the pelvic cavity between the bladder and the rectum (Fig. 4-5, Fig. 4-6). It is about three inches long and two inches wide at the top. It becomes narrow at its base, where it is normally about half an inch to one inch across. The size of the uterus varies, depending on the age of the female and her reproductive state.

At birth, a baby's uterus is enlarged due to hormones she receives from her mother while still in the womb. The uterus becomes smaller during childhood because it lacks this hormonal stimulation. As discussed earlier, the estrogens secreted at puberty signal the uterus to grow until it reaches its mature size. After childbearing, it reaches its largest dimensions, then remains large until after a woman experiences menopause, or the cessation of her menstrual cycle.

Female Reproductive System: Side View
Figure 4-5

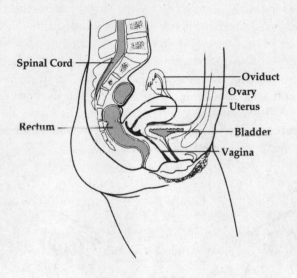

Female Reproductive System: Front View
Figure 4-6

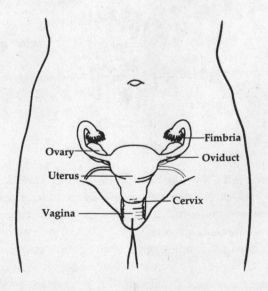

The uterus is divided into three portions (Fig. 4-7). The fundus of the uterus is the upper division, lying at the top between the oviducts. Extremely muscular, it is responsible for the strong contractions that press the baby down through the pelvis during childbirth. Below the fundus lies the body of the uterus. The fundus and the body expand enormously during pregnancy to accommodate the baby's growth. The body of the uterus narrows near its base at a place called the isthmus. The isthmus thins out and lengthens during pregnancy and aids the body of the uterus as it grows. The isthmus is often not considered as a separate part of the womb, but is merely seen as the dividing line between the body of the uterus and the cervix, or neck, of the uterus.

Divisions of the Uterus
Figure 4-7

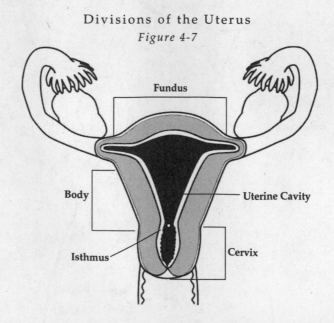

The cervix is the lowest part of the uterus and is attached to the front wall of the vagina. The cervical canal is about an inch long. The cervix has fewer muscle cells than the rest of the uterus and more collagen fibers. Within the canal is a mucous membrane, with glands that secrete a fluid that changes in appearance and chemical composition prior to ovulation.

The uterus is normally maintained in its position by the muscles of the pelvic floor and is capable of a wide range of movement. The only immovable or fixed portion of the uterus is the cervix. The remainder of the uterus is free to expand, contract, tip forwards or backwards, be pushed upwards by a full bladder or downwards by the rectum if it is distended. During lovemaking, the uterus changes its position several times and contracts during the phases of sexual arousal that accompany orgasm.

A fertilized egg, or early embryo, usually implants itself in the body of the uterus a good distance away from the cervix. This is the ideal place for the ovum to attach, because it allows for the greatest degree of expansion and the most developed blood supply.

The two layers that make up the uterus are the myometrium and the endometrium. An outer later, called the perimetrium, covers the womb's external surface (Fig. 4-8).

Layers of the Uterus
Figure 4-8

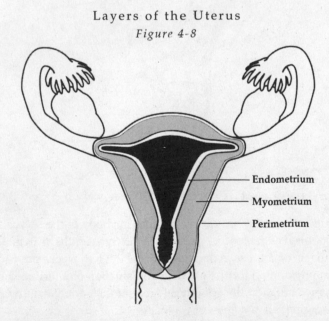

— Endometrium

— Myometrium

— Perimetrium

The myometrium, which means "muscle layer," consists of many interwoven fibers of muscular tissue. It makes up seven-eighths of the thickness of the walls of the uterus and has the capacity to expand greatly in size. There are three layers of muscle. The inner layer is composed of circular fibers. A thick intermediate layer has fibers laid out in a figure-eight pattern surrounding the blood vessels that contract to stop the flow of blood after a baby is born. An outer layer extends lengthwise across the uterus like wide rubber bands. This layer is four times more plentiful in the area of the fundus, to aid it in the expulsion of a baby (Fig. 4-9).

Muscles of the Uterus
Figure 4-9

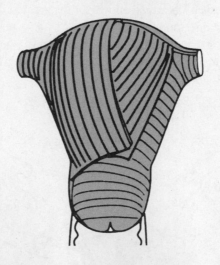

THE BUILD-UP OF THE UTERINE LINING

The endometrium, or "inside layer," lines the body of the uterus and is richly supplied with blood vessels. It is about five-eighths of an inch thick and made up of soft tissue that grows for about two weeks prior to ovulation in preparation for the possible implantation of a fertilized ovum. During menstruation the superficial layer of the endometrium is shed, like the peeling off of a layer of wallpaper.

The menstrual cycle consists of four distinct phases that mainly affect the tissue structure of the endometrium (Fig. 4-10 and 4-11). The regenerative phase begins as soon as menstruation stops and lasts for two days. At this time, the glands and cells that are left start to multiply and rebuild the endometrium. Any blood that remains is absorbed, as in the healing of a wound. The proliferative phase (notice the word *pro-life* here) begins two days after menstruation ceases and lasts until ovulation, for about fourteen days. To proliferate means "to grow rapidly in the production of new cells." This is just what happens as estrogen stimulates the lining of the endometrium to rebuild itself until it is about an eighth of an inch thick.

Monthly Changes of the Uterine Lining
Figure 4-10

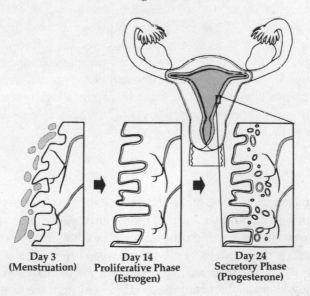

Day 3	Day 14	Day 24
(Menstruation)	Proliferative Phase (Estrogen)	Secretory Phase (Progesterone)

The premenstrual phase, or secretory phase, starts after ovulation. Progesterone secreted from the corpus luteum causes further growth in the endometrium cells, an increase in the blood supply to the lining of the uterus, and the secretion of fluid from glands that have developed in the lining of the uterus. The endometrium reaches a thickness at its peak of about a quarter of an inch. The lining of the uterus actually is a glistening red at this point after having been so well prepared to receive the awaited guest, a fertilized ovum.

The high levels of estrogen and progesterone at this time in the cycle inhibit the release of any more FSH or LH, so that no new primary folli-cles start to mature. Progesterone keeps the uterus quiet by acting on the myometrium, or muscular layer, of the uterus as a precaution against the possible expulsion of a fertilized egg. It also begins to stimulate growth in the ducts of the breasts, which some women experience as tenderness and/or swelling in this area.

When fertilization does not take place, phase four, or the menstrual phase of the cycle, starts. The corpus luteum is active for about ten to twelve days following ovulation, secreting estrogen and progesterone to enable the endometrium to prepare itself to receive a fertilized ovum. When fertilization doesn't occur, the corpus luteum begins to disinte-grate, and the amount of estrogen and progesterone secreted decreases. The corpus luteum ends up as a white scar, called the corpus albicans (white body), eventually becoming a wrinkled indentation on the surface of the ovary. About two days before the end of the normal menstrual cycle, the corpus luteum stops secreting hormones altogether, and the level of estrogen and progesterone sharply falls, bottoming out on about the twenty-sixth day of a thirty-day cycle.

THE LINING IS DISCARDED

When hormonal stimulation of the endometrial lining stops, the cells in this area shrink to about two-thirds of their normal size. About one day before the onset of menstruation, the blood vessels that supply the lining of the uterus are closed off. In the absence of a blood supply, the cells lin-ing the uterus die and separate from the rest of the uterus. These dead cells, along with a small amount of blood released from the capillaries (tiny blood vessels) of the endometrium, are expelled by contractions of the uterus as the menstrual flow (Fig. 4-11). During menstruation a little more than an ounce of body fluid and the same amount of blood leave the uterus in a flow that lasts for about five days. The first menstrual cycle is the menarche, and the last is termed menopause.

An abnormally large amount of menstrual flow is called *menorrha-gia*. This condition can be caused by disorders of the glands that secrete hormones affecting the menstrual cycle, various diseases, or abnormali-ties of the reproductive system. Any excessive bleeding should be reported to your health care provider.

Menstrual Cycle
Figure 4-11

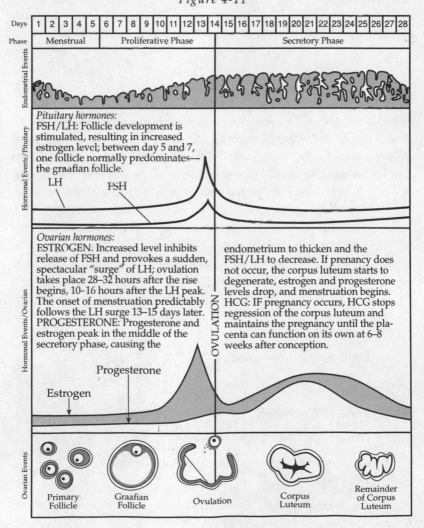

Days	1	2	3	4	5	6	7	8	9	10	11	12	13	14	15	16	17	18	19	20	21	22	23	24	25	26	27	28

Phase: Menstrual | Proliferative Phase | Secretory Phase

Endometrial Events

Hormonal Events/Pituitary

Pituitary hormones:
FSH/LH: Follicle development is stimulated, resulting in increased estrogen level; between day 5 and 7, one follicle normally predominates—the graafian follicle.

LH   FSH

Hormonal Events/Ovarian

Ovarian hormones:
ESTROGEN. Increased level inhibits release of FSH and provokes a sudden, spectacular "surge" of LH; ovulation takes place 28–32 hours after the rise begins, 10–16 hours after the LH peak. The onset of menstruation predictably follows the LH surge 13–15 days later. PROGESTERONE: Progesterone and estrogen peak in the middle of the secretory phase, causing the endometrium to thicken and the FSH/LH to decrease. If prenancy does not occur, the corpus luteum starts to degenerate, estrogen and progesterone levels drop, and menstruation begins. HCG: IF pregnancy occurs, HCG stops regression of the corpus luteum and maintains the pregnancy until the placenta can function on its own at 6–8 weeks after conception.

OVULATION

Progesterone

Estrogen

Ovarian Events

Primary Follicle | Graafian Follicle | Ovulation | Corpus Luteum | Remainder of Corpus Luteum

Amenorrhea is the absence of menstruation. This condition can be primary, meaning that menstruation has never occurred, or secondary. Secondary amenorrhea is normal during pregnancy and lactation. It can also result from poor nutrition, anorexia, stress, intense and prolonged physical exertion, medication, a low percentage of body fat, and hormonal disorders. Primary amenorrhea can result from some of these same conditions or from malformed or underdeveloped reproductive organs. Medical assistance is needed when prolonged amenorrhea exists.

COPING WITH MENSTRUAL CRAMPS

Menstrual cramps are not a figment of the imagination, but are instead linked to real causes. Treatment for painful menstruation has become more effective through the use of antiprostaglandins, which act to inhibit contractions of the uterus. The advantage of using antiprostaglandin medication for normal menstrual cramps is that it can be taken as needed (as opposed to every day with birth control pills or hormones) for as little as one day a month. Prostaglandin inhibitors include: ibuprofen (Motrin, Advil), ketoprofen (Actron), fenoprofen calcium (Nalfon), mefenamic acid (Ponstel), naproxen (Naprosyn), and naproxen sodium (Anaprox, Aleve). Discuss these medications with your health care provider, and be sure that you understand the benefits and risks in taking them.

Other methods of relieving uncomplicated menstrual cramps are:

• using a heating pad.

• massaging the lower abdomen.

• taking a warm bath.

• experiencing orgasm to relieve pelvic congestion.

• doing stretching exercises to relieve tension.

• drinking red raspberry leaf tea; peppermint tea for digestive upset.

• becoming pregnant.

Mild discomfort often accompanies the onset of the menstrual flow. Low back pain, tenderness in the lower abdomen, diarrhea, and cramping of the uterus are not uncommon during the first twenty-four hours. The difference between mild discomfort and painful menstruation is whatever a woman explains it to be. No one outside a woman's body can determine how much pain is present, because pain is a subjective experience that can't be measured like one's heartbeat or temperature.

Dysmenorrhea is the term for painful menstruation. The prostaglandins secreted by the body are the primary culprit behind painful periods. Other possible causes are inflammation of the pelvic cavity or reproductive system, constipation, hormone imbalances, emotional stress, fibroid tumors, endometriosis, and ovarian cysts. The actual causes of painful menstruation are poorly understood at this time, however. If a woman's menstrual cramps are not relieved by mild painkillers or become disruptive to her daily schedule, dysmenorrhea is said to exist.

The two types of dysmenorrhea related to a hormonal imbalance are called spasmatic dysmenorrhea and congestive dysmenorrhea. Spasmatic dysmenorrhea is caused by an imbalance of progesterone, with too much of it being secreted in relation to the level of estrogen. This condition can be treated with hormones and is likely to be less severe after a woman bears a child. It is most common between the ages of fifteen and twenty-five.

PMS ISN'T JUST A STATE OF MIND

Congestive dysmenorrhea is associated with premenstrual syndrome, or PMS. It is probably caused by too much estrogen in relation to progesterone. The symptoms include a feeling of heaviness due to fluid retention in the breasts, ankles, and abdomen. It usually begins during the week prior to the onset of menstruation and can include many other symptoms: headache, breast soreness, a craving for sugary foods, fatigue, depression, irritability, dizziness, complexion changes, and forgetfulness.

The actual causes and best treatments for PMS are still undergoing debate. Some say that it isn't caused by a deficiency of progesterone, but by vitamin or mineral deficiencies, low blood sugar, low thyroid function, poorly functioning prostaglandins, and/or sleep deprivation. Diet and vitamin therapies have relieved the symptoms of PMS for many women. Based on a diet for hypoglycemia (low blood sugar), the therapy recommends whole grains, no caffeine, lots of water, no sugar, and frequent small meals, supplementing with from 300 to 800 milligrams of vitamin B6 daily during the week before the onset of menstruation. Other women have found that their symptoms are only relieved by taking progesterone in its natural form. The hormone is derived from yams or soybeans and made into a powder that can be absorbed from vaginal or rectal suppositories.

The controversy over PMS will continue until accredited institutions perform adequate studies that clearly demonstrate what it is and how best to treat it. Consumers should be careful about taking progesterone or vitamins in large amounts until the effects of such substances on the human body are known. In the meantime, a diet low in sugar and high in calcium seems to help the body cope with hormonal changes before menstruation. Caffeine, alcohol, nicotine, nitrates and nitrites, salt, monosodium glutamate, chocolate, and artificial sweeteners should be avoided as well. Getting the proper amount of rest, eliminating stress, and managing the stress that can't be eliminated are also important ways to decrease the severity of PMS symptoms.

It is estimated that nearly 80 percent of all women experience PMS to some degree. That makes PMS a fact of life for the majority of women, if this is accurate. One of the most effective ways of coping with the mood swings and physical symptoms is to understand our own cycles and realize that the hormonal fluctuations we experience are real.

It is not as if most women are *looking* for excuses to hide behind or gain sympathy. The ovary literally explodes with ovulation each month, and the reproductive system is actively engaged in performing its responsibilities every day. We don't often think about all of the things going on inside us, but we need to accept that what we can't see produces changes that affect our *entire* body.

Our cyclical nature is an integral part of who the Lord created us to be. We can learn creative ways to deal with this aspect of our sexuality. As we look over the complex process of the menstrual cycle, we can either be amazed at the balance of its design or deny the wisdom at work in our bodies; we can be realistic about making plans that fit in with what our bodies are doing at specific times of the month or work at full-steam, only to collapse with fatigue; we can eat nutritious foods that will strengthen our bodies or follow our cravings for junk food that increases premenstrual tension; we can be honest with our husbands about how we're feeling and why or pretend that everything is fine because we don't want to be seen as "the weaker sex."

To live in harmony with the way the Lord has created us means we can acknowledge that our bodies' cycles *do* affect us. We can live with our cycles while consciously helping our bodies cope with the changes we experience from month to month.

MENSTRUATION AND LEVITICAL LAW

When a woman has her regular flow of blood, the impurity of her monthly period will last seven days, and anyone who touches her will be unclean till evening. Anything she lies on during her period will be unclean, and anything she sits on will be unclean. Whoever touches her bed must wash his clothes and bathe with water, and he will be unclean till evening. . . . If a man lies with her and her monthly flow touches him, he will be unclean for seven days; any bed he lies on will be unclean. . . . You must keep the Israelites separate from things that make them unclean, so they will not die in their uncleanness for defiling my dwelling place, which is among them.

LEVITICUS 15:19-21, 24, 31

Today it is difficult to imagine what it was like to be a woman living in the desert, with no running water or flush toilets, no packages of sanitary napkins or tampons, and no soap or deodorant. The Lord in His wisdom gave His people a set of laws, recorded in Leviticus, that comprise the first public health code to be used by a group of people in history. Our Creator, who had made the human body, was intimately familiar with every cell, every process, and every organism. The fifteenth chapter of Leviticus speaks directly to the contaminating properties of bodily discharges; the menstrual flow is included in this category.

It was not until the mid-1800s that Ignaz Semmelweiss discovered the importance of soap in preventing the cross-contamination that results from not washing between examining a person who has just died of an infectious disease and examining another patient. Soap is a relatively new "invention," and the concept of cleanliness in preventing disease was not widely accepted until the 1880s. Dr. Semmelweiss was ridiculed for his theory and was ostracized by his profession. It is often only in retrospect that such discoveries make sense to us. Today we cannot imagine what hospital wards must have been like without antiseptics, clean sheets, and sterile instruments, just as we cannot imagine life without disposable toilet and menstrual paper products.

The menstrual flow is made up of body fluid containing cells that have sloughed off from the endometrium and blood from the capillaries of the uterus lining. This discharge leaves the body in a clean state. Once it becomes exposed to air, however, it becomes an ideal medium for bacteria to grow in.

With no soap to keep the vaginal area cleansed and little water available to even rinse off the menstrual flow, we can easily understand why these verses in Leviticus emphasized the danger inherent in such situations. If we were to be this cautious today about sexually transmitted diseases and their symptoms, we could quickly curtail the rate at which such infections are spread—especially if monogamy also prevailed. AIDS would cease to be a public health menace; genital herpes would be curtailed; and chlamydia and gonorrhea would no longer be making thousands of women sterile each year. The Lord explicitly and clearly informed the Hebrew nation about the dangers of discharges, skin lesions, and sexual relations outside marriage, in specific language.

The laws in Leviticus are further proof of the Lord's sovereign nature. We can read these chapters today and marvel at the way God provided practical help and protection to preserve the health of His people. Now that we understand more about microbiology, we are able to reasonably protect ourselves from many diseases and infections that can be curtailed through proper hygiene. Menstruation is no longer a cause for separation from everyday life and need not be considered a contaminating body condition. Daily bathing or showering with soap and water has made all the difference.

The toxic shock syndrome scare that linked the deaths of women using superabsorbent tampons to a fatal disease reminds us of the power of microorganisms to multiply and devastate. Toxic shock syndrome, or TSS, is a disease caused by a bacteria called staphylococcus aureus. It has been estimated that fifteen out of every one hundred thousand girls and women who are menstruating will get this disease each year.

To prevent TSS, the Food and Drug Administration issued the following guidelines:

- The low risk of getting TSS can be almost entirely eliminated by not using tampons.

- The risk can be reduced by using tampons on and off during the menstrual cycle (such as wearing them during the daytime only) and by not leaving a tampon in for more than four hours at a time.

- About one in every three females who have had TSS get it again and should not wear tampons until more research has been done.

The warning signs of TSS are:

1. sudden fever that is usually 102 degrees or higher, and

2. vomiting or diarrhea.

If these signs should occur during a period, the tampon should be removed and a doctor called right away. Other symptoms include a sudden drop in blood pressure accompanied by dizziness and a rash that looks like a sunburn.

AVOIDING TOXIC SHOCK SYNDROME

If you choose to wear tampons rather than sanitary pads during your period, you can reduce the risk of developing toxic shock syndrome by:

- washing your hands before and after inserting a tampon.

- washing the external genital area twice a day while menstruating.

- not leaving a tampon in place for more than four hours.

- alternating tampon use with sanitary pads for a twenty-four-hour period.

- wearing tampons only when you are flowing heavily.

- avoiding superabsorbent brands of tampons, which are more likely to cause tiny cuts in the skin of the vagina when inserted.

LOVEMAKING AND MENSTRUATION

Though making love during menstruation may be uncomfortable and seem unaesthetic, in a healthy woman there are no medical contraindications to this practice. Many women prefer to not have intercourse when they feel discomfort or are self-conscious about what they consider to be messy or malodorous lovemaking. This is not an ideal situation for a woman to be fully sexually responsive, and each couple needs to be completely frank with one another about their feelings regarding sexual expression during menstruation.

Alternative expressions to intercourse might be preferable—for instance, seminudity instead of full nudity to enhance a woman's feeling of attractiveness. Some couples choose to view menstruation as a break, a time for "courtship activities"—going out for a date, playing Scrabble, or walking in the park hand in hand. All women benefit from having times like this, whether for the purpose of avoiding intercourse during menstruation or not.

Other women experience a heightened desire for lovemaking during their periods, especially when their flow tapers off after the first few days. Be open about your level of interest if this is true for you. If your husband is unresponsive, find out how he feels about making love during this phase of your cycle. Your husband may just not be informed enough to know that bathing before going to bed sufficiently cleanses you and that on light days there is only a trace of blood. He may be pleasantly surprised to discover that this phase of the month can be a time of increased responsiveness for *both* of you. It is important to remember, however, that pregnancy can result from lovemaking during menstruation among fertile women, unlikely as it may seem.

Be confident in determining your own preferences and needs as a couple in this area, knowing that there is no single "correct" way to approach the subject. What matters is how the two of you feel.

The rhythms of regeneration, proliferation, ovulation, the premenstrual phase, and menstruation form a pattern that repeats itself several hundred times during a woman's fertile years. These cycles make up an intricately designed framework within which our other reproductive functions may be creatively expressed and experienced.

> In the life of each of us, I said to myself,
> there is a place remote and islanded,
> and given to endless regret or secret happiness.
>
> SARAH ORNE JEWETT

Chapter Review

Personal Reflections

1. Living with a cyclical nature can be:

2. When I'm experiencing distressing PMS symptoms, God's strength is especially evident to me when:

3. My best coping strategies for PMS and menstrual discomfort are:

4. Stress affects my ability to cope with hormonal ups and downs by making me more vulnerable to:

5. Getting the rest I need is particularly important at times of the month when I am:

6. When I feel frustrated with the ongoing realities of my sexual design, I think God helps me most as I:

Related Bible Passages for Further Study

- Psalm 5:1-3

- Psalm 17:6-8

- Psalm 18:30-33

- Psalm 28:7-9

- Romans 8:37-39

- 2 Corinthians 4:16-18

$\mathcal{G}$IVING AND RECEIVING THE GIFT

Sexual freedom comes into its own in a life of fidelity.
A personal relationship, sustained in commitment and sup-
ported by a faith that God intends permanence for marriage, is
the best environment for sexual freedom. For here alone sexual
experience can find the uncluttered trust and personal security
to grow into the adventure of sexual discovery.
Sexual freedom is the liberty to explore the possibilities
of sexual intimacy in the openness of trust, the security of
unreserved acceptance, and the assurance of fidelity.[1]

LEWIS B. SMEDES

What a lovely, pleasant sight you are, my love, as we lie here
on the grass, shaded by cedar trees and spreading firs.

SONG OF SONGS 1:16-17 NLT

Women's sexuality is not something we can understand in merely mechanical terms. For us, sexual arousal cannot be achieved the way a computer can be programmed to perform a certain function. Though a host of popular books attempt to provide step-by-step instructions for "satisfying sexual success," real-life experience tells us it is pretty ridiculous to expect the same reactions every time we want to make love.

Our sexual responsiveness varies with the time of day, the time of the month, the time of year, and the time of life. It is affected by our hormones, physical health, emotional status, personal circumstances, stress level, and situations we have encountered in the last ten minutes and the last ten years. Sometimes arousal seems to take place almost automatically, initiated by the whisper of a word, the catching of a glance, a whiff of aftershave. At other times, extended caressing and stroking produce . . . absolutely nothing.

It seems we cannot reliably predict our responses any more than we can forecast the weather. This is why the whole idea of a magical, foolproof kind of foreplay totally misses the mark. There just is not one "right way" to proceed every time we want to be sexually expressive with our husbands. Instead, there are countless variations to be tried and tested. And later tried again.

Each one of us needs to determine what works best in our own relationships, regarding our own bodies, with our own husbands. This means everything—positions used for intercourse, how best to reach an orgasm, what clothes to wear to bed (if any), what perfume to wear, when to refrain from lovemaking, and how frequently to engage in it.

Interestingly, the Bible is remarkably silent on these things. We are not told what to touch and how to touch, how to kiss or where to kiss, or how to make love to a man. The Lord has given us the basic rules, which He fully expects us to abide by. But beyond this, it is safe to assume we are free to use our imaginations. So, in order to relax and respond in mutually satisfying ways with our mates, the pressure to perform according to someone else's mythical sexual standard must be tossed out, removed, abandoned, forgotten. Forever.

THE ULTIMATE EXPERTS

Many books and articles available today tell us in painstaking detail how to drive a man wild in bed, how many children to have, or how to achieve the best orgasm. Each month, countless magazines and talk shows announce the latest trends, trouble spots, and top ten "how to have a happier sex life" secrets. Some of the information can be educational. But it can also make us feel that somehow we just aren't measuring up to what we should be as women. I don't know about you, but I am tired of being told what I should be doing differently (or better) in the bedroom.

For this reason, I want you to consider *The Christian Woman's Guide to Sexuality* as a resource only. If it enables you to live life more passionately as a woman, a wife, and a follower of Christ, that's great. I wrote this book to encourage you in the Lord, as a way of saying, "Keep going! Don't give up! You can do it!" But if you are not in agreement with me or cannot relate to something I say, continue praying. And please don't stop here.

The person who decides what activities are pleasing to the Lord and right for your life is *you*, along with your husband. As a couple, you are the ultimate experts concerning how you approach the sexual aspect of your relationship. But don't forget—your husband does not live inside your mind, and he cannot fully comprehend the way you experience your sexuality. *You are the best authority on what is sexually arousing to you.*

Perhaps one of the reasons you bought this book was to better understand your sexuality. Maybe you are getting married soon, and someone recommended that you do some reading before your wedding. Or you could be tired of what most of the media has to offer and are looking for a biblical perspective that will help you make sense of your love life. Regardless of your reason, I am glad that you think your husband's and your sexual happiness is worth your time and energy.

By sharing your reactions and perceptions with your husband, you will enhance his ability to understand and meet your sexual needs. The same thing is true for him. How does your husband experience his sexuality? What are his reactions and perceptions regarding your love life? Are you familiar with his thoughts, feelings, concerns, expectations, struggles, and desires in this area?

The most important part of human anatomy affecting sexuality is the brain. Our minds empower our bodies to be sexually responsive through the way our nervous system functions. Research even suggests that the grand finale of lovemaking—orgasm—takes place to a large degree in our minds rather than in our pelvis. This is why it is important to realize that how we *think* influences how we *respond* to lovemaking. Our minds have a tremendous impact on how we interpret and respond to sexual arousal.

This is true for both sexes. Because there are several similarities between our husbands' sexuality and our own, it is possible for us to identify with a certain amount of what they experience (Fig. 5-1).

Physiology of Sexual Arousal and Lovemaking:
Characteristics of Both Sexes
Figure 5-1

— MUSCULAR TENSION

— INCREASED BLOOD FLOW TO BREASTS AND GENITALS

— CHANGES IN PULSE, BLOOD PRESSURE, AND BREATHING RATE

— RELEASE OF SECRETIONS FROM THE GENITALS

— MUSCULAR CONTRACTIONS ACCOMPANYING ORGASM

— SIMILAR ORGANS FOR RECEIVING AND TRANSMITTING SEXUAL STIMULI:
    THE PENIS AND THE CLITORIS

Beyond these similarities, it is clear that our husbands' sexual responses substantially differ from our own. To draw closer to our husbands and respond to their sexual makeup with sensitivity and honesty, we need their input to help bridge the gap between us.

H. Norman Wright writes:

For women sex is only one means of intimacy out of many and not always the best one. For many men, sex is the only expression of intimacy.

Men tend to compress the meaning of intimacy into the sex act, and when they don't have that outlet, they can become frustrated and upset. Why? Because they're cut off from the only source of closeness they know.

Men are interested in closeness and intimacy, but they have different ways of defining and expressing it. Here again is an area where men and women need to talk, listen, and understand the other person's view of sex and in some way learn to speak the other person's language.[2]

Needless to say, this can be challenging. Understanding the way a man thinks and communicates about his sexuality can be as difficult as deciphering hieroglyphics. Unlike most men, for example, we haven't necessarily been conditioned, biologically or culturally, to find naked bodies belonging to the opposite sex particularly enticing. We may tend to avert our eyes from museum sculptures that display the obvious difference between us and them in marble. Some of us might roll our eyes in mock disgust if a muscular man wearing next to nothing strutted by us on the beach.

The majority of males, however, have learned from an early age to think of scantily clothed female bodies as attractive objects of sexual desire. I am not suggesting here that girls need more exposure to male nudity. I am just making the point that many women are somewhat repulsed by their husbands' intimate body parts initially, if not permanently, in part because of the way we are taught to think about men's sexuality.

As Christian women, we can discover ways to respond to our husbands' bodies with as much pleasure as they respond to ours. Though they may have a head start, much of their conditioning is less than positive. We can begin from a biblical basis (see chapter 1 if you need a quick review) and learn from there.

Understanding the sexual language our husbands "speak" allows us to talk to them about our joys and frustrations with greater clarity, to take things less personally when they seem ready for lovemaking much sooner than we are, and to appreciate the fact that they communicate sexually in a strikingly different way than we do.

"MY LOVER IS MINE. . . ."

The Bible encourages us to view our husbands' sexuality as if it were part of our own—because it is. First Corinthians states: "The wife's body does not belong to her alone but also to her husband. [Keep reading!] In the same way, the husband's body does not belong to him alone but also to his wife" (1 Corinthians 7:4).

In Song of Songs, the Shulammite woman expresses this another way when she exults, "My lover is mine and I am his" (2:16). This is incredible. We can be as receptive to responding to our husband's anatomy and sexuality as he is to ours. It is a marital delight we can share *together*. The needs of one are designed to be balanced by the needs of the other.

For many years, the reciprocal nature of marital sexuality has been underestimated. This is no less true today, even though we live after the sexual revolution. We may be so focused upon giving ourselves to our husbands that we fail to recognize that receiving the gift of their sexuality is an important part of marriage, too. This servant attitude reached its zenith during the Victorian era, which saw it as a woman's duty to be on the receiving end of her husband's passions and to bear the children that resulted. "Good" women were discouraged from enjoying sex.

We can be thankful that era is over. We acknowledge that lovemaking is for the purpose of receiving, as well as giving, pleasure. In fact, the best part of making love for many husbands is knowing that their wives enjoy being sexually aroused by their masculine physiques. Sexual ecstasy is not nearly as fulfilling when the experience is one-sided, so it seems safe to assume that most men find it deeply satisfying to be married to women who react to their masculinity and sexual overtures with sincere affirmation and approval.

So allowing ourselves to receive sexual pleasure becomes one of the best ways to give sexual pleasure to our husbands. Mutuality in lovemaking means that there is an open interchange taking place, back and forth, as two bodies are joined as one. What happens sexually is done or felt by each toward the other. Isn't it amazing to think that the Lord built this concept of mutuality right into our minds and bodies? He seems to have intended us to desire it and to be fulfilled by it in our marital relationships when He created us.

PLAY ME A LOVE SONG

Our bodies are like instruments tuned to play love songs in harmony together. Each of us carries a melody that is unique and different from all the rest. A symphony is held within our bodies, waiting to be expressed at appropriate moments within the exclusive bond of married love. Mike Mason described this phenomenon perfectly when he wrote:

> What great and profound truths, what startling confessions and intimacies pass between the hearts of a man and woman when they are in bed together! It may have taken several hours of sensitive closeness and patience, or tentative explorations, and literally hundreds of kisses and hugs and strokings and subtle contacts and pressures between the two bodies of wife and husband before they were able to enter into a place of such extraordinary honesty and simplicity and naked safety, into that still point of absolute trust at the heart of the sanctuary of sex.[3]

The songs our bodies long to sing together were created to be fully expressed only when we feel cherished, protected, and safe. But there is still a degree of risk involved in sharing our hearts and bodies with our husbands, making it difficult at times to play—or hear—the music. This is true for a number of different reasons.

Sexual intimacy makes us vulnerable. When we share our bodies with our husbands, we are inviting them to share parts of ourselves we keep guarded and hidden from all others. The nature of our sexuality significantly differs from our husbands in this respect. Making love requires our bodies to be intimately entered, with lovemaking taking place on the inside of us rather than just on the outside. This produces feelings of vulnerability, because we are sharing a part of ourselves that we need to protect and guard from others. It takes time and trust to become vaginally responsive during lovemaking.

Sexual intimacy connects lovemaking with other aspects of our reproductive design. We cannot escape the facts of our physical structure when we make love. The same passageway that we menstruate and give birth through is the organ with which we hold and caress the penis during lovemaking. If we are uncomfortable with other sexual functions of our bodies, we also may feel ill at ease during lovemaking. Making peace with the way God has designed our bodies places us on more comfortable terms with the full complement of our sexual design (see chapter 3).

Sexual intimacy reveals the physiological realities associated with our husbands' bodies. During lovemaking, there is no getting around the reality of how the Lord designed the male body. Being comfortable with the physical realities of one another's genitals, including the way they look, function, smell, and feel fosters sexual intimacy between married lovers. Our husbands' bodies are likely to seem surprisingly foreign to us initially, causing us to look away or avoid intimately touching them. As we mature, though, we can explore the masculine features of our husbands' sexuality and learn to be as comfortable and familiar with their bodies as we are with our own.

Sexual intimacy reminds us of our creatureliness. When we engage in sexual activity, our body chemistry changes in ways that can make us feel animal-like and instinctive, as opposed to being "civilized" and in control of what we do and say every moment. The physiology of lovemaking results in a feeling of abandonment and physical excitement unlike any other human experience.

The more we try to maintain control over how our bodies respond during sexual arousal, the less likely they are to be aroused at all. But our socialization has taught us to be in control of sexual situations rather than following the dictates of our bodies. And that's normally a good thing. Self-control is necessary, evidence that we can respect our boundaries and live in harmony with others. When it comes to lovemaking within marriage, however, open sexual expression can become remarkably beautiful when we surrender our control over our physiological responses—and the uninhibited expression of our sexuality is often full of surprises.

Sexual intimacy is designed to be mutual, reciprocal, and complementary. Most women do not feel sexually responsive to their husbands 100 percent of the time. If we did, how would we ever manage to get anything done? Our days are filled with busyness. So when the end of the day arrives, it often becomes easier to satisfy our husbands' sexual needs rather than taking the time and energy to become aroused ourselves. Many women would prefer a back rub or a nice long evening of hugs to the excitement of lovemaking after a long, busy day. And that is okay. But if this becomes the norm, it may be time to try something new.

Sexual intimacy often results in unpredictable outcomes. When we experience a state of sexual arousal, we are liable to say and do things that can seem embarrassing or ridiculous later. If we want lovemaking to be expressive and playful—as well as to be an exclusive bond we share with our husbands outside the demands and stress of our everyday activities—privacy is essential. A good lock on the bedroom door and soft music playing in the background offer a sense of security when there are others living in the house. It is especially important not to say things to our husbands later that make fun of their sexual responses. It is also wise to avoid sharing the intimate details of our sex lives with anyone except our husbands. These are a few examples of ways privacy and trust can be lovingly developed.

Sexual intimacy takes us beyond ourselves. Making love is an adventurous experience each time we participate in it. That is because lovemaking involves personal risk as it unites us with our husbands. The biblical reality of what it means to become "one flesh" is mysterious. At times it even seems almost supernatural. It can be difficult to tell where the "I" ends and the "you" begins. Through lovemaking, two separate individuals are transformed into one flesh, inexplicably, and the pleasure we receive from this experience seems equal to the pleasure we give. Within marriage our sexuality finds its proper expression as we use it for the purpose for which it was created.

Sexual intimacy is enhanced when boundaries are respected. Sharing sexual intimacy requires mutual respect for the ground rules. Over the course of marriage, our union's boundaries will be tested. The degree to which they are respected will depend on the choices we make. Daily. When sexual boundaries are respected, marital intimacy has a chance to grow beyond us into something spectacularly rich, satisfying, and fruitful. When these rules are broken, the physical, emotional, and spiritual intimacy we share with our husbands is harmed. Pornography, emotional affairs (alien bonding), and adultery are examples of out-of-bounds activities that can kill a marriage. Stay away from these self-destructive behaviors if you want to keep your love life strong, resilient, trusting, and healthy.

MOVING TOWARD MUTUAL UNDERSTANDING

In summary, our beliefs, values, and attitudes about sexuality have a tremendous impact on how we feel about our bodies and our husbands' bodies. Our emotions, in turn, directly affect our ability to give and receive sexual pleasure.

To demonstrate this more clearly, try to imagine what happens within your body when your husband gives you a tender kiss that has more than a hint of passion in it. Add to this the sensation of his hand stroking the back of your neck and his soft cheek brushing against yours as he whispers, "I love you, honey." In and of themselves, these combined actions can produce terrific sensations and act as a prelude to lovemaking. But, since the circumstances surrounding this behavior are not stated, how could we possibly tell where things might be headed?

What if he had kissed you just as you were about to hop out of the car on your way to a dentist appointment? How might your reaction differ if all of your children were watching from the table as you were getting ready to serve dinner? Or if you had just cuddled up together at a hotel on a romantic weekend away from the kids? As you can see, the circumstances surrounding the kiss—and how you feel about them—play a large part in determining your body's responses to your husband's affection.

Because we filter our physical responses to sexual intimacy through our thoughts and emotions, our minds hold the key to how we perceive our body's ability to be sexually responsive. An inability to be sexually aroused, for both women and men, is caused much more often by a neutralizing emotional reaction to lovemaking than it is by a lack of hormonal stimulation, underdeveloped genitalia, or disturbances of the nervous system.

Each of us experiences sexuality in ways as special and individually unique as we are. The 1-2-3 approach to sexual intimacy never works out well in the long run, because the patterns of our responses fluctuate unpredictably across the long span of life's changing seasons. By learning about human sexuality from a Christ-centered viewpoint that matures right along with us, we grow in our understanding of what promotes satisfying sexual intimacy and brings us enduring satisfaction.

> Sex was not invented in a dark alley behind a porno shop. It was made in heaven—where purity reigns. As Christians, we must look at sex through the eyes of God. Despite the bad press given it by misguided believers, sex is God's gift to humanity. In marriage, let us celebrate sex. May husband and wife never be ashamed to enjoy together what God was not ashamed to create. [4]
>
> RANDY C. ALCORN

Chapter Review

Personal Reflections

1. Telling my husband about what pleases me sexually is easier when:

2. Thinking of myself as the person who knows the most about what is sexually pleasing to me gives me the confidence to:

3. At times my husband's sex drive is difficult to understand unless I consider:

4. I am most/least interested in receiving the gift of my sexuality if:

5. Sexual intimacy for me and my husband means:

6. If I could ask God two things about His design for mutuality within our sexual relationship, they would be:

Related Bible Passages for Further Study

- Psalm 8:3-5

- Proverbs 5:15-19

- Song of Songs 3:8-17

- Matthew 19:4-6

- 1 Corinthians 6:18–7:1-5

- 1 Thessalonians 4:1-4

$\mathcal{W}$ELCOMING YOUR HUSBAND

Our human sexuality, our maleness and femaleness,
is not just an accidental arrangement of the human species,
not just a convenient way to keep the human race going.
No, it is at the center of our true humanity. We exist
as male and female in relationship. Our sexualness,
our capacity to love and be loved, is intimately
related to our creation in the image
of God. What a high view
of human sexuality![1]

RICHARD J. FOSTER

I t seemed as if she had waited for this night forever. As she slipped on her silky nightgown, she dreamed of being held in her husband's arms and the intimate ways he would express his love for her. The picture in her mind was a combination of scenes from the movies she had seen and the books she had read with fascination over the years. Songs from the wedding drifted through her mind while she dabbed her neck with perfume and brushed her hair. She imagined her husband waiting in the room beyond—he was still a mystery to her even though she felt closer to him than any other person she had ever known. Would he find her body pleasing? What would it feel like to make love to this man? How would their relationship change over time? How could she possibly grow to love him more in the years ahead if she felt so much love tonight? Two weeks alone on this beach on the Caribbean! She felt overwhelmed by happiness as she opened the door to walk into this aspect of her life she had been anticipating for so long. . . .

THE MYTH OF INSTANT SEXUAL HAPPINESS

What did you imagine would be awaiting this young bride on her honeymoon and in the years ahead? Only in fantasy would one expect her *every* hope, *every* desire, and *every* secret longing to be fulfilled. What we see in movies or read about in romance novels often leads us to think we should expect the same thing immediately after we try it for the first time ourselves. In reality, most women discover that lovemaking is initially disappointing compared to the romantic portrayals of sexual intimacy at the local cinemaplex.

Developing a satisfying love life requires communication and commitment, time and energy, patience and respect, tenderness and understanding—based upon a foundation of truth as we live within God's boundaries for our lives. Making love is an art we learn gradually, over a lifetime, as our bodies relax and become familiar with our husbands' bodies, as two distinctly different personalities blend together and grow, year by year by year, to complement one another. This is costly. Pretending that it is not perpetuates an imaginary ideal that can make us feel inadequate when our expectations are not met.

The true goal of sexual sharing is to *know* our husbands, as the Hebrew word *yadah* implies, through becoming one flesh with them. A biblical approach to sexual intimacy emphasizes this goal over every other. In determining what we want to achieve when we make love with our husbands, it is the primary reason for our sexual sharing. All others pale in comparison. And some do not matter at all.

Sexual pleasure in and of itself is only superficially gratifying, leaving our deepest needs for intimacy and safety unfulfilled. If we are to give and receive the gift of our sexuality as the God-made aspect of our lives it is, we must try to find a balance between complete self-absorption and total selflessness. Both extremes impede sexual intimacy and transform sexual sharing into a dissatisfying, empty experience.

By exposing popular sexual myths, learning information on the anatomy and physiology of sexual arousal, and moving away from a goal-oriented "sexual performance" model, we find greater freedom to enjoy sexual intimacy with our husbands regardless of the length of time we have been married.

Myth #1: Lovemaking is always more enjoyable for men than it is for women. It takes time for a woman to learn how to complement, rather than match, her husband's sexuality. In discovering how her body responds to her husband's body, a woman can find an almost endless variety of ways to make love creatively and pleasurably. Lovemaking is a learned skill. It is developed and enhanced through experience instead of inherited or acquired by instinct. A man and wife actually *teach each other* how to respond to one another's bodies and how to make their sexual relationship mutually satisfying.

Women have been created with the ability to enjoy lovemaking as much as men do, but there is a difference. Lovemaking for the majority of men is almost automatically enjoyable, whereas women normally require more time to become comfortable with their bodies and learn what works and what doesn't during lovemaking. Time, energy, and motivation are required to understand the art of sexual responsiveness.

Lovemaking is often initially uncomfortable for women, as the hymen that partially covers the entrance to the vagina is gradually stretched to accommodate a man's penis. And anxiety or nervousness can cause the muscles of the pelvic floor to become tense, making sex uncomfortable, until a woman learns how to creatively release and use these muscles responsively during intercourse.

New sensations are experienced that can be confusing and even alarming at first as a woman learns to relax and yield her body to lovemaking. Many women are surprised to discover that the vagina is a tender and sensitive organ that is not necessarily as responsive to stimulation as the clitoris is. The muscles surrounding the vagina, termed the pubococcygeus or PC group, are believed to be more sensitive to pressure than vaginal tissue is in terms of their ability to convey pleasurable sensations during lovemaking.

The responsiveness of the PC group is directly related to their strength and flexibility. The strength of the PC group can be promoted by doing pelvic floor exercises (see chapter 13). The PC muscles' ability to relax and contract may be self-taught by discovering how these muscles work.

Some women find that a particular area of the vagina is capable of producing pleasing sensations when pressure is applied to it during lovemaking or when their husbands touch them there. This area, about the size of a dime, lies just behind the urethra on the front wall of the vagina and feels like a sponge. When stimulated, it enlarges and grows

Map of Sexual Response
Figure 6-1

FEMININE RESPONSE

EXCITEMENT/ arousal	PLATEAU/ pleasuring	ORGASM/ release	RESOLUTION/ recovery
External Signs			
- Clitoris becomes larger - Outer lips open, flatten - Inner lips swell, darken - Nipples become erect - Breasts become larger	- Clitoris withdraws under its hood - Inner lips turn red, enlarging about one minute prior to orgasm - Pelvis moves rhythmically - Muscles become tense	- No noticeable change in external genitals - Facial muscles become tense - Gasping may occur	- External genitals return to normal size and color - Skin may perspire - Body relaxes - Breasts and nipples return to normal state
Internal Signs			
- Uterus rises in pelvis - Vaginal lining lubricates	- Pulse, breathing rate, and blood pressure become elevated - Inner 2/3 of vagina widens - Outer 1/3 of vagina swells and tightens, forming the orgasmic platform - Uterus rises higher	- Pelvic floor contracts 3 to 12 times - Uterus contracts rhythmically - Heart and breathing rates rise - Entire body responds with pleasure	- Vagina relaxes, thins out - Uterus drops back into normal position overlying bladder - Cervix drops into seminal pool to encourage conception

to the size of a nickel or a quarter. Women who have strong PC muscles bring this area into better contact with the penis by tensing their pelvic floor during lovemaking. Since this "urethral sponge" responds best to deep pressure, lovemaking positions can be used that enable the penis to

Map of Sexual Response
Figure 6-1

MASCULINE RESPONSE

EXCITEMENT/ arousal	PLATEAU/ pleasuring	ORGASM/ release	RESOLUTION/ recovery
External Signs			
- Penis becomes erect as it fills with blood - Scrotum rises, thickens	- Penis becomes darker, swells - Scrotum becomes thicker - Muscles tense, pelvis moves rhythmically - Pre-ejaculatory fluid drips from penis	- Penis contracts rhythmically, expels semen - Facial muscles tense, gasping occurs	- Erection subsides - Scrotum thins out, droops - Muscles relax - Skin may perspire
Internal Signs			
- No significant changes	- Testes become larger - Pulse, breathing, and blood pressure elevate - Prostate and seminal vesicles contract prior to ejaculation	- Entire seminal duct system contracts - Pelvic floor tightens - Pulse, breathing, and blood pressure rise more - Feels pleasure concentrated in genital area	- Testes return to normal size, drop - Relief is felt as blood leaves genital area

apply greater pressure to this area: rear entry, woman above, and man above, with a woman's knees brought toward her chest or a pillow used under her hips.

Sexual expression rooted and grounded in love can be very fulfilling, even when lovemaking is awkward, humorous, or unexpectedly embarrassing. Each encounter can be a new revelation rather than an end in itself, a fresh look at the person with whom you have made a covenant to share life's journey. Perfection is not the goal, because being the "best" is not what a woman is aiming for. Love, the kind that flows from a heart that has received much from God, is the purpose and the end to which we are called within marriage.

Myth #2:"Vaginal" orgasm is more fulfilling, more complete, more feminine, or more mature than "clitoral" orgasm. This belief can be traced to Sigmund Freud, the controversial creator of psychoanalysis. He believed that any orgasm resulting from directly touching the clitoris was "childish" due to its association with genital exploration during infancy and later in masturbation. He stated that it is only when a woman grows up and graduates from her earlier levels of sexual experience that she becomes capable of achieving the "mature" kind of orgasm Freud associated with sexual intercourse.

There are several problems with Freud's theory. In studying human sexuality, researchers have identified four phases of sexual response. These are defined as the excitement phase, characterized by arousal; the plateau phase (pleasuring); orgasm (release); and the resolution phase (recovery). Figure 6-1 outlines these phases and the physical events associated with them. Notice the differences and the similarities between the sexual responses of males and females and how the Lord has designed our bodies to correspond with our husbands'. You can also see that the characteristics of a woman's orgasm consist of a combination of fairly predictable physical activities. These activities take place with varying intensity from woman to woman and within the same woman at different times.

While some women may never have an orgasm and feel quite satisfied in their sexual relationships, other have found that having an orgasm is one of the most physically enjoyable aspects of sexual sharing. Whether a woman has an orgasm through vaginal or clitoral stimulation is beside the point. Lovemaking is to be mutually pleasing and beneficial between husband and wife; the Bible is not explicit about the specifics. We are not meant to compare ourselves against a "standard model" of how to achieve an orgasm, and the Lord has clearly given most women the ability to experience this phase of sexual response, if they so desire. This is a matter for couples to discuss privately so they can develop an awareness of one another's preferences and needs.

There is no discernible difference between an orgasm produced by stimulating the vagina and one that results from clitoral stimulation. Most women have a preference, but this seems to be purely a personal matter. The differences are subjective, a matter of opinion, and quite frankly, nobody else's business.

Myth #3: Having an orgasm at the same time as one's husband during lovemaking is the best way to achieve an orgasm. Herbert Miles in his excellent book *Sexual Happiness in Marriage* states that in his surveys of sexual behavior only 13.7 percent of the couples that he studied reported that they regularly had an orgasm at the same time. The vast majority of couples seem to prefer experiencing this phase of sexual response at different times.

This is likely due to the fact that having an orgasm is an intensely personal experience, and it is difficult to focus on one's partner during that time. Also, keeping track of one's "timing" can be terribly distracting, with each partner thinking *Is it happening yet?* instead of abandoning himself or herself to the joys of lovemaking.

A sense of oneness during lovemaking is not merely the result of performing sexual acrobatics. It is produced by an intense desire to pleasure one's partner. Once again, *it is self-defeating to try to live up to someone else's ideas of what "good sex" is, because we fail to discover our own uniquely personal ways of expressing our sexuality.* What is meaningful and special to one woman might seem boring or shocking to another.

Having an orgasm at the same time is not the "best" way of achieving an orgasm for all couples. For the 13.7 percent of the couples who said it was in Miles's study, this indeed was an enjoyable aspect of lovemaking. But we should avoid the perspective that what makes us feel best will also be what is "best" for others.

Myth #4: Lovemaking should last as long as possible if intercourse is to be truly fulfilling. This belief is probably related to the idea that it is best for a woman to have an orgasm during intercourse or for a couple to experience orgasm at the same time. Since many women require fairly direct stimulation of the clitoris in order to have an orgasm, lovemaking must take place over an extended period to sufficiently stimulate the nervous tissue of the clitoris. When a couple is focused on this "goal" to the exclusion of genuine enjoyment during lovemaking, the experience can become one of work rather than play.

The "average" male reaches the point of ejaculation within the first two to four minutes of lovemaking. For a man to partake in extended lovemaking, he may have to forego a great deal of pleasuring beforehand. When he does make love, if he is emotionally as well as physically aroused, he usually must think of something else (other than his wife or the pleasure that he feels) in order to avoid having an orgasm.

How strange it is that lovemaking is often turned into an athletic event to determine if a man can "go the distance" while performing like a superlover and at the same time keeping his mind *off* his wife. It is his wife that he needs to be thinking about, not playing a mind game that transports him away from a sense of oneness with his partner. When a man has an ejaculation the instant he starts making love, some training is in order. But for the man who wants to make love freely, why should he have to live up to some sort of image that forces him to distance himself from his wife during lovemaking?

The majority of time that most couples spend in sexual sharing takes place throughout the pleasuring or plateau phase of sexual response rather than during intercourse. Characterized by caressing, kissing, rubbing, squeezing, and stroking, this phase creates an emotional openness and often results in a couple moving ahead to intercourse. It is as if the Lord designed us with a built-in need as women that would require us to have a time of physical closeness and skin-to-skin contact with our husbands prior to being able to experience sexual release through orgasm.

The extensive amount of touching and fondling that takes place during pleasuring promotes bonding, or feelings of attachment, between a wife and her husband. During this phase, a woman becomes increasingly more able to relax her body and enjoy pleasurable sexual sensations. (See Figure 6-2.) This is partially because stroking the skin enhances the autonomic nervous system's ability to counteract stress, thereby allowing blood to flow into the genitals.

When the plateau phase produces an atmosphere of intimacy as well as heightening sexual arousal, intercourse becomes the natural extension of lovemaking rather than an end in itself. When the "act" of intercourse becomes the goal of all sexual sharing and all or most sexual encounters between a husband and wife, it is possible for a couple to miss out on the joys and satisfaction that accompany the pleasuring phase. *When the pressure to perform according to a mythical standard is removed, a couple is free to become more creative, expressive, and confident in the sexual aspects of their relationship.*

Typical Pattern of Sexual Response
Figure 6-2

EXCITEMENT PHASE	PLATEAU PHASE	ORGASM PHASE	RESOLUTION PHASE
Main Characteristic: *Arousal*	Main Characteristic: *Pleasuring*	Main Characteristic: *Orgasm*	Main Characteristic: *Recovery*
Sign in Male: *erection*	Intercourse may proceed at any time.	Sign in Male: *ejaculation*	This phase is reversible for many women.
Sign in Female: *lubrication*	This phase usually makes up the majority of lovemaking time.	Sign in Female: contractions of the pelvic floor muscles	Most men experience a period that does not allow them to become erect, called the refractory period.

...... : female

_____ : male

Orgasmic contractions

Arousal in the male is approaching "the point of no return."

Male reaches the point of "ejaculatory inevitability"

Women may resume sexual response cycle at any time.

Males require at least a 10–30 minute rest before resuming lovemaking.

This diagram represents a typical sexual response pattern for men and women. Many variations in the length and intensity of each phase are possible. What is most important is to learn to please one another through mutually satisfying sexual sharing.

Myth #5: Deep thrusting of the penis is an important aspect of intercourse. This, of course, is not necessarily true. Many women find that the most sexually responsive parts of their anatomy are the clitoris, the external portion of the vagina (approximately the first two inches), the PC muscles, and the breasts.

When a woman becomes sexually aroused, it is likely that the outer third of her vagina will swell, causing it to become "tighter" and more restricted in diameter. This creates what is known as an *orgasmic platform*. (See Figure 6-3.) There is a dual purpose behind this physiological event. The tightening that takes place allows a woman to grip the penis more firmly while experiencing greater pleasure during lovemaking, and a seal is formed so that when semen is deposited in the vagina, there will be a better chance of it remaining there to promote conception.

Orgasmic Platform / Seminal Pool
Figure 6-3

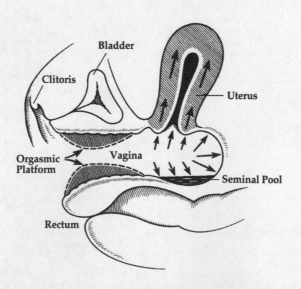

When the penis is forcefully thrust deeply into the vagina without a woman's guidance, there may be very little satisfaction in lovemaking; when movements of the penis are directed toward stimulating sexually responsive areas, there tends to be greater friction exerted against the orgasmic platform and the urethral sponge. Another advantage to a woman providing feedback for her husband during (or after) lovemaking is that she can obtain better contact with the clitoris if she finds this area is more sexually responsive than vaginal stimulation alone. By using a variety of positions, pelvic movements, and rhythms, a woman may be pleasantly surprised by her degree of responsiveness.

The rhythm of lovemaking, the depth of penetration, and the length of time spent making love with one's husband will vary with a woman's mood, level of sexual desire, the setting, the time of the month, the amount of energy she has, and the ability she has to communicate her needs to her husband.

Lovemaking need not always be cautious, slow, or concentrated on stimulating specific areas. In fact, there are times when it is terrific to get quite carried away. Since we have been created with the ability to experience such variety in this area of our lives, why always settle for a heavy-duty approach to lovemaking when it can become more like an intimate conversation?

Myth #6: Men have a greater "sex drive" than women. Notice the period that lies at the end of that sentence. That little bit of punctuation is what makes it a myth. It is not true that men have a greater "sex drive," *period.* Men's and women's bodies have been designed to be affected by thoughts and feelings, culture and environment, values and beliefs, lifestyles and attitudes. While it is often true that men have a greater desire to express their sexuality through intercourse than women do, it is equally true that many women have a greater need to express their sexuality through caressing and nongenital forms of sexual sharing than their husbands do.

It is easy to adopt an outlook that views only intercourse as the end-all and be-all of sexual interaction. After all, that is exactly what our culture has conditioned us to believe. But we cannot dismiss the fact that the Lord has created our bodies with a fabric of skin that responds favorably to sexual touch. When we place the focus of sexual sharing on orgasm or intercourse, we can miss out on the marvelous ways our Creator has established for us to express our love through touch and nongenital sexual sharing.

This aspect of sexuality is experienced by many women as a physical need as deep as a male's need for intercourse. Does this mean that women are less sexual than men, or is it that we are actually made to complement one another in these areas?

This myth can also be disputed when we consider that sexual desire fluctuates during the life cycle. There may be times when women experience a more intense desire to make love than their husbands. Most males reach a peak of feeling the need for sexual release when they are in their late teens to mid-twenties, whereas females are often "late bloomers," having a greater desire for sexual interaction in their thirties and forties. While these patterns vary from person to person, we can be encouraged by the fact that sexual desire isn't static, but changes with the seasons of our lives.

When we consider that marriage is intended to last for life, it is reassuring to know that men and women can enhance one another's sexuality by "peaking" at different times. Just as a husband's interest might be waning, it is not unusual for the wife's to become more intense and renew the relationship. It is inappropriate to compare male and female sexuality in terms of which gender has the greatest sex drive when the Lord created us to express our sexuality *differently* from one another, with a man and woman each contributing their own unique blend of feelings and abilities to the marital relationship.

Myth #7: What men like best about sex is intercourse. This commonly held belief does not fit the Christian model of sexual expression within marriage. For the hedonist, penile stimulation may be the pinnacle of sexual experience; but for a Christian husband, the sexual responsiveness of his wife may bring him greater joy and satisfaction than do mere physical sensations alone.

Women often wrongly assume that their husbands are more interested in their own bodies than in the bodies of their wives. What a surprise it is when a woman discovers that the source of her husband's sexual fulfillment springs from *her* openness and excitement!

There is a tendency to view male sexuality as selfish and female sexuality as sacrificial. Song of Songs refutes this line of thinking. It is Solomon's *reaction* to his wife that seems to give him the greatest pleasure—the more she responds to him, the more joy he seems to experience. He barely speaks of his own reactions, but refers over and over again to how delightful his wife is (Song of Songs 1:9-11, 15; 4:1-15; 6:4-9; 7:1-9). When he finally does speak of himself, it is in reaction to the Shulammite's openness with her body (5:1). The belief that men "will take whatever they can get sexually" can lock us into a stereotype of men that discounts biblical truth about God's design for human sexuality.

Because of the way our culture portrays male sexuality, men are expected to want to have sex with the greatest variety of partners possible in order to prove their masculinity. By seeing our husbands as God

created them to be—with the ability to express their love toward their
wives through the physical design of their bodies—instead of assuming
that all men are sex-starved and always "on the prowl," we can invite
them to become all they can be in Christ. By encouraging them to be
accountable for their thoughts and actions related to their sexuality—to
get the help they need to heal from their sexual brokenness related to past
events or current struggles—our marriages take on a new level of transparency, permitting us to honestly confront our differences and meet one
another's sexual needs in a way that honors God.

Sexual desire was designed by our Creator for the purpose of nourishing and strengthening the marriage bond, not diminishing it. But we
live in a sexually charged culture that sends us mixed messages about our
sexuality. As a result, our husbands' desire for us can be confusing. For
example, how many times do we react to our husbands by thinking, *He
only wants me for my body*, or, *He isn't interested in what I've gone through
today—all he wants is sex*? How many times have we rebuffed our husbands when a hand has reached out to touch a breast or lips have yearned
to be kissed?

If we aren't comfortable with our husbands' sexuality or are worried
about the source of their focus on our bodies, we will not feel comfortable
with lovemaking. The way we view their sexuality directly enhances or
detracts from our willingness to welcome them with our bodies. Many
wives silently declare the honeymoon is over when they realize just how
often and how intensely their husbands desire to be physically close to
them. It may be okay *initially*, but somewhere along the line it is not
unusual for women to begin to wonder when things will settle down.

Even the Shulammite struggled with her husband's continuous
desire for her (Song of Songs 5:2-3). Her relationship to Solomon deepened when she realized that she yearned for her husband as much as he
wanted her. Their relationship matured after she dreamed that she had
rejected him; after this event, she spoke lovingly of his body for the first
time in a manner similar to how her husband had spoken of hers (5:10-
16; 4:1-15).

In the following verses, the Shulammite's attitude toward her body's
ability to attract her husband and his overwhelmingly joyous response is
a lovely reminder of the dual nature of sexual intimacy. What is he
responding to? His sexual union with his wife. Most importantly, God's

benediction at the passage's closing reassures us of His blessing on this scene and invites them to fully celebrate their sexuality.

[The bride to Solomon:]

> *Awake, north wind,*
>   *And come, south wind!*
> *Blow on my garden, that its fragrance*
>   *may spread abroad.*
> *Let my lover come into his garden*
>   *And taste its choice fruits.*

[Solomon to his bride:]

> *I have come into my garden, my sister, my bride;*
>   *I have gathered my myrrh with my spice.*
> *I have eaten my honeycomb and my honey;*
>   *I have drunk my wine and my milk.*

[The Lord:]

> *Eat, O friends, and drink;*
>   *drink your fill, O lovers.*

SONG OF SONGS 4:16; 5:1

What do you like the most about your husband's sexuality, his body, and his lovemaking? Have you reached a place in your relationship where you can see your husband's body as a gift to you? Do you feel free to stroke and touch him intimately as you respond to his sexual desire for you? Are you drawn to his differences, or do they confuse or repel you? Do you harbor inner doubts about his sexual purity or commitment to fidelity within your marriage? How will you resolve your differences and respond to any doubts you are currently struggling with?

If we get our ideas about love from journalists and entertainers, we will become hopelessly muddled. If we get them from Jesus Christ, we will have a clear and convincing pattern to follow as we obey his command to love one another.[2]

EUGENE PETERSON

Chapter Review

Personal Reflections

1. Romantic ideals of sexual love depicted in books and movies have made it easier/harder for me to come to terms with my husband's:

2. Of the seven myths covered in this chapter, I was most surprised by:

3. My husband's desire for sexual interaction sometimes makes me feel:

4. From a sexual standpoint, welcoming my husband to me means.

5. My greatest concern about my husband's level of sexual desire is:

6. Believing that God created the patterns of male and female sexual response helps me to understand:

Related Bible Passages for Further Study

- Psalm 96:4-6
- Psalm 103:1-5
- Proverbs 4:5-9
- Song of Songs 7:10-13; 8:10
- John 14:27
- James 3:13-18

$\mathcal{N}$ATURALLY YOURS

The struggle to feel good about your body is a process
of becoming open with yourself and your spouse. It also includes
honesty concerning your feelings about yourself, feeling comfortable
with being in the nude, caring for your body, and allowing
yourself to receive affirmation through touch and verbal feedback
through others in your world. A new sense of comfort with and
acceptance of your body can bring increased freedom and pleasure to
your sexual experience. In all this, it is crucial to maintain a healthy
perspective on where your value as a person is centered. Christ's mes-
sage is loud and clear—man looks on the outside, but God looks on
the heart. We cannot disregard either part: the part man looks at—
the outside, nor the part God looks at—the heart.[1]

JOYCE AND CLIFFORD PENNER

Your breasts like clusters of fruit" . . . "your mouth like the best wine" . . . "How beautiful you are and how pleasing, O love, with your delights" (Song of Songs 7:7, 9, 6).

Solomon's inspired love song plaintively underscores a fact we sometimes forget: a woman's natural adornments and attributes are intended to be a bountiful, aromatic treasure in her mate's eyes. The natural beauty we are created with possesses a powerful ability to attract our husband's interest. A clear-eyed gaze, freshly washed hair, and the sweet fragrance of a recently bathed body are more appealing to most men than over-perfumed skin, heavy eye makeup, oversprayed hair, and a body swathed from head to toe in a lace-trimmed cotton nightgown. In fact, when we get right down to it, do any of us really think that our husbands care about what makeup or lingerie we have on once lovemaking starts?

The point of what we wear and put on is often to make ourselves feel more attractive. And that's not all bad. Few women are completely satisfied with the way they look without any clothes or makeup on. Cosmetics companies and clothing manufacturers have made fortunes by taking advantage of this fact—as if external things are what sexual attraction is all about. But when we consider what we are underneath it all, the pressure to live up to beauty experts' expectations eases.

PROMOTING FEMININE HYGIENE

In an intimate situation with one's husband, the natural odors and lubricants of a woman's body are more sensual than the most expensive commercial products. When we become sexually aroused, our bodies are designed to prepare for lovemaking by making the vagina more slippery, moistening it with a fluid secreted by the Bartholin's glands. It is a strong signal that our bodies are responding to our husbands and lets them know when we are becoming sexually aroused.

As women, though, we have been socialized to find this kind of thing somewhat embarrassing, not stimulating. Reminding ourselves that this natural reaction to lovemaking was designed into our bodies for the purpose of making sex more comfortable and pleasurable helps to counteract our discomfort. Knowing this natural lubrication is a healthy sign that we're sexually responsive, rather than a warning to head for the nearest washcloth, enhances our ability to accept our bodies' responses to lovemaking. It may even be a good idea to think of this unique fluid as a kind of spice that enlivens sexual sharing instead of as a messy nuisance to put up with prior to lovemaking.

Vaginal odors and post-coital secretions are another aspect of female sexuality that can make a woman feel self-conscious about her genitals. Because the vagina is a self-cleansing body organ, daily bathing of this area is a sufficient means of getting rid of the bacteria that exaggerate the odor of vaginal secretions. Regular douching is not recommended as a means of cleansing the vagina because it alters the acid-base balance of the vaginal lining. When the pH of the vagina is thrown off by douching, "good bacteria" are destroyed. Harmful bacteria and other potentially troublesome organisms can thrive in the absence of bacteria designed to keep the vaginal tract healthy. A condition known as vaginitis results—irritation and inflammation of the vagina.

Oils, bubble bath detergents, and deodorant soaps should be avoided, especially by women who have recurring bladder or vaginal infections. Simply cleansing the genitals with water is normally sufficient. In addition to a daily shower or bath, getting up and using the toilet after lovemaking is an easy way to promote a feeling of cleanliness. Urinating after intercourse rinses out the lower portion of the urethra, discouraging the growth of bacteria that may have been introduced into this area during lovemaking. Toilet tissue or a washcloth moistened with warm water can be used to quickly wipe away secretions. If your bathroom is equipped with a bidet, you no doubt have already discovered that it was well worth the investment.

Vaginal health is also promoted by avoiding tight, restrictive clothing, by wearing cotton underwear and panty hose with a cotton panel between the legs, by using "breathable" sanitary pads and panty liners, and by sleeping without underwear at night. Air circulation discourages bacterial growth and prevents the accumulation of excess moisture in the vaginal area. As long as vaginal discharge is not foul-smelling or producing itching, painful irritation, or redness, it's perfectly harmless.

I recently read a book, published in the 1930s, that gave advice on how to achieve sexual happiness within marriage. This practical little volume contained many useful ideas, including the importance of bathing before going to bed together. The authors, a married couple, recommended changing one's daily bathing routine so that it would take place at the end of the day as a kind of "fresh start" that recognizes the value of structuring one's day around lovemaking instead of work. Isn't this an intriguing idea? It definitely feels refreshing to get into bed with newly washed skin after a long, stressful day. So why not take an additional bath or shower late in the day, even if we cannot completely surrender our early morning shower habit? Showering together on occasion can be a pleasant prelude to lovemaking; bathing at the same time is also an interesting way to save on energy costs and water bills. Plus, who knows what might happen while we are rinsing or drying off?

THERE'S NOTHING LIKE THE REAL THING

One of the nicest things about sexual sharing within marriage is that it allows us to do away with a wide variety of social pretenses. As a couple grows to be increasingly more intimate, they stop trying to impress one another and can just "be themselves." Once a woman knows that her husband cares for her, she no longer has to go to extremes to feel attractive to him.

Consider the following example: A young woman has been asked to go out on a date by a young man she has had on her mind for quite a while. It is easy to imagine the kinds of things this young woman thinks about throughout their evening together, because we were once in her position. Because she sincerely wants to get to know him better, she stays on her best behavior and tries to be congenial, attractive, and generally impressive. And, if the young man is interested in her, he is also doing his best to display his finest attributes.

As their feelings for one another deepen over the following months, they allow themselves to become more transparent, taking greater risks in conversation as they share previously undisclosed hopes and dreams. They begin to think less about themselves and more about one another. The young woman spends less time in front of the mirror before she sees her boyfriend and is not as concerned about whether he will see her in worn-out clothes or without makeup. She wants him to know her real self—not a manufactured identity.

Knowing that we are loved enables us to reveal our true identity to another. If I have not let you see me as I am, how will I know that you will not reject me once you see the *real* me, minus my makeup, best clothes, and carefully controlled conversation?

After the wedding, there is no room for our transparent selves to share our beds with a superficial, manufactured type of sexuality between the sheets. Adam and Eve were naked before one another in body, mind, and spirit—without walls, without cover-ups, and without pretense. The female body as the Lord created it is fully capable of satisfying our partners without any add-ons.

There is just one small catch to all of this: our natural sexuality requires a certain measure of basic body care. Poor hygiene, carelessness about wearing clean, pressed clothes, lack of exercise, compulsive overeating, chronic self-starvation, or neglecting one's health in other ways can steal our natural beauty. The right balance between accepting our natural, God-created beauty and doing what we can to be well-groomed and emotionally, physically, and spiritually healthy comes when we earnestly desire to take care of ourselves. Because we have a balanced, biblical estimate of our self-worth, we understand the value of honoring God with our bodies and accept the responsibility of reasonably caring for them.

RELAX AND ENJOY

Have you ever been surprised by the strength and magnitude of your body's reactions to your husband's touches? It was with amazing tenderness that the Lord must have created our bodies—as well as with an incredible sense of humor.

Women do not seem to be nearly as automatic as men in their sexual responsiveness. One moment a woman might be totally disinterested in sexual sharing, and then suddenly she can be transported to the brink of ecstasy. I do not think anyone will ever be able to completely figure this phenomenon out; so we may as well relax and enjoy the element of surprise. Perhaps we were made this way to make life more interesting, less boring, or sometimes simply hilarious. At any rate, loving husbands will grow to recognize the unpredictability in their partners. And then they will plan accordingly.

Creating a safe, secure atmosphere that fosters emotional closeness is a fundamental part of this process. A wise husband knows that his wife's lack of sexual arousal is genuine and, when appropriate, will seek to discover the source of her disinterest. At other times, he will figure out that he really has been a grump or a big baby, so he will apologize and say a few words to set things straight. He may even come up with some pretty remarkable ways to convince her that she will really be missing out if she turns down yet another wonderful opportunity to spend some quality time together.

Once we are emotionally open to sexual interaction with our husbands, we become aware of sensations that will let us know that our bodies are interested, too. The feelings accompanying sexual excitement are usually a pleasant means of encouraging us to want to be physically close to our husbands as we draw nearer to them in intimate ways.

In addition to vaginal lubrication, the signals of sexual arousal in women include swelling of the lips around the vagina and a feeling of warmth as blood rushes into the pelvic area; a tightening sensation in the breasts as the nipples and areola (the pigmented ring around the nipples) become erect, and the breasts increase in size; an increase in the heart and breathing rates; and swelling of the clitoris, which is probably the most noticeable sensation of all for many women. It is as if the body is awakening from its quiet state and discovering its sexual abilities all over again.

The ability to experience and enjoy the sensations associated with sexual arousal is strongly related to the way we feel about our husbands prior to lovemaking. Generally speaking, genuine emotional intimacy precedes genuine physical intimacy. Our bodies do not respond willingly without our wholehearted emotional assent. With this internal voice of approval, we are much more likely to find ourselves enjoying intimate times with our husbands.

PAYING ATTENTION TO WARNING SIGNS

Mutual satisfaction in lovemaking is unlikely when we do not feel okay about being sexually responsive. But our discomfort is not a threat to be ignored, stuffed down, or forgotten. We can view it as a golden opportunity to discover the source of what we are sensing.

If a woman has had premarital sexual experiences, it is not unusual for her to associate intense feelings of sexual arousal with fear, shame, or guilt. Once she is married, these negative feelings may interfere with her ability to relax and enjoy the sensations she is experiencing with her husband.

Victims of incest, rape, or childhood sexual abuse may find themselves recalling long-forgotten memories that impede their ability to have satisfying sexual interaction with their husbands. Within marriage, if a woman's husband has ever had sex with her without her invitation, has had an adulterous affair, or has used pornography as a means to provoke her sexual interest, her reactions might be pain, anger, fear, shame, or deep sadness.

If you have difficulty with sexual arousal and responsiveness in your marriage, please don't discount your emotional discomfort. It is there for a reason, if only as an indicator that you need a temporary time out from sexual interaction due to stress or seasonal changes in your life. If the discomfort persists, see chapter 10. Seek God's wisdom and discernment concerning how to respond to your current circumstances.

If your uneasiness with lovemaking continues for several weeks or longer, consider consulting a Christ-centered counselor, preferably a woman, who would be able to help you understand your feelings about your body's reactions to sexual arousal. Don't worry: you are not abnormal. Nor are you alone. Literally thousands of women have struggled with the same feelings.

Be confident in the Lord's ability to *cleanse, heal,* and *restore* you as you are transformed by the renewing of your mind and conformed to Christ's image. As we face our fear and brokenness with the Holy Spirit's help, we can learn to embrace God's merciful design for our lives in all of its liberating fullness.

THE POWER OF SEXUAL LOVE

Sex is powerful, naturally. Some men and women abuse this power by using their sexuality to manipulate, denigrate, or fascinate another human being, by primarily pleasuring themselves rather than finding their greatest source of sexual pleasure in faithfully loving their spouse. When our sexuality is infused with the Holy Spirit, however, lovemaking becomes a profoundly mysterious, tender, and generous experience. John and Paula Sandford eloquently explained some dramatic spiritual dynamics that take place during our physical bonding:

> We have found in counseling that too few husbands know the virtue of nudity with their wives. Our spirits pour forth to one another much like electricity. We need the current of each other. Clothes tend to insulate. A husband needs the power of his wife's body against his, quite apart from sexual union.
>
> All too few husbands and wives understand that verse, "Let her breasts satisfy thee at all times." During the day husbands need to hug their wives long enough to let that current which flows from her to pierce the heart to refresh and strengthen. Woman was taken from the rib of man. Man protects woman by his strength and logic, but woman protects the heart area of man. Her breasts satisfy him when

held against his chest. Her energy fills and warms his thinking with wisdom and gentleness. In sexual embrace, husbands most often fail to feed, sensitively and quietly, a long time upon their wives' breasts. Men need to touch, hold, and kiss the breasts long enough. The command is to "*let* her breasts satisfy thee at *all* times." It is fulfilling and satisfying to both partners. A man who is fully satisfied in his wife's embrace, who truly feeds on her love, is not easily tempted to [go to] another. Who would take a bologna sandwich [in preference] to a banquet? Only his own wife is a fully satisfying banquet to his heart and soul and spirit and body. Let husbands pray that God will reveal to them the gift and power of their wives' love from them. It is not that we are too sexual, but not sexual enough, because we do not discover how to meet and nourish, cherish, embrace, and feed upon one another's love as we ought.[3]

Sexual sharing that honors the Lord does not use the power of sex to break God's rules or harm one's partner. A husband who is living out his Christian beliefs never needs to "conquer" his wife. A wife who is seeking to follow the Lord's will in her life never needs to seduce her husband. A couple that seeks sexual wholeness in their relationship never needs to resort to the use of pornography to "liven things up."

The purpose of our sexuality is to promote unity, or oneness, within marriage. The oneness comes not only through the act of making love, but in our ongoing respect for keeping God's rules and our mutual high regard for one another—our different growth patterns, emotional needs, body experiences, spiritual makeup, and personal vulnerabilities.

Our hope as wives, and as Christ's followers, can be that we express our sexuality in mutually satisfying ways with our husbands as we acknowledge the beauty of God's natural design for sexuality within marriage and the way He created our minds, hearts, and bodies to respond to the sexuality of our husbands.

Marriage is always a risk. I cannot even predict the future course of my own marriage. Our first twenty-six years have been years of anger, tears, forgiveness, immaturity, love, and astonishing growth. We have learned to respect and trust each other's strengths and abilities (fortunately, they complement each other). We have also learned a certain amount of honesty about our weaknesses and have learned to laugh about them, with genuine amusement and less defensiveness. We have decided, quite illogically, that we deserve each other, yet that God has, in putting us together, given each of us far more than we deserve. And while we cannot predict the future, we no longer fear it.[2]

JOHN WHITE

Chapter Review

Personal Reflections

1. I would describe my comfort level with my body's natural responses to lovemaking as:

2. Thinking that I don't need any add-ons to be sexually desirable to my husband helps me accept:

3. Given the amount of time and energy I spend on my physical health and personal appearance, I would say that at this point I need to pay more attention to:

4. Mutuality in lovemaking, to me, means:

5. Knowing that sex is a powerful force in our marriage relationship that either of us can exploit keeps me aware of my need to:

6. God revealed His pattern for oneness in our marriage most recently to us when we:

Related Bible Passages for Further Study

- Psalm 85:7-12
- Psalm 119:9-11
- Proverbs 4:25-27
- Song of Songs 2:3-6
- John 12:44-46
- 1 Peter 1:13-16

8

$\mathscr{S}$PEAKING WITHOUT WORDS

Your hands lie open in the long fresh grass,—
The finger-points look through like rosy blooms:
Your eyes smile peace. The pasture gleams and glooms:
'Neath billowing skies that scatter and amass.
All round our nest, far as the eye can pass,
Are golden kingcup-fields with silver edge
Where the cow-parsley skirts the hawthorn-hedge.
'T is visible silence, still as the hour-glass.
Deep in the sun-searched growths the dragon-fly
Hangs like a blue thread loosened from the sky:—
So this wing'd hour is dropt to us from above.
Oh! clasp we to our hearts, for deathless dower,
This close companioned inarticulate hour
When twofold silence was the song of love.[1]

DANTE GABRIEL ROSSETTI

This close-companioned inarticulate hour when twofold silence was the song of love." What a beautiful way to describe the language a man and woman speak with their bodies when they make love. Speaking without words through the sexual design of our bodies is what being lovers is all about. Becoming fluent in the language of lovemaking takes time and patience as one tries out new sounds and expressions. Each of us sounds awkward at first as we say something we have never said before or try a different way of saying something familiar.

Every time a kiss is shared or two bodies are joined in lovemaking, a conversation takes place between a wife and her husband, informing each other of their love. When a woman looks into the eyes of the man she has vowed to spend her life with and responds to him with her body, she tells him what she thinks and how she feels about him. Love communicated through sexuality is a profoundly simple language. All we need to do is let our bodies do the talking.

THE LANGUAGE OF LOVE

Our Creator has given us the ability to be sexually expressive and creatively responsive with our bodies when we feel loved and accepted by our husbands. Our natural, inborn responses do not require years of study to develop. If we learn to listen and respond to the messages our bodies send us, we will find that we do not have to work at acquiring new skills, because we are already capable of speaking a love language spontaneously in articulate and meaningful ways.

When a woman feels awkward or embarrassed about speaking with her body, she will receive little satisfaction in sexual intimacy. On the other hand, if her husband's body does most of the talking, the resulting one-way conversation will fall disappointingly short of the dialogue God intends for them.

Because our sexuality is made up of much more than our physical actions, the "speech" we use during lovemaking is a unique form of communicating who we are. Lovemaking is an experience involving our bodies, our minds, and our spirits as two are blended into one flesh. Our sexuality is a dynamic force that, when unleashed, makes time seem to stop and causes us to forget everything else for a few moments. As we bring ourselves to the experience of lovemaking, we find it was not designed to be engaged in out of a sense of duty or responsibility. Sexual fulfillment results when we stop controlling our responses and enjoy the way God has designed our bodies—with hilarity at times, with passionate exultation at others.

The desire to stay in control of the conversation during lovemaking can stifle the dialogue. A woman's past experiences, a lack of trust in her husband, or the belief that it is not proper for a Christian woman to experience or express sexual pleasure can keep her from full and active sexual sharing.

We have been given the freedom to say yes to the gift of our sexuality within the holy bond of marriage. By giving ourselves permission to release the fear we hold in our hearts, we remove a significant stumbling block to our ability to be sexually loving and lovable. We are better able to make the decision to speak articulately with our bodies, to talk freely without reservation, because we know God has designed the gift of our sexuality. Accepting the ways our bodies behave and sound during love-making is not only possible, but is preferable to holding back the wonderful sensations He has created us to experience.

As your heartbeat quickens and your breathing becomes louder, relax and let it happen. If you feel like moving your pelvis with pushing or thrusting motions, go right ahead if this pleases your husband. The words of the English language (or any other for that matter) cannot fully describe the joy or the ecstasy that can take place during lovemaking when it is relaxed and mutually satisfying. When we stop trying to be what we are not and accept our own styles of response, we begin to understand the tremendous range of expression we are capable of: shouting, whispering, chatting, enunciating, crying out—a woman's body speaks in all these different ways.

PERSONAL IMPRESSIONS

Our speech tends to be sloppy when we are careless, distracted, fatigued, or uneducated. Just as with verbal expression, the physical expressions of our sexuality benefit from our being able to understand the phrases, patterns, and words we are using. The effects of stress upon sexual expression are presented in chapter 10, which suggests ideas on how we can improve our sexual conversations through recreation and relaxation. But what about the results of ignorance on speech patterns?

In this analogy, your body is equivalent to the medium of spoken language. Like words, it is the tool that conveys a vocabulary of love to your husband, the means through which you send messages about how you think and feel about yourself, as well as what you think and feel about your husband. If you take the time to understand what your feelings are about your husband's body, as well as about your own body, you can strengthen your sexual relationship.

The next time you take a shower or bath—whichever is the most relaxing for you—spend some time deciphering the way you talk about your body to yourself. As you lather your skin, look at it. What are your personal impressions of this magnificent covering God has given to you for protection and sensation? If there are folds of fat, do you view them as smooth and feminine or lumpy and ugly? Do you often think about how unattractive you are and how you wish you could look? Do you ever think, *If only my breasts were bigger (or smaller or fuller or firmer)*, or, *If only my buttocks and hips weren't so wide (or so flabby or muscular or bony)*?

Do you enjoy your body and appreciate it for all it's worth? Try that now, as your washcloth glides over the amazing fabric that covers the entire surface of your body. How does the soap feel, and what sensations does the water produce? Do you take delight in the fact that the body God has given you is able to provide you with pleasurable sensations as you bathe? In everything, we can give thanks to God and praise Him for the loving-kindness He bestows upon us.

Have you ever witnessed the vitality and exuberance of a toddler in the bathtub? (Or had to mop the floor up after the adventure was over?) Splashing, soaking, swishing, blowing, reveling in the wetness, a young child springs with enthusiasm from one bubbly escapade to the next with apparent disregard for how loud, messy, or silly it is. Caught up in the moment, a child at this age is a bundle of spontaneous energy ready to explore the world with each new opportunity.

Is there a childlike curiosity in you that invites you to splash? To revel in the wetness of the water? Go ahead and blow at the bubbles and see what new shapes you can make. Growing up does not have to mean that simple pleasures in life such as bathing become dull or tedious. As the water wakes up your skin, sing . . . laugh . . . turn your head toward the shower spray and gargle. It's great to be alive, isn't it?

As you step out of the tub, look into the mirror and say the words that come to mind right out loud. Verbalize the first things you think of—there is no need to filter out words that are unkind or sound stupid. Then, after you are finished, think about what you've said. These words form the basis of your opinion of yourself. They have a very real impact upon your ability to feel "at home" in your body. Do you realize how significant and valuable you really are?

During our vacation last summer we had the chance to return to our native state and spend some time on the shore of Lake Michigan. How I love the air there, so cool and fresh as it blows over the water and creates waves that move back and forth over the rocks and shells. The constant friction of the water moving the stones rubs away all their rough edges. Over hundreds of years these rocks become so smooth that they look as if a sculptor has worked diligently to create them.

As I walked along the shore, this picture from the Psalms passed through my mind: "Love and faithfulness meet together; righteousness and peace kiss each other. Faithfulness springs forth from the earth, and righteousness looks down from heaven. The Lord will indeed give what is good. . . ." (Psalm 85:10-12). Picking up one stone after another, I marveled at how beautiful each one was and at the amazing process that made them. Each one was a work of art, but had no monetary worth, no price tag to signify its value. So unappreciated and yet so significant, these stones had survived eons of hardening, shaping, and smoothing.

The rocks in the sand were warm as I picked them up. I brushed one against my cheek and kept turning it over and over in my hand. Then, as I looked out over the vastness of the water, I remembered the postcard I had just bought describing Michigan's state rock, the Petoskey stone.

When we returned to our cottage, I picked up the Petoskey we had found at a sand hill the day before. I read the card once more. It informed me that what I held in my hand was petrified coral, an ancient piece of history about three hundred million years old, using current dating methods. I will never forget that moment, and the Petoskey stone I held that day will always be one of my prized possessions. Why? Because God used that small gray rock to teach me an important lesson.

However old the rock was, it was beyond my ability to truly comprehend it. Someday my life would be older. I realized in a new way that God, who had created this rock so long ago, loves me with an *everlasting* love. Eternity became much more real to me that day.

Can you too appreciate how wonderful and mysterious it is to be loved by such a God . . . to be significant to the Creator of the universe . . . to have been given the gift of *life*? Our God is a living God who speaks to us today through His Word and through His creation. In the words of this brief poem, the anonymous writer captures what it means to be heading toward eternity with our Beloved. Anticipation of that great event can bring us joy in the here and now.

> *Think of stepping on shore, and finding it heaven!*
> *Of taking hold of a hand, and finding it God's hand,*
> *Of breathing new air, and finding it celestial air,*
> *Of feeling invigorated, and finding it immortality,*
> *Of passing from storm and tempest to unbroken calm,*
> *Of waking up, and finding it Home!*[2]

HOW DOES YOUR BODY SPEAK?

As you talk to yourself about the areas of your body specifically created for expressing sexual love, do you feel comfortable thinking about them? Do you enjoy sharing these areas with your husband? Are you familiar enough with your body to use it to speak expressively to your husband?

Solomon extolled the joys of conjugal sexuality as he shared this poignant advice on the importance of being faithful to one's wife:

> *Let your fountain, the wife of your youth, be blessed, rejoice in her, a lovely doe, a graceful hind, let her be your companion; you will at all times be bathed in her love, and her love will continually wrap you round. Wherever you turn, she will guide you; when you lie in bed, she will watch over you, and when you wake she will talk to you.*
>
> PROVERBS 5:18-19 NEB

Another version reads, "May her breasts satisfy you always, may you ever be captivated by her love." Bathing your husband in your love, letting your love continually wrap him around—this is a lovely description of the essence of a woman's sexuality expressed through sexual sharing.

The next time you are with your husband, notice how your body responds and communicates to him. Look at your breasts. Did you know that most women's breasts are not identical? When your husband touches your nipples, how do they respond? In both men and women, muscle fibers lying beneath the nipples cause them to become erect when they're

Female Reproductive System
Figure 8-1

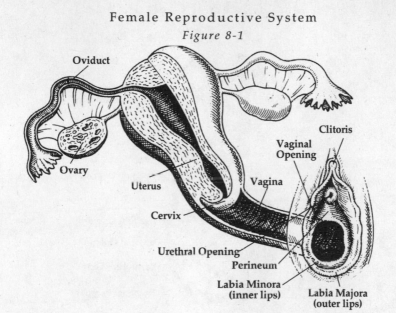

stimulated. This makes the nipples easier to grasp and is a way of telling your husband you are responsive to his touches.

Have you found pleasure in sharing your breasts with your husband? Are you able to let him know what pleases you? Stroking, rubbing, and squeezing the nipples with the lips, tongue, fingers, or hands can produce a variety of sensations capable of heightening your sexual arousal. If you have not explored these different types of touching, perhaps you could guide your husband in touching you, teaching him what feels most pleasurable to you and encouraging him to caress you in satisfying ways.

Some women are unfamiliar or uncomfortable with their genitals. Our genitals are discreetly concealed between our legs and are difficult to see, but our husbands have seen and touched their genitals for as long as they can remember. Because we urinate sitting down and use toilet paper afterwards, we have minimal contact with this area of our bodies compared to our husbands.

Your genitals may not seem a very real part of you if you never look at them or were taught as a child that this area was "dirty." The following diagram is intended to help you become more familiar with your body without shame being attached to the learning process (Fig. 8-2).

Female External Genitalia
Figure 8-2

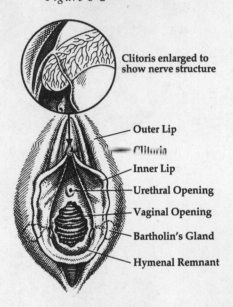

Clitoris enlarged to
show nerve structure

Outer Lip

Clitoris

Inner Lip

Urethral Opening

Vaginal Opening

Bartholin's Gland

Hymenal Remnant

Nerve Endings Sensitive to Sexual Stimulation
Figure 8-3

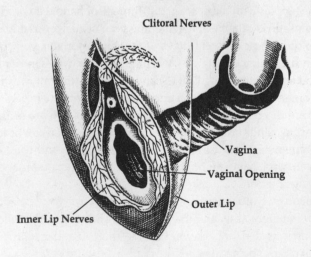

Clitoral Nerves

Vagina

Vaginal Opening

Outer Lip

Inner Lip Nerves

Male Reproductive System
Figure 8-4

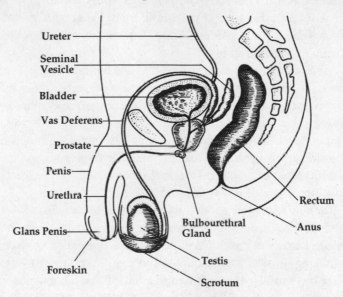

Ureter

Seminal
Vesicle

Bladder

Vas Deferens

Prostate

Penis

Urethra

Glans Penis

Foreskin

Bulbourethral
Gland

Testis

Scrotum

Rectum

Anus

Your husband will become more familiar with your body as you share what you learn about it with him. If you wish, you may use a mirror to help you to identify each structure.

You will see a fold of skin lying over the clitoris, which helps to protect the glans of the clitoris from excessive stimulation during lovemaking. The clitoris itself is a loose fold of skin with many nerve endings extending deep beneath its surface. This delicate structure is designed to bloom like the soft petals of a flower as it swells with blood during sexual arousal. The number of nerve endings in the clitoris vary greatly from woman to woman, accounting for some of the differences that exist in the responsiveness of this organ among women (Fig. 8-3). Some women require very direct stimulation of the clitoris to reach orgasm, while others merely press their thighs together or receive indirect stimulation during lovemaking in sufficient amounts to reach this response.

As you become better acquainted with your body, why not become more familiar with your husband's body as well? Ask him to show you how he likes to be stroked and kissed. What areas does he say are the most sensitive? What types of touch give him the most pleasure?

Notice the texture of skin on the different areas of his body. As you consider the ways his body complements yours, what impresses you most about your differences? Your similarities? What positive feelings do you have about your husband's body? Is there anything about his physical form that embarrasses you?

Think about how perfectly suited his genitals are to yours. As his body responds to yours, and yours to his, express your approval in ways that show your acceptance of his masculinity. Encourage him to tell you what he finds enjoyable; surprise him with the pleasure that you receive from touching him; listen to what your body is "saying" as it seeks to lovingly respond to the pleasurable ways your husband's body expresses his love for you.

Who would have thought that two people could converse so silently, with a love language that is theirs alone?

Teaching each other about the sexually responsive areas of your bodies will help to dispel any fears and ignorance about one another's differences. Each of us has different tastes and a unique set of responses to lovemaking—just as we like different foods. What if twice every month you cooked a meal that your husband totally disliked but was too embarrassed to tell you about? *The only way for you to discover what your husband enjoys is for him to communicate his preferences to you.* Learning to be sexually intimate with one another is no different. You each have the right and the responsibility to inform one another of your preferences before engaging in any sexual activity that might cause one of you to feel uncomfortable or embarrassed. In this way, the two of you can develop many creative approaches to lovemaking.

If you have been unfulfilled by the way your husband touches you or responds to you, it may be because you have yet to explore the types of touch that feel best to you or to learn which areas are the most responsive during lovemaking. Either you or your husband can try using different types of touch to discover these areas. In many women, the clitoris is by far the most sensitive area, but there is no one "right" way to touch it.

The glans of the clitoris is almost unbearably sensitive during the peak of sexual arousal in much the same way that the penis is. Stroking, rubbing, or pressing along the sides, the base, or the top of the clitoris all create different sensations. Together, you and your husband will discover what feels best as you relax and enjoy the pleasurable sensations this part of your body was designed to produce.

You may also wish to explore the effects vaginal stimulation produces by having your husband touch this area. You will discover that the walls of your vagina are able to stretch open or close tightly through your use of the pelvic floor muscles that surround it. This area is capable of birthing a baby with a head size of up to fifteen inches in circumference. This is due to the pleats, or rugae, that allow this muscular membrane to stretch so well.

The muscle group that makes up the pelvic floor is actually what is stimulated through the vaginal wall during lovemaking, producing pleasurable sensations for both the wife and her husband (Fig. 8-5). These muscles are the tissue that contracts during orgasm and grips the penis during intercourse. Can you tighten these muscles around your husband's fingers or penis when he touches you there? Just squeeze them as if you were closing the openings to your bowels and bladder very tightly. He will feel a ring of muscles tighten about one and a half to two and a half inches up within your vagina. Ask him to press the top, sides, and bottom of the ridge that he feels and let him know what sensations this produces. Have him try stroking the tightened area along the rear wall of the vagina (toward your rectum) and along the front (underneath your bladder). Then he may go deeper beyond the muscular area to see how your vagina widens and expands.

Vaginal Muscles
Figure 8-5

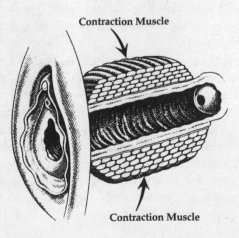

Contraction Muscle

Contraction Muscle

What areas are most sensitive? Let him know if any of the sensations are especially arousing or uncomfortable. Compare light touch to firm pressure, and share what feels best. Take your time. There is no need to hurry, and you need not be embarrassed about guiding your husband's hands as you teach him how to please and satisfy you.

WHAT CAN YOU SAY WITH YOUR BODY?

Boredom in the bedroom can be like boredom in any conversation. What if you had exactly the same dialogue with someone every time you were with that person? You probably would stop listening and focus your attention on something more interesting. We seem to have a built-in need for variety as well as stability. And in lovemaking, it is no different.

There are an endless number of ways to say, "I love you," through intimate sexual interactions with your husband. Varying positions, as well as settings, can allow you to say new things with your body when you make love. When a couple naturally arrives at a new idea together and is not afraid to experiment, memorable interludes result.

Creativity, as well as spontaneity, is part of what makes sex enjoyable. Varying the time of day, when possible, allows you to see how changes in your energy level affect your responsiveness. Music, candlelight, and clothing may be used to enliven lovemaking. Powders and perfume or aromatic candles can make you feel more sensuous as well. Showering together, being playful with one another, and sending out the signal that you are interested in making love ("Now? Here?") are a few additional ways to spark memorable interludes, though you will likely think of many more.

By varying the positions you make love in, you will find that different postures produce different sensations, allowing for a different range of movement. Though it may seem a bit strange for such a private, intimate subject to be presented in technical terms, it can be helpful for those of us who have a tendency to settle for the "same old, same old" lovemaking routine to review our options. Please feel perfectly free to skip this section—or any of the others in this book, for that matter.

In a face-to-face position with the husband above, an intimacy is shared that makes a woman feel protected. This position, however, is restrictive to movement at times. The wife can put her legs nearly together, on the inside of her husband's thighs with his legs on the outside, to allow him greater freedom of movement and to decrease the depth of penetration. Another variation would be for the wife to elevate her hips by putting a pillow underneath them, which would allow for deeper penetration. If a woman raises her knees up toward her chest, or even puts her legs up toward her husband's shoulders, this also enables him to move more freely. Each of these positions allows for different sensations and a different tempo.

When the wife is in the above position for lovemaking, her husband can view her body even after intercourse begins. She may choose to sit or squat, kneel or lie down. Because a woman's body is usually smaller than her husband's, a woman has a wide range of possible movements as she finds the rhythm of lovemaking conversation that fits her mood. Manual stimulation of the clitoris is generally easier in this position as well. If your husband enjoys looking at your body and seeing how you respond to him during lovemaking, this position is an excellent way of meeting his needs. You can also face away from him if you are on top by turning toward his feet.

Other variations include sitting down or standing up. A woman can sit on a chair, edge of the bed, or other supportive surface and have her husband kneel or stand in front of her during lovemaking. This is an especially useful position during late pregnancy when pressure on the abdomen is uncomfortable. Where she places her legs or knees will vary the angle and depth of lovemaking.

Lying side by side during lovemaking produces greater friction within the vagina because of the pressure exerted there by the thighs. If a woman turns around so that her back is toward her husband, they may lie in an X-shape or "spoons together" position. Other variations of the husband-behind position can be accomplished in a standing or kneeling position as well. The main disadvantage to this posture is that eye contact between the couple is lost, but the pleasure that's gained through the angle of lovemaking can increase sexual enjoyment for both partners. The closer a woman's chest is to her knees while kneeling, the deeper the penetration will be. In these positions the husband has a greater range of control over the depth and rhythm of lovemaking as he responds to his wife's behavior and expressions.

Marriage is to last a lifetime. There is no reason to hurry and try to achieve some sort of world's record for the number of positions tried in a single week or month or year. Many intimate conversations will take place over your years together, and some years will bring more satisfaction than others. There will be plenty of chances to try new and exciting things during your relationship. You are able to say so many things with your body. At times you will talk slowly and marvel at the ability of your body to make love-talk throughout an entire evening with your husband. And there will be moments when all you will have time for is a five-minute explosion of joy.

As you learn to listen to your body and hear what your husband's body is saying in response to yours, you will know when and how to vary your movements, how long you both want lovemaking to last, and what you're interested in trying at a given time. No two conversations will ever be exactly the same. It's truly fascinating to discover the strength and beauty of one's sexual responsiveness. The intensity of feeling that a woman is capable of can be just as surprising at sixty-two as it is at twenty-two.

AFTER THE CONVERSATION HAS ENDED

The sense of satisfaction and the fullness of heart that accompanies love-making especially comes during the resolution phase of the sexual response cycle. Basking in the afterglow that sexual release brings provides couples with a unique opportunity for bonding.

The term *bonding* refers to the process of attachment fostered between two human beings as they participate in reciprocal interactions through the experiences of touch, sight, sound, and speech. You may be familiar with this word in the context of the bonding that occurs between parents and their infants, but bonding takes place between husbands and wives also. It is part of the glue cementing two people together in such a way that even the stresses and strains of daily life cannot easily pull them apart.

Since God designed us to be emotionally and spiritually vulnerable to one another during sexual expression, the unique bond created by lovemaking is particularly evident in the moments that follow intercourse or orgasm. When the physical intensity of lovemaking has subsided, it is as if we lie naked before our lover in more than just a physical sense. If we are willing to be mutually transparent along with our husbands, our hearts are joined to theirs in a remarkable way as we reflect upon the closeness that results when two are joined as one. Relaxing in the afterglow of lovemaking while being held in the arms of one's husband is one of life's most sublime experiences.

The next time you drift off to sleep as you snuggle against your husband, praise God for the beautiful gift He's given to you to enjoy as a married woman—the incredible feeling of tranquillity following your silent conversation of love. What a blessing it is to drift along quietly in the moments that follow lovemaking, without guilt or fear. The tenderness and warmth of these times in our lives are a welcome shelter from the stormy world outside.

> But how does one learn this technique of the dance? Why is it so difficult? When the heart is flooded with love there is no room in it for fear, for doubt, for hesitation. And it is this lack of fear that makes for the dance. When each partner loves so completely that he has forgotten to ask himself whether or not he is loved in return; when he only knows that he loves and is moving to the music—then, and then only, are two people able to dance perfectly in tune to the same rhythm. [3]

ANNE MORROW LINDBERGH

Chapter Review

Personal Reflections

1. Spending time and energy on developing a "language of love" with my husband seems:

2. When I stood in front of the mirror after bathing and looked at my body, the first words that came into my mind were:

3. For me, letting go of control during lovemaking is:

4. Trying new positions for lovemaking often leads to:

5. The best way to describe the feeling I have after my husband and I make love is:

6. God's approval of sexual intimacy within marriage tells me that:

Related Bible Passages for Further Study

- Psalm 34:1-8
- Psalm 37:4-6
- Psalm 95:1-7
- Romans 14:7-8
- 1 Corinthians 13:4-7
- Galatians 5:1

$\mathcal{L}$EARNING TO LISTEN

Is there such a thing as working at sex? I believe there is.

I reject the popular theory that sex is "doing what comes naturally."

That may be true of animals. But we are concerned not with

the mere releasing of tension but with a means of communication in

which each partner seeks to give pleasure to the other. A few couples

are instinctively sensitive and skillful. Others take years to

learn to satisfy each other. Methods of learning vary. . . . There is

absolutely no "right way" to achieve mutual sexual satisfaction. I am

not suggesting that you never refer to a good sex manual. I am say-

ing that an essential prerequisite for successful sex in marriage

is finding the methods which give both of you contentment,

ihappiness and peace. It is the approach which recreates for you that

assurance that, through the body, you are no longer two, but one.[1]

JOYCE HUGGETT

As you may already know, not all lovemaking conversations flow smoothly. Sometimes it's difficult to whisper, let alone speak, with our bodies. Sexual communication between spouses requires a willingness to be not only informed about our bodies but to be informative with them. Expecting our husbands to tenderly initiate lovemaking 100 percent of the time is not realistic. Men are affected by the stressors in their lives, too. They become impatient and tired just like we do. Though we may think men are always "ready, willing, and able" and women are more typically the passive followers regarding sex, is this true in every situation? Of course not.

Imagine the following scene: A woman thinks about spending some intimate time with her husband off and on all day. In anticipation of what will happen after a candlelight dinner she plans for that evening, she rushes home to get the groceries into the refrigerator, feeds the kids a carry-out meal, and then whisks them off to spend the night at Grandma's house. While she is gone, her husband arrives and notices the evening newspaper's announcement about his favorite symphony's evening performance downtown. (This could just as well be his favorite sports team, jazz group, or a movie.) Wanting to surprise his wife, he leaves to get the tickets.

When he arrives back home, he finds his favorite foods waiting on the table. His wife greets him with a lingering kiss in the front hall. But as she continues caressing him, she feels his body tense up and asks him what is wrong. Handing the tickets he picked up to his wife like a bouquet of flowers, he informs her the concert will start in one hour. She is not impressed.

What would you do? Have you ever been in a similar situation? Has your husband ever become preoccupied with his own plans while neglecting to ask you about yours?

SIDE BY SIDE

"Submission is the inward compulsion of love in response to love," wrote Joyce Huggett.[2] It is our responsibility to teach our husbands how we feel, what we think, what we know. We have so much to offer them, as they do to us. From the standpoint of Genesis, "a woman's place" is standing next to her husband, side by side. She fits her life in with his as his loving companion, co-minister, and counterpart. Matthew Henry poignantly pointed out: "The woman was made of a rib out of the side of Adam; not made out of his head to rule over him, nor out of his feet to be trampled upon by him, but out of his side to be equal with him, under his arm to be protected, and near his heart to be beloved."[3]

The experience of being made one flesh through the physical joining of our bodies is a powerful symbol of the mutual give and take our marriages require. The finest measure of our thought life and behavior as

Christians is whether the qualities of the Holy Spirit are made manifest in the things we think, say, and do. When we are unsure about the acceptability of our love life to God, it can be beneficial to apply this yardstick from Galatians: "But the fruit of the Spirit is love, joy, peace, patience, kindness, goodness, faithfulness, gentleness, and self-control. Against such things there is no law" (Galatians 5:22-23). Does the sexual area of our lives bring this kind of spiritual fruitfulness?

Prior to spelling out what the fruits of the Spirit are to be in the lives of all believers, Paul lists the acts of the lower nature. Compare these two lists. The following questions can help us to understand whether our sexual behavior is pleasing to the Lord:

Is it *loving?*

Is *joy* expressed in our attitude toward each other? (*Strong's Concordance* defines joy as "calm delight.")

Do we feel God's *peace* before, during, and after we're sexually intimate?

Are we demonstrating *patience* with one another?

Do we see God's *goodness* manifested in the physical love we share with one another?

Are we *faithful* to each other?

Are we being *gentle* with each other?

Are we able to *control* our thoughts and actions, remaining within God's boundaries for our sexuality, when we are together or apart? Through self-control, do we serve one another's needs when we are making love?

If we desire to keep in step with the Spirit, we will want to say yes to each of these questions. Our love lives are not excluded from the rest of our walk with Jesus. The time we spend in lovemaking can be as pleasing, as sanctified, and as blessed as any other aspect of our marriages.

HELPING OUR HUSBANDS TO MEET OUR NEEDS

Unless we're comfortable with our bodies and can lovingly guide our husbands as we teach them to view our needs from a woman's perspective, we may wonder why people consider sex such a great thing. Sex may seem like something done *to* us rather than something we do.

A participant in one of my seminars on women's sexuality confidentially shared her frustration with me. She began by saying that her husband was so thoroughly enthralled with lovemaking he had a tendency to head straight for her erogenous zones almost every time they touched. Often she tried to redirect his hands, hinting at possible alternatives to his approach. She did not know what she wanted—or did not say anything because she thought he should know what she wanted. She simply kept assuming he would figure it out someday. At other times, she tried to rush through lovemaking because she was too tense or upset with her husband's intense focus on sex to enjoy it at all. Then when her husband asked, "What's wrong, honey?" she told him everything was fine or turned her back to him, stuffing down her anger and frustration. She finished, "I'm starting to think it's useless to try and explain my needs to my husband when I've already told him a zillion times how I feel."

I think many of us can relate to this statement. When it comes to intimate sexual sharing with our husbands, what *do* we need, expect, want, or desire? What may happen if we ignore our frustrations, concerns, and disappointments? Or if we expect our husbands to solve the regularly recurring situations we face as couples without taking responsibility for our side of the relationship?

One of the myths discussed in the sixth chapter was that men have a greater sex drive than their wives—period. The wife in this situation appears to have chosen to believe this myth. Instead of learning about her own capabilities for sexual response, she views her husband as a guy who's always "on the prowl." She spends a good deal of time running in the opposite direction.

It is safe to assume that many (most?) women desire to be stroked, caressed, and embraced skin-to-skin before, during, and after lovemaking. Sometimes what a woman needs is a nurturing back rub without lovemaking. At other times, what she wants is just to hold hands and talk for a while. Unless she expresses what she needs and wants, however, her husband may rush into things too quickly, especially if his need is primarily for the release that lovemaking brings to him. And he may also be more likely to turn over and fall asleep after lovemaking, leaving his wife alone to ponder the meaning of it all in the dark.

TEACHABLE MOMENTS

Each woman needs to discover what her own erogenous zones are instead of expecting to react as a textbook case. Since every woman responds in her own unique way to sexual stimulation, we need to feel comfortable sharing our reactions with our husbands if sex is to be mutually satisfying. The solution lies in our taking responsibility for exploring our range of reactions—and our husbands' willingness to be teachable.

A good place to start is with a complete massage like the one described in chapter 12. Ask your husband to do this for several nights in a row, agreeing not to touch your breasts or genitals for the time being. The goal of this exercise is for you to focus on the pleasurable sensations your body feels as you receive the gift of touch from your husband. If your husband becomes sexually aroused during the massage, you may wish to meet his need for sexual release (with or without engaging in intercourse) after he is finished. Or the two of you can agree ahead of time to limit your touching to include nongenital stroking only. This exercise can be applied by either spouse and need not concentrate on the woman alone.

Once you feel relaxed with your body's responses to your husband's touches, perhaps you will want to progress to kisses, though you may not have spent an hour kissing since high school. The kisses can travel over the surface of the body instead of being confined to the face and neck—whatever is pleasing to you.

Over time you will want to progress to caressing the breasts and genitals. A good position for this would be with you sitting nearly upright or semi-reclining, propped up at the head of the bed with lots of pillows. Place a rolled up pillow under each of your knees as well so that your legs, buttocks, and pelvic floor muscles are relaxed. If you find there is only a little natural lubrication at first, a small amount of cold-pressed almond oil on your husband's hands will increase your comfort and enjoyment as well as your husband's ability to feel each area distinctly. Guide your husband's hands, helping him to understand the amount of pressure that feels best to you, as well as the types of stroking you want him to use and what areas you would like him to avoid.

The difference between sensations inside and outside your vagina and the role of your pelvic floor muscles in sexual responsiveness can be determined with your husband's assistance. As he softly touches this area, consciously pull inwards and then bulge outwards while contracting and releasing the muscles surrounding your vagina. You may also find that lying on your stomach with a pillow under your hips and your legs relaxed open will increase your enjoyment.

Instead of taking an aggressive role during intercourse, your husband may gently guide his penis with your help into just the outer entrance of your vagina. By using pelvic floor contractions to alternately grip and release your husband's penis, lovemaking can proceed according to the depth and rhythm you desire. Using your pelvic floor muscles, you can communicate your responsiveness. (Your husband will undoubtedly enjoy these "inside kisses" also.) If he is sitting upright, supporting his weight by his arms placed to the side and behind him, you can easily use your own hip movements to control the tempo of lovemaking. He may also lean back against the pillows and manually stimulate your labia and clitoris in this position. Trying different positions at different times will enable you to understand how sensations during lovemaking vary, allowing you to be more expressive and aggressive.

In these and other ways, you can develop your own unique love language as a couple over the years as you share your bodies with each other. Knowing there is freedom to privately explore your own distinctive style without feeling the need to perform removes the pressure of thinking you have to live up to someone else's standard of sexual finesse.

ALTERNATE EXPRESSIONS

At times during every woman's life cycle she may be unable to participate actively in lovemaking, and some days the pressures of daily living drain her sexual desire. Because the Bible clearly promotes the value of sexual release without pauses—except for the purpose of spending time in prayer and fasting by mutual consent—it is important to examine the role pleasurable touch plays in satisfying a couple's sexual needs.

"Do not deprive each other," states Paul (1 Corinthians 7:5). But what is a couple to do when a woman takes several months to recover after giving birth? Or during lactation when a mother's estrogen levels fall and her sex drive plummets? Or following a disabling accident . . . or after surgery that temporarily requires her to avoid activity that hinders the healing process?

Clearly, our bodies are designed to achieve orgasm without engaging in sexual intercourse. If sexual expression within marriage is to be consistent and mutually satisfying, each couple may consider the needs of both partners when intercourse itself is undesirable or not feasible. *A husband and wife can wisely choose to avoid neglecting this vital part of their relationship even during times of stress, illness, recuperation, and childbearing.*

The hormonal differences between men and women account for some of the contrast in their sex drives as well. Presumably, many men have consistently higher expectations for the frequency of sexual sharing, partly because their bodies produce high levels of testosterone, the hormone closely linked to the desire for sexual release. Because of this and other factors influencing a man's sex drive, it is safe to assume that a majority of healthy men benefit from having regular, frequent sexual interaction with their wives.

In looking at a woman's ovulatory cycle, we see that her hormone levels vary significantly from one time of the month to another. Peaks in sexual interest reportedly correspond to the timing of ovulation and the days that immediately precede menstruation, with many women preferring not to make love during their periods. So where does this leave most husbands whose bodies are geared for a high level of interest in sex at almost any time of the month? Or what about wives whose husbands' sex drives are consistently lower than theirs?

As with other areas of our lives, a balance is necessary. Individual couples find that time spent together meeting one another's sexual needs draws them closer together and powerfully nourishes the bond they share. *How these needs are met vary between couples and with the same couple at different times.*

Life is not static. When a couple is able to discuss openly their sexuality within the context of their daily lives together, their need to be flexible and understanding toward one another becomes evident. In developing a love life that is mutually satisfying, a husband and wife grow to complement one another physically as well as emotionally and spiritually. Their creative use of loving touch expands over the years to include embraces that fulfill their need for sexual release whenever there is a need for sexual activity for one partner and a need for rest from sexual release on the part of the other.

Speaking without words in the sexual dimension of our lives can take into account that some conversations allow for one partner to listen while the other is speaking. We have the freedom to meet one another's sexual needs when one partner is unable to play an active role in the conversation. Adopting a mentality that views intercourse as the end-all and be-all of sexual interaction restricts many couples to either periodic or permanent abstinence.

This view does not have a biblical basis. Unfortunately, many books fail to address this issue, and the statistics of extramarital sex during times when a couple is unable to make love, such as during the time surrounding childbirth, prove that many husbands and wives believe avoiding intercourse means avoiding sexual expression altogether.

We can see once again the Lord's love for us in speaking through Paul's letter to the Corinthians. *God designed men and women to be sexual together within marriage—and He gives us permission to meet one another's sexual needs with joy.* The need a husband may have for regular release from sexual tension calls for a loving response on his wife's part as she balances her needs with his. A woman does not have to engage resentfully in intercourse when alternative expressions can provide the release her husband desires, and a husband does not need to resent his wife for not wanting or being unable to make love. A husband with a low sex drive or permanent sexual dysfunction, due to paralysis for example, can satisfy his wife by pleasuring her through physical touch.

Breathe a sigh of relief as you reflect upon what this means to you and what effect regular sexual sharing may have on your husband as you aim to spend time together. As you discuss what you have learned, explore ways you will each be comfortable with as you create more opportunities for sexual expression with one another even though one of you assumes a less active role. This may end up being one of the best talks you will have about your sexuality if you are honest about how frequently you desire intercourse and about your need for loving touch, and if you share your outlook on sexual intimacy without intercourse. If you are unsure about my interpretation of the Bible's teaching in this area, please check it thoroughly for yourselves so that you feel confident as you develop your own unique approach to meeting one another's sexual needs.

Gifting your spouse, volunteering whether he deserves it or not, for no reason whatsoever, for no payment in exchange, gratuitously, perfectly freely, for his sake alone, regardless of his work, his worth, or his investment in the relationship; giving him something for nothing—this is Grace. This displaces the marriage contract again and again with newness. And this images in action the divine face of the Lord Jesus Christ. As Jesus loved, so do you show the same love to your spouse.[4]

WALTER WANGERIN, JR.

Chapter Review

Personal Reflections

1. Knowing that God cares about every aspect of who I am—physically, emotionally, and spiritually—encourages me to:

2. Taking responsibility for my share of our sexual relationship at this point in our marriage will mean:

3. Telling my husband what I need concerning sexual intimacy is:

4. There have been times when I've tried to communicate with my husband about my sexual needs and preferences, but he didn't seem to listen, and so I:

5. The idea of one of us meeting the other's need for sexual release without having intercourse makes sense when I consider:

6. Perhaps the reason God's Word describes the importance of sexual intimacy in marriage without offering a detailed list of do's and don'ts is:

Related Bible Passages for Further Study

- Psalm 128
- Psalm 131
- Proverbs 8:1-11
- 1 Corinthians 7:1-6
- Galatians 6:1-26
- Philippians 2:1-4

$\mathscr{P}$RESSING ON

As for God, his way is perfect; the word of the Lord is flawless.
He is a shield for all who take refuge in him.
For who is God besides the Lord? And who is the Rock
except our God? It is God who arms me with strength
and makes my way perfect.

PSALM 18:30-32

We cannot live our lives constantly looking back,
listening back, lest we be turned to pillars of longing and regret,
but to live without listening at all
is to live deaf to the fullness of the music.[1]

FREDERICK BUECHNER

When Adam awoke to view his partner in Eden for the first time, he must have beheld her with the wonder we feel upon viewing a shimmering waterfall cascading over a rocky cliff, or an ancient range of mountains covered by glaciers gleaming in the sun, or turquoise waves rolling over a coral reef, or the endless expanse of a midsummer sky eerily lit with the northern lights. With a mixture of awe and excitement, we behold the majesty of creation from our tiny reference points, humbly moved by God's power as we view His splendid handiwork.

Eve was such a vision. Adam must have shouted for joy. He probably noticed her humanness after seeing nothing but animals. Her physical beauty was so similar to his own. Creative intelligence, a hallmark of their Creator, must have been evident in her eyes as she returned his gaze. Her smile likely radiated a warmth that Adam had not seen in any of the other creatures. She stood tall and moved gracefully toward him with a gait nothing like the loping, lurching travel of the others. But when she touched him . . .

She was the perfect partner. These two were unique in all creation. God blessed them and spoke freely with them. Their creation was conceived and carried out in love. After declaring the woman's identity an integral part of his own—"bone of my bones and flesh of my flesh"—the first man (Hebrew *Ish*), who had named all things, named the first woman (*Ishah*). He had been alone in his humanity, but now there was another with whom he could share himself. He found his counterpart in this woman of his flesh and bones.

The maleness of the one and the femaleness of the other combined to form the first human relationship. Humanity was expressed in duality, not in singularity—in complementary companionship rather than in isolation. Self-knowledge became shared knowledge. Their bodies were the same, yet different—designed to fit together, provide mutual comfort, and bring children into the world.

Naked in body, mind, and spirit before God, these two were also physically naked before one another. Nothing stood between them. Shame and guilt were unknown. Before one another and before God, with their gazes unimpeded by clothing or deceit, every detail of their individual uniqueness stood revealed, as Moses described: "The man and his wife were both naked, and they felt no shame" (Genesis 2:25).

This brief, concise statement underscores what all this must have meant to the man and woman. To our minds, it is difficult to comprehend the intimacy of their relationship. We cannot completely relate to that innocent time when sexuality was experienced without lust or greed or envy. Eve had no other woman to compare herself to. There were no other men for Adam to compete with. They shared an open, exclusive, one-of-a-kind relationship far removed from us in space and time.

Though we may experience the remnants of Eden's glory, we cannot return to its innocence. But we can appreciate the sexual design of our bodies and the purposes for which they have been created—to be joined together with our husbands within marriage, sharing the delight and comfort of one another's companionship; to replenish the earth; and to honor God with our bodies by giving our lives to Him to be used for His purposes and glory.

For this appreciation to be genuine, we need to choose honestly to face our sin and imperfection. We need to refuse courageously to pretend that the past doesn't matter. And we need to receive willingly God's complete forgiveness as He heals, mends, and remakes our hearts.

LIVING OUT OF EDEN

Perfect relationships are no longer possible this side of heaven. Many of us have been wounded by sexual sin. Few adult women have not been touched in a sexual way by someone other than their husbands. Fewer still have never fantasized nor thought about another man in sexual terms.

Beyond this, many women living in the United States today have experienced sexual assault or abuse—between 25 and 38 percent (estimated).[2] Millions of women have experienced divorce. Countless Christian wives today are dealing with, or have yet to face, the consequences of their husbands' involvement with pornography, sexual addiction, homosexuality, Internet liaisons, or an extramarital affair. We no longer reside in the Garden.

You would be an unusual person if you said that your sex life is satisfying to you all the time. If you have never felt guilty about your sexuality or endured a broken romantic relationship or glanced at a sex magazine or fantasized about kissing your favorite actor—well, that would be quite exceptional, too. The point is: we're human. And, because of our shared nature, we *all* fall short of God's glory. Without exception.

Some of us have felt at times as if we will never be whole again or be able to make love passionately with our husbands. Because there may still be that nagging doubt that we have been completely forgiven, we hold back from giving ourselves openly. We associate painful memories from our past with sexual sharing. We carry anger, hurt, fear, shame, resentment, or guilt as leftover baggage from the sexual experiences and relationships we experienced outside our marriage.

These experiences and emotions affect our ability to welcome our husbands wholeheartedly to the marriage bed. But because sexual sharing was designed to take place openly and lovingly within marriage, between partners with a lifelong, exclusive, mutual, unchanging, high regard for one another, we feel a deep inner dissatisfaction. We cannot experience sex as God created it to be because our hearts have been broken. We want to protect ourselves from being hurt again; we don't feel we can trust our husbands with our bodies; we're ashamed of the associations we have with sexual pleasure; we feel torn between wanting to hide and wanting to open up.

All too frequently, we see our husbands as the cause of our conflicting, self-protective feelings. Our husbands cannot love us perfectly. Christ alone can. Even though we know that no human being is capable of completely meeting our needs, we may not fully accept it. Sooner or later (and it is usually sooner), our mates disappoint us. Over time we may harden our hearts (if they were not that way already), structuring our sexual expression in ways that are predictable, to be run according to schedule, without the risk of self-exposure or rejection. We want to remain in control. Then we wonder why we feel that we have fallen into some kind of rut. And that is where the vicious circle starts. Resentment, bitterness, and despair creep in like "little foxes" to spoil the vine of marital sexuality. Intimacy becomes one more burden that must be borne rather than the gift of God it really is.

If we shut the Lord out of this area of our lives, we end up locking ourselves into feeling condemned, cheated, or wronged. We may get so stuck in the vicious cycle of defeat and despair that an extramarital affair ("I was only looking for *real* love"), divorce ("If I just had another chance"), or retribution ("I'm going to make him pay for this") actually seem an appealing, less painful alternative.

But Jesus offers a different way out. If our desire is to love our husbands and honor the Lord with our bodies, He will lead us into sexual wholeness. Through Christ, we have been given the opportunity to be healed in every area of our lives as we are reconciled to God through the finished work of the Cross. It is almost unbelievable. To feel so dead or empty inside and be shown the path of life and freedom is like a dream come true. We hear the words, we read the Word, yet we may still not believe it. *God has promised that He will restore our minds and our hearts through His Holy Spirit operating in our lives.*

I am not saying that this transformation will be easy. Nor will the changes take place instantaneously, without any real work involved. But all it takes to get started is this simple prayer: "Yes, Lord, here I am. I give You my heart, mind, body, spirit, will, and life. You are all that I need, Jesus. I'm Yours."

CLEANSED THROUGH CHRIST

"If we say we have no sin, we are only fooling ourselves and refusing to accept the truth. But if we confess our sins to him, he is faithful and just to forgive us and to cleanse us from every wrong" (1 John 1:8-9 NLT). "I— yes, I alone—am the one who blots out your sins for my own sake and will never think of them again" (Isaiah 43:25 NLT).

Praise God that His Word is true. If we "walk in the light, as he is in the light" (1 John 1:7), we have fellowship with the One who sits at the right hand of the Father. The blood of Jesus cleanses us from every sin (1 John 1:9), and our lives become "hidden with Christ in God" (Colossians 3:3).

We do not have to approach the promises of God timidly. We don't have to hide anymore. Our Lord has promised that He will cleanse us and forgive us if we acknowledge our sexual brokenness to Him. Through Jesus, we can be released from the oppressive yoke of bondage that sin places on our hearts, minds, and spirits.

Those of us who have been held captive by the weight of premarital and extramarital sexual experiences, relationships, and/or fantasies can be set free from fear and oppression. We can ask the Lord to take away the hurt and anguish we have suffered from broken or imperfect relationships, unmet expectations, clouded thinking, or victimization. We can give up our attempts at control to Christ and learn to depend on the Lord as the solid source of our identity and self-esteem.

Reading Psalm 51—perhaps the Bible's clearest expression of what it means to cry out to God for help in dealing with sexual brokenness—is an excellent place to get started. After reading it, you may want to pray the following prayer if you need healing in this area of your life:

Dear Heavenly Father,

I thank You for the hope that You have restored to me today. Through Your Word, I know that I am forgiven of sin that I confess to You. Lord, I ask You to forgive me for (be specific here). I acknowledge and accept Your forgiveness. I also ask that You help me forgive (person's name), because You have asked that I forgive others as You have forgiven me. Make me the partner for my husband that You would have me be. Teach me to love him as You have loved me.

I bind my heart, mind, spirit, and body to Your will for my life and marriage. I thank You for the gift of my sexuality and ask that You restore me to sexual wholeness. Grant me the grace, wisdom, and strength I need to make choices that honor You. I pray this in the name of Your Son, Jesus Christ.

Amen.

MOVING ON

People sometimes say they forgive us, but they keep reminding us of the wrong we did. God's forgiveness is not like that. When He forgives, He truly forgets our offense. In fact, He sees us as if we had never done the wrong. That's what we mean by the term justification.

The living out of our belief in this reality is an ongoing moment-to-moment process that continues throughout the remainder of our lives. This process as it is described in the Bible is called sanctification. Paul referred to it when he wrote about "pressing on" in the following passage:

Not that I have already obtained all this, or have already been made perfect, but I press on to take hold of that for which Christ Jesus took hold of me. Brothers, I do not consider myself yet to have taken hold of it. But one thing I do: Forgetting what is behind and straining toward what is ahead, I press on toward the goal to win the prize for which God has called me heavenward in Christ Jesus. All of us who are mature should take such a view of things.

PHILIPPIANS 3:12-15

It is not always easy to put the past behind us. We are like the child who has fallen down and skinned her knee. Every time she scratches the scab off the wound, it reopens and begins to bleed again. Emotional wounds, especially deep ones, take time to heal. We must make a conscious effort to walk away from the memories that tie us to past events, threatening to pull us backwards away from what's ahead. We need to look at the past only long enough to learn from it, and then move on.

"Obedience must be the struggle and desire of our life," said hymnwriter Phillips Brooks. "Obedience, not hard and forced, but ready, loving, and spontaneous; the doing of duty, not merely that the duty may be done, but that the soul in doing it may become capable of receiving and uttering God."[3]

Paul tells us to "strain toward what is ahead." This is not an automatic process that suddenly overtakes us upon our conversion. We must choose each day, moment by moment, to turn our backs on the habits, relationships, behaviors, and pain that rob us of our present joy in Jesus' presence—the people and things that make it difficult for us to stay headed in a new direction.

Paradoxically, the road trip we are on requires both weakness and endurance. We cannot do it on our own. And we cannot do it perfectly. As we depend upon God's grace and strength, we aim for a destination that sometimes seems far beyond our reach. That is where the need for faith and stamina comes in. The decision to keep going is not made once or twice. It is made thousands of times, in big and small ways, as we learn to lay down our tendency to seize control of our lives and as we surrender our self-rule to Christ's lordship.

Other people can offer us their support and sustenance, but they cannot complete the journey for us. When the way seems lonely—and there *will* be moments when only God knows what we are going through—we can choose to turn to the Lord for help, trusting Him to supply refreshment. In addition, practicing spiritual disciplines will build our stamina and draw us close to God.

Reading the Bible. Numerous passages remind us of our heavenward call in Christ. Instead of wondering if the Lord is able to lead us home, we can build up our stamina daily through reading His Word. When feelings of fatigue, sadness, regret, discouragement, or loneliness sap our strength, various psalms are especially vital reminders of God's care and comfort.

Sharing our concerns with the Lord in prayer. Remember Jesus in the Garden of Gethsemane as He shared with His Father His inner turmoil about His betrayal and its consequences? We are given God's promise in the Bible that He will draw near to us when we draw near to Him and that He will hear us when we call upon Him with a sincere heart. Learning to wait upon the Lord with listening ears and an open heart brings a fresh perspective on our situation.

Talking to a Christ-centered counselor. When lingering depression about the past exists, sharing our concerns with someone gifted in the ministry of counseling can be a valuable source of help. We need to find a person with whom we are comfortable. A referral from a trusted friend, pastor, physician, or colleague can be a good source of information concerning counseling support. After one or two visits, it is usually apparent if the counselor is satisfactory or not. Beyond this, the number of appointments needed may be determined by mutual decision between counselor and client.

Joining a support group. Many churches and counselors offer support groups as a way of promoting personal accountability and responsibility. Victims of incest, sexual assault, adultery, and spouse abuse; women with a history of substance abuse, sexually transmitted disease, and sexual addiction; teen moms, single parents, infertile couples, and widows—these and many other "subgroups" find rich solace through local Christian ministries devoted to specific community outreach.

Considering time our ally, not our enemy. Time is one of the greatest sources of healing. If the past still hurts, it is essential for us to realize that it will not hurt to the same degree one year from now. Or ten years from now. Or twenty-five years from now. The passage of time helps us forget the specific details of past events, reminding us that we are continually moving away from what is behind us.

Be patient as God tends the wounds of your past, always keeping in mind that He desires to bring about your sexual wholeness. Trust Him to complete His perfect work in your life. Walk with boldness and confidence into the future, and don't think that it is strange when the Lord reminds you of what you need to work on along the way. Eventually your wounds will heal completely, although the scars will faintly remain until the day when you are changed in God's holy presence.

> Let your understanding strengthen your patience.
> In serenity look forward to the joy
> that follows sadness.[4]

PETER DAMIAN

Chapter Review

Personal Reflections

1. Believing the Lord loves me unconditionally comes more easily when I:

2. It is difficult for me to accept God's forgiveness concerning:

3. At times I am surprised by how clearly a painful event related to sexuality pops into my mind, making me feel:

4. Knowing that nothing can separate me from God's faithful care helps me realize:

5. The greatest source of sexual shame in my past is:

6. If I were to ask God about how to regard my sexuality at this point in my life, I think He would say:

Related Bible Passages for Further Study

- Psalm 34:1-8
- Isaiah 61:1-3
- Luke 4:14-21
- Luke 7:36-50
- Hebrews 4:14-16
- 1 John 1:5–2:2

$\mathscr{C}$OPING WITH STRESS

We seem to live in the midst of a battle—there is such
a din, such a hurrying to and fro. In the streets of a crowded
city it is difficult to walk slowly. You feel the rushing of the
crowd and rush with it onward. In the press of our
life, it is difficult to be calm.

In this stress of wind and tide, all professions seem
to drag their anchors, and we are swept out into the main.
The voices of the present say—Come! But the voices of the past
say—Wait! With no less calm and solemn footsteps, nor less
certainty, does a great mind bear up against public opinion,
and push back its hurrying stream.

HENRY WADSWORTH LONGFELLOW

Through developing an appreciation of the variety of ways our
bodies interact with our emotions, thoughts, culture, and environment,
we learn to understand why our interest in sexual sharing fluctuates. If
our basic physical needs go unmet, for example—such as the need for
good nutrition and plenty of rest—this can inhibit sexual responsiveness.

Try to imagine your body as it directs and "prioritizes" its many
activities: providing nutrients to cells for energy and growth, maintaining a steady temperature and metabolic rate, promoting oxygen intake
through heart and lung activity, coordinating the complex processes by
which our brains and nerves communicate, and removing waste products
through our circulatory and digestive systems. Compared to these essential activities, sexual sharing is relatively unimportant.

To a large degree, our lifestyles either enhance or take away from our ability to carry out these basic functions. It is perfectly normal to feel disinterested in lovemaking when we are not healthy or if we are in pain, tired, or emotionally drained. Many factors influence sexual desire and how our bodies respond to lovemaking (Fig. 11-1).

Factors That Inhibit Sexual Expression
Figure 11-1

- Hunger	- Negative social learning	- Ignorance about how the body functions sexually
- Fatigue		
- Pain	- Preoccupation with other matters	- Feeling ashamed or embarrassed about one's body
- Depression	- Poor body image	
- Alcoholic beverages	- Misconceptions about a biblical view of sexuality	- Mistrust of husband's motives
- Medications		
- Anxiety		- Tension
- Fear	- Guilt over past experiences	- High level of stress
- Feelings of rejection	- Fear of pregnancy	- Conflicting sexual needs
- Low self-esteem	- Inability to communicate one's needs	
- High progesterone levels, hormonal changes	- Not enough time	- Misunderstanding husband's needs and concerns
- Illness	- Lack of privacy	

By acknowledging the reality of how our bodies function, we can discover ways to be more realistic about what they are capable of. We can also adapt our lifestyles to accommodate our physical and emotional needs and accept our limitations as well as our abilities. It is just good, plain common sense to pay attention to what our bodies "tell" us and meet our requirements for a variety of foods, adequate rest, and refreshing recreation. After meeting these basic needs, nonessential activities such as lovemaking take place with greater ease.

THE EFFECTS OF STRESS

Stress is a major roadblock to good lovemaking. In and of itself, stress is a helpful response, enabling us to cope with changes in our environment. But over a period of time, stress reactions can become chronic, deplete our energy reserve, and hinder our ability to fight off infection.

Through a complex system of nerves that exit from the spinal cord, our brains regulate many activities taking place within our bodies. From the moment our brains begin to function during the first month of pre-natal development, our nervous systems work to control our vital func-tions until the last current of "electricity" disappears from the brain and the heart stops beating.

As God created us, the body takes care of its vital functions at the subconscious level. Stop and think for a moment about the last time you tried to match your breathing rate to the oxygen level in your blood-stream when you hurried up three flights of stairs. We never have to think twice about such a thing because our brains monitor our oxygen levels automatically. In order to maintain a "steady state" within our bodies, our nervous systems must be able to regulate bodily processes whether we are working, thinking, dreaming, laughing, or doing som-ersaults.

The nervous system monitors our reactions to incoming information in numerous ways. We are only comfortable within a certain temperature range—protection against chilling and overheating. When the air gets too chilly, we put warmer clothing on. A body position held too long causes discomfort and signals us to shift our weight as a way of protecting our joints from damage. A finger that momentarily touches a hot pan is pulled quickly away in order to prevent the skin from burning. In these and other ways, the nervous system interacts with our environment through our perceptions about how and what we are feeling, thinking, and sensing at any given moment.

Fear sets our nervous system off like an alarm and provokes a reflex outside our control. Called the "fight or flight response," this reflex gears our bodies to confront the source of alarm or to flee from it. The fight or flight response is an important component of our autonomic nervous sys-tem. It enhances our ability to respond to what goes on around us—essen-tial for our survival in a dangerous world.

Think about the last time something unexpected and frightening hap-pened to you, such as when the phone rang in the middle of the night or when a car swerved into your lane and nearly hit your vehicle. Did your mouth dry up? How about your hands—did they get cold and tense?

Could you feel your heart pounding away on the inside of your chest? Good! That means you are perfectly normal: Your body responds to emergency situations in the appropriate way.

Like it or not, when the fight or flight reflex is turned on through the sympathetic nervous system, several things happen within our bodies. Stress hormones are released into the bloodstream, redirecting our blood supply away from our inner organs to larger muscle groups; our heart and breathing rates increase; our blood pressure rises; and our emotional state becomes acutely aware of potential danger. What an amazing process this is for helping us live in an erratic, unpredictable, ever-changing world.

But what about the times when stress hormones are secreted in non-threatening situations? What happens when your alarm clock jars you out of a restful slumber? When you drink three cups of coffee shortly thereafter? What does your heart rate do when you lose your temper in a traffic jam on the way to work or you try to beat the light because you are late to an appointment? How about the times you become angry at the latest bad news on television or when you shout at your husband or the children? These things can stimulate your sympathetic nervous system too, even though they don't pose the same threat as more dangerous situations.

Bit by bit the sympathetic nervous system, or SNS for short, can be provoked throughout the day, allowing levels of stress hormones to build up without our awareness. If our lifestyles provoke the flow of stress hormones on a frequent or continual basis, chronic stress results. Because our stress response to daily situations is not as strong as the response to a truly life-threatening situation, we tend to deny the significance of less serious stressors. In the long run, however, the chronic stress produced by constant lifestyle challenges can become far more destructive to our health than the acute stress of a brief crisis episode.

But don't despair. The Lord has designed us with the ability to maintain a balance in our nervous systems (Fig. 11-2). While the SNS *gears our body for action*, the parasympathetic nervous system, or PNS, *calms us down*. Consequently, we can counteract the daily stresses of life through regularly scheduled periods of rest and relaxation.

Jesus realized the importance of setting aside time to be alone with His Father, away from the demands of ministry to the multitudes. We also

Nervous Systems
Figure 11-2

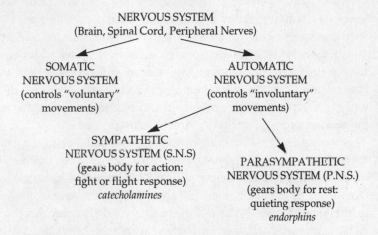

need a time of peace and quiet on a daily basis—as well as basic nutrients, exercise, sleep, and the appropriate expression of our emotions.

We have five main ways to reduce the effects of stress:

A balanced diet: By avoiding excessive sugar, alcohol, caffeine, processed meats, and monosodium glutamate, we can enhance our ability to cope with daily pressures. Several of these substances have been shown to produce changes in heart rate and contribute to other problems, such as tooth decay, obesity, alcoholism, headaches, and nervousness. In addition, drinking six or more glasses of water daily, including foods rich in complex carbohydrates (whole grain products, fruits, and vegetables), lowering fat intake, and eating calcium- and protein-rich foods promotes health and increases our ability to withstand stress.

Exercise for fun and enjoyment: Competitive activities or a mind-set that makes us push ourselves to the limit can increase stress hormone levels in our bodies. As a result, the activities we participate in for enjoyment as well as for fitness are the best forms of exercise. Swimming, walking, dancing, cycling, running, rope-skipping, and cross-country skiing are all excellent cardiovascular fitness activities. These forms of exercise can significantly reduce our stress level and improve our sense of well-being, especially when engaged in regularly for a thirty-minute period at least three times a week, if we keep our focus away from "beating the clock."

A regular bedtime followed by uninterrupted sleep: Irregular sleep patterns and frequent changes in bedtime schedules can disrupt the body by interfering with our ability to dream and reach specific brain wave patterns during rest. Dreaming allows us to release tension and anxiety. Our metabolism slows down, and our muscles relax when we achieve a deep-sleep state. Since our bodies and minds renew themselves in many different ways when we sleep, getting the rest we need enables us to be refreshed each night. Adequate sleep and physical rest also may reduce the severity of premenstrual syndrome in many women.

Appropriate expressions of emotion: It has been said that if we try to bury the feelings we are uncomfortable with, we bury them alive. In other words, simply denying negative feelings does not make them disappear. When we face the reality of our emotions and share them with the Lord, we learn to trust Him more deeply. Many of the psalms vividly portray this principle. As David poured out his heart to God, we witness his heart changing in dramatic ways as he is humbled, strengthened, and renewed in the Lord's presence. This theme is repeated many times throughout the Bible. Psalm 139 tells us that the Lord knows our words even before they are on our tongues and that no matter where we are, in the heavens or in the depths, our God is there. Like David, we too can invite the Lord to know our anxious thoughts and lead us in the everlasting way of His truth. Learning to be open before our Father is an essential part of our relationship to God.

Quiet times for relaxation: We can promote our ability to handle stress on the physical, emotional, and spiritual levels when we take time out to reflect on the majesty of God. Taking fifteen to twenty minutes out of a hectic day to relax in a comfortable position while setting our minds on Christ refreshes our bodies, minds, and spirits.

When we sit with our feet up in a recliner, soak in a warm bath, or lie comfortably on a soft supportive surface, we help our body relax by releasing the muscular tension that accumulates during the day. With closed eyes, taking deep breaths, we can think about how much the Lord loves us. Spending time in peaceful communion with Jesus in this way is yet another means of learning about Him. Rather than only asking for His help and intervention, we benefit from taking the time out to enjoy the ever-present comfort of the Holy Spirit.

Relaxing in this way can stimulate the PNS as a means of countering the effects of stress hormones. When the PNS is switched on, bodily processes slow down and powerful chemicals called endorphins are released. Endorphins diminish pain and promote a feeling of tranquillity. They're also released after times of physical exertion. Our Creator has wisely granted us the ability to reduce the effects of stress when we take time out to draw near to Him and rest in His presence.

STRESS AND SEXUAL RESPONSIVENESS

As women, chronic stress inhibits our ability to be sexually responsive. When the SNS is stimulated by stress hormones, blood flow to the genitals is greatly restricted. This response is much more obvious in a male than it is in a female. Perhaps you have noticed such an event in your husband when you were caressing one another, and suddenly he jumped up thinking someone was at the door. In an instant, all sexual interest was gone as the blood left his genitals and rushed to his legs and arms.

What about other areas? Increased muscle tension in the pelvic floor can make intercourse painful. Instead of feeling pleasantly sensitive, the breasts tighten, and touching them causes irritation. Stress hormones are a potent way to delay sexual gratification when danger is present. The SNS in effect "turns off" sexual responsiveness, while the PNS better enables it to become "turned on" (Fig. 11-3).

Body Factors and Sexuality
Figure 11-3

BODY FUNCTION	FIGHT OR FLIGHT EFFECTS	QUIETING RESPONSE EFFECTS
Heart rate	Faster	Slower
Breathing rate	Increased	Decreased
Blood pressure	Elevated	Lowered
Sweat production	Increased	Decreased
Metabolic processes	Speeded up	Slowed down
Circulation in large muscles	Greatly increased	Remains steady
SNS activity	Increased	Decreased
PNS activity	Decreased	Increased

ADDITIONAL FACTORS RELATED TO SEXUAL FUNCTION	FIGHT OR FLIGHT EFFECTS	QUIETING RESPONSE EFFECTS
Blood flow to genitalia	Decreased	Steady (increased when stimulated)
Tension in pelvic floor	Tense	Relaxed
Skin temperature	Lowered	Elevated
Vaginal responsiveness	Sensitivity decreased	Sensitivity increased
Muscle tension	Increased	Decreased or directed to specific areas when stimulated
Breast sensitivity	Reduced	Promoted
Emotional state	Distracted, agitated	Calm, able to focus on pleasurable sensations
Level of sexual response	Greatly minimized	Pleasurable sensations maximized

In addition to relaxation, there are several other ways of stimulating the PNS. The response that opposes the fight or flight reflex is called the quieting response. One of the best ways of provoking it is through touch. Think about the sensations you feel during a back rub or when someone else brushes your hair. Those sensations are related to PNS activity.

Twelve Ways to Prompt the Quieting Response

1. Warm, leisurely shower or bath

2. Slow breathing: 6-12 breaths per minute

3. Soothing environment: candlelight, dimmed lighting, adjusted room temperature, pillows, loose clothing

4. Relaxing sounds: music, nature sounds, silence

5. Comfortable position with release of muscular tension

6. Avoidance of worry

7. Reflection on the beauty and majesty of God and His creation

8. Listening to an audio tape of someone reading psalms

9. Resting in bed while awake

10. Massage: back, neck, face, scalp, arms, legs

11. Contemplative prayer

12. Sitting quietly for fifteen minutes, without distractions
    or interruptions

As you relax, know that the Lord is with you. Avoid any thoughts that distract you from delighting yourself in God and resting in His presence. Find Bible passages that give you confidence and reassurance—God's promises of peace—and think about them. Give thanks to and praise the Lord for His blessings, entrusting Him with every burden weighing you down. Psalm 23 describes this well as it paints a pastoral scene of the Lord tenderly caring for us as our Shepherd. You may find it helpful to picture yourself in one of these ways as you relax in God's gentle protection— leaning on the everlasting arms, lying down in green pastures, walking beside the still waters, resting under the shadow of His wings (Deuteronomy 33:27; Psalm 17:8; 23:2; 91:4).

"To learn sense is true self-love," wrote Solomon (Proverbs 19:8 NEB). Our physical, emotional, spiritual, and sexual health is promoted when we choose to live wisely, according to the way God has designed our bodies, minds, and spirits to function. Learning to live sensibly requires knowledge and self-discipline as we balance our needs for activity and rest, talking and listening, working and playing, serving others and taking time out for ourselves. Finding this balance—and maintaining it—is challenging; neglecting or denying the need for this balance can turn even the most fruitful life into an arid wasteland. Anne Morrow Lindbergh observed: "Traditionally we are taught, and instinctively we long, to give where it is needed—and immediately. Eternally, woman spills herself away in driblets to the thirsty, seldom being allowed the time, the quiet, the peace, to let the pitcher fill up to the brim."[1]

We are aware of our hunger and our needs, but ignorant of what will satisfy them. With our garnered free time, we are more apt to drain our creative springs rather than refill them. With our pitchers, we attempt sometimes to water a field, not a garden. We throw ourselves indiscriminately into committees and causes. Not knowing how to feed the spirit, we try to muffle its demands and distractions. Instead of stilling the center, the axis of the wheel, we add more centrifugal activities to our lives—which tend to throw us off balance.[2]

Woman must be the pioneer in this turning inward for strength. In a sense, she has always been the pioneer. Less able, until the last generation, to escape into outward activities, the very limitations of her life forced her to look inward. And from this gaze she gained an inner strength that man in his more outward life did not find as often. But in our recent efforts to emancipate ourselves, to prove ourselves the equal of man, we have, naturally enough perhaps, been drawn into competing with him in his outward activities, to the neglect of our own inner springs. Why have we been seduced into abandoning this timeless inner strength of woman for the temporal outer strength of man?[3]

The hectic pace many of us so easily fall into demands constant reevaluation. When we start to feel dry, we need to recognize the critical importance of asking God to refill our inner springs and waiting upon His presence as He does so.

We can choose how to respond to life's daily stresses. Will we "learn sense" as Solomon advised and thereby resist the outward pull of our culture? Or will we be "seduced into abandoning this timeless inner strength of woman for the temporal outer strength of man?" Our created nature causes us to thirst for the fountains of God. In His presence we will be refreshed and renewed as we freely drink from the streams of life that flow into our lives at His command.

> *The fruit of righteousness will be peace; the effect of righteousness will be quietness and confidence forever.*
>
> ISAIAH 32:17

Thy whole creation speaks thy praise . . . that so our soul rises up out of its mortal weariness unto Thee, helped upward by the things Thou hast made and passing beyond them unto Thee who hast wonderfully made them: and there refreshment is and strength unfailing.

AUGUSTINE

Chapter Review

Personal Reflections

1. When I start to live out of balance, I've usually neglected:

2. For me, the greatest challenge to waiting on God to refill my inner springs lies in my choice to:

3. I'm most vulnerable to denying my need to slow down and live sensibly on a daily basis if I:

4. Stress affects my sexual responsiveness most in the area of:

5. For me, the quieting response is prompted best by:

6. Jesus promised His followers that He would give them "a spring of water welling up to eternal life" (John 4:14). This promise encourages me to remember to rest in His presence when:

Related Bible Passages for Further Study

- Psalm 23

- Psalm 33:13-22

- Psalm 36:5-10

- Psalm 42:1-5

- Isaiah 35

- Matthew 11:28-30

ℋOW TO GIVE A GREAT BACK RUB

*As we grow older, skin offers the most natural medium
for communicating basic emotions, such as love. It is our chief organ
of contact with others. Skin cells offer a direct path into the deep
reservoir of emotion we metaphorically call "the human heart."*

*Touching includes risk. It can evoke the cold, armorlike resistance
of a hurt spouse refusing to be comforted or the lonely shrug of a
child who insists, "Leave me alone!" But it can also conduct the
electric tingling of love-making, the symbiosis of touching and
being touched simultaneously. A kiss, a slap on the cheek—
both are forms of touching, and both communicate.*[1]

DR. PAUL BRAND AND PHILIP YANCEY

H ave you ever had the luxury of receiving a massage from a registered physical therapist or a certified massage therapist? If so, you are
already aware of the stress-relieving qualities of therapeutic massage.

I know what you may be thinking: *Why would a Christian woman even
consider going to a massage therapist?* Well, I admit that I used to think it was
pretty strange too until my sister-in-law and one of my best friends (both
Christians) became massage therapists and applied their skills to me one
day. It was absolutely wonderful. Now if I could just convince my husband to go through the training.

Seriously, I can't think of anything quite as relaxing as a properly
administered back rub. Part of the reason for this is that few things stimulate the PNS better. Massage can also be an excellent prelude to love-

making. Loving touch aimed at nurturing one's partner in nonsexual ways is an invaluable means of conveying love and affection. Learning the art of massage can benefit a marriage in multiple ways.

Emotional attachment to our loved ones is promoted through the built-in gift of touch God has given to us. Did you know that we were created with a need for touch in order to survive? Babies who receive an insufficient amount of touching may actually waste away and die of a disease called failure-to-thrive syndrome.

Loving touch is a primary means of expressing our attachment, concern, appreciation, sympathy, and involvement toward another person. It does not matter whether the person is two or ninety-two—touch speaks a language of its own. Consider all of the "touch" phrases we commonly use to refer to human interaction:

"I'll be in touch with you soon."

"That scene was really touching."

"Reach out and touch someone."

"Let's stay in touch."

"He really rubs me the wrong way."

"I'll handle that matter for you."

"Is she ever a soft touch!"

Human relationships thrive on touch when it is done appropriately and with respect. We have many examples in the Gospels of Jesus touching those around Him and of His disciples touching Him. I especially like the references to "the disciple whom Jesus loved" leaning back against Jesus at the Last Supper and to His taking the little children in His arms. The "laying on of hands" has great significance throughout the New Testament and continues to be used today in many different denominations during Communion, baptism, ordination, prayers for healing, and requests for special anointing. Through touch we let others know *we care*.

Nonsexual physical expressions of love are a key way of nurturing our husbands and our children. Think for a moment. Have you ever heard a friend complaining that her husband was giving her too many back rubs?

CARING COMMUNICATION THROUGH TOUCH

Between a husband and wife, the gift of touch is as significant as it is in any human relationship. If married partners only touch one another in sexual ways or in order to attempt to stimulate one another toward sexual arousal, a marriage can suffer.

Many women have told me of their resentment that their husbands only touch them when they want "something in return." It is certainly true that many men have been raised in homes where cuddling, hugging, snuggling, and putting arms around male family members was uncommon. Discovering new ways of expressing love through touch can be a growing experience for anyone reared in a "low-touch" atmosphere. But learn we must. We cannot afford to abandon the caring communication *everyone* needs, whether they're aware of it or not.

It is unrealistic to think that your husband will know how to give you a good back rub if he has never received one himself. Thus, a good way to begin to foster more loving communication through touch in your home is by learning how to give your husband a good massage. In this way, your hands will teach him gently about your love for him and will also "tell" him how you would like him to touch you. Taking the time to learn this skill is well worth the time and effort. Eventually you will take turns and may even find yourself trying to think up ways to be the second recipient. It is difficult to get up after being the first one to receive the massage!

The principles upon which an effective massage is based are fairly simple to learn and easy to remember. In following these steps, you will rapidly develop an excellent technique and have your husband expressing his appreciation to you even with your first attempt. These steps are:

1. *Reduce the friction* caused by your hands with an agent such as cornstarch or oil. The types of oil that work best are vegetable, nut, or cold-pressed seed oils such as peanut, almond, safflower, or corn oil. You may use them alone or in combination with one another. Scented oils may be obtained through some health food stores or specialty soap shops in eight-ounce or larger containers.

2. When you are ready to begin the massage, *put on some relaxing music and ask your husband to remove his clothing.* Give him a gigantic terry towel or flannel blanket to wrap around himself. When he lies down on his stomach for the back rub, be sure to keep him covered from the buttocks downward. By keeping areas covered

that are not a part of the area you are concentrating the massage on, you will keep the focus on the back rub and away from his sexuality. Massage can be incorporated into lovemaking at other times. For learning these techniques and as a means of stress reduction, however, it is helpful to agree on avoiding sexual stimulation.

3. *Have him lie on a comfortable surface* at a height that will help you to avoid back strain as you work. If he is lying on his stomach, place a small pillow under his abdomen to reduce back strain for him, if needed. You may also place a rolled towel under the front surface of his ankles to enable his legs to relax. When he is lying on his back, he may enjoy having a doubled up pillow under each knee to reduce back strain.

4. When you massage, *use strokes that conform to the contours of your husband's body* while at the same time applying pressure deep enough to promote circulation but not uncomfortable. Use your hands to "talk" to your husband lovingly, smoothly, and rhythmically.

5. *Stroke in particular patterns* at speeds described in the text. Rhythm and repetition are essential. Stroke without interruption over a specific area until you have completely massaged it.

6. *Pray for your husband while you're touching him.* Let your hands express how you feel about him and view them as a means of conveying not only your love for him, but the Lord's love for him as well. Ask him to do the same for you whenever he gives you a massage. Bless one another through soothing forms of touch.

7. *Obtain feedback from him* to find out what parts of the massage he liked the best and if he would like you to continue by concentrating on specific areas.

8. *Finish the massage one area at a time* by placing your hands flat on the surface that you have completed, pressing in slightly, then lifting up and off the surface. For example, when you have completed the back, place one hand between the shoulders and one

hand at the base of the spine, press, then lift both hands at the same time. This quiet signal tells him you are done.

BASIC MASSAGE TECHNIQUES

Now that you have learned these tips, you are ready to begin massaging. You may want to begin with just the back and gradually add other areas as your hands become stronger: the shoulders and neck, arms and hands, legs and feet, scalp and face. Doing a complete massage is time-consuming. You might vary the area you massage and length of time you spend on each, depending on your schedule. When specific areas of the body are tense, such as during a headache or after doing yard work, concentrating on those areas are a better use of your time.

The circular and patterned movements you will be using are directed toward the head and heart, while the long, flowing, relaxing strokes move toward the periphery of the body. In this way, circulation is promoted and relaxation is enhanced. In addition to putting on some soothing music, you might take the phone off the hook to better separate yourselves from the stress of the world outside. This can really be a special time between the two of you, as corny as it may seem. Most of us just get too busy and can use such moments to better appreciate the wonder of our relationships.

The Back

1. *Circle sweeps:* With your husband lying on his stomach, place both of your hands at the base of his back on his waist. Be sure to have enough oil on your hands so they glide smoothly over the surface of his skin. Begin to stroke up along the spine (but not on it), using circular movements that move up, over the surface of the back, toward the sides, then back around to the midline. Make the strokes six to eight inches in diameter, and move in an upward direction to the shoulders. It will take four or five circles spiraling upwards to cover the surface of the back.

   Once your hands have reached the top, place them at the base of the neck, palms down, and apply gentle pressure as they glide down to the base of the back. Repeat this sequence for two to five minutes or until you feel the muscles in the back release their tension. It may help to think of this counting sequence as you rub: 1 (up), 2 (out), 3 (down) repeated slowly for four or five strokes; on last stroke—1, 2, 3, center, down, 2, 3, 4.

2. *Hands together:* Now focus your strokes on one side of the back at a time. Place your hands next to one another on the right side of the spine at the base of the back. Put your right hand slightly higher than the left so your right thumb is nearly over the left thumb near the left forefinger. In this way, your left hand will follow the strokes your right hand makes, just as if it is imitating what the right hand is doing. Begin stroking, using the circle sweeps pattern, making sure to glide smoothly over the skin while applying a greater degree of pressure than before. Continue to rhythmically stroke the right side, including the shoulder, for two to three minutes. Repeat this sequence for the same length of time along the left side, leading with your left hand.

3. *Walk-ups:* In this pattern, you will be working closer to the spine, one side at a time. Place the three middle fingers of your right hand next to the right of the base of the spine so they are almost flat. Then put the three middle fingers of your left hand under the base of your right fingers, with your left hand underlying your right palm. Your fingers will be working as a unit and will be touching the back with their fleshiest part. Using circles two inches in diameter, spiral up along the bones of the spine, being sure to avoid putting pressure on the spine itself. You will actually be rubbing only the muscles that lie alongside the bone. The large nerve roots that exit from the spinal cord will be stimulated as well. Each circle can be done in one count, and it will take about sixteen to twenty circles to reach the base of the neck.

    Continue upwards along the neck using your right hand only, until you reach the skull. Slide back down to the base of the spine with your hands flat and in the same position you used for Step 2 of the massage. Repeat on the left side, leading with either your left or right middle fingers—whichever is most comfortable. Alternate back and forth in this manner for three to five minutes.

4. *See-saws:* Place your hands parallel to each other over the top portion of the buttocks in a horizontal position. Your right hand should be on top, with your right thumb lying next to the small finger of your left hand. Following the contour of your husband's body, draw your hands out to the sides. Then slide them over across the back to the opposite sides. Your hands meet only when at the center of the back. The count would be: 1 (right hand moves left/left hand moves right), 2 (right hand moves right/left hand moves left), 1, 2, 1, 2, etc., until the hands reach the shoulders. The movements are nice and easy, and the count is fairly slow. Slide your hands down along the center of the back, in a parallel position, to resume your starting point. Repeat for two to three minutes.

5. *Thumbs-up:* Place your wrists about two inches apart, with your thumbs pointing upwards and your fingers directed toward the sides of the back. Your right fingers will be pointed to the right side and your left fingers to the left. With your hands resting gently on the surface of the back, use the pads on your thumbs to press up along the sides of the spine about three inches at a time in wide arcs. The count for this movement is: 1, press, 2, out—a two-count pattern. Lift the thumbs slightly to return to midline after each stroke while keeping the fingers of both hands resting lightly along the sides. It will take ten to twelve strokes from the base of the spine at the top of the buttocks to the base of the skull. (When you reach the neck, you will be using your thumbs only, with your fingers lifted out and away from his neck. Repeat for several minutes.)

6. *Repeat favorite pattern:* Ask your husband which pattern he enjoyed the most and repeat it for a few minutes. Be creative, as you may develop several patterns of your own after you discover what he likes best.

7. *The harp stroke:* When you have completed Steps 1 through 6, you can finish the back rub with downward stroking along the cen-

tral area of the back. Beginning near the neck, draw the fingers of your right hand down the back in a stroke that begins at the top and lifts off near the buttocks. As the right hand lifts, the left hand repeats the stroke, so that the pattern is continuous. It will take two counts to complete each stroke. Repeat this for one or two minutes. Place your right hand at the top of the back, your left hand at the base, and apply a slight pressure to signal the end of the back rub.

The Shoulders and Neck

The muscles of the shoulders and neck often carry more than their share of tension compared to other areas of the body. This massage can be done almost anywhere. It is not necessary to massage skin-to-skin, although it is preferable.

1. *Feather stroke:* You may begin this stroke at the top of the head or under the ears by placing your hands lightly on the surface of the skin. With your hands next to one another, or on opposite sides, smoothly stroke downwards, then outwards. Cover the top of the shoulders; then repeat this pattern while moving closer to the center of the back each time. It will take three to five strokes to reach the midline. Repeat this sequence for one to three minutes. (You will be stroking downwards to the level of the shoulder blades each time.)

2. *Kneading dough:* Follow Step 1 with a more vigorous massage that will remind you of kneading bread dough. Start with your hands on both sides of the base of the neck with your thumbs pointing toward the spine and your fingers lying across the sides of your husband's neck. Gently squeeze the muscles lying at the base of the neck while rubbing the muscles carefully between your thumbs and fingers. Move along the muscles that lead from the neck to where the arms are joined to the shoulders. Use circular motions of the thumbs to press his muscles toward your fingers. When you reach the edge of the shoulders, use a long stroke to return back to the neck. Ask your husband how vigorously he

wants you to rub and pray that your hands become stronger! Repeat for several minutes until he indicates the tension is gone. If indicated, spend time on smaller areas that seem to be especially tender or tense. Rub in this manner along the sides of the neck, if needed.

3. *Repeat Step 1.* End this massage by placing your hands on your husband's shoulders, applying pressure for a moment, then lifting off.

The Arms and Hands

The arms and hands massage is a natural extension of the neck and shoulder massage if you have time to do it. Ask your husband to remove his watch and rings. As with the neck/shoulder massage, this massage can be done with your husband sitting up, with the exception of Step 2, which requires a prone position.

1. *Repeat Step 1* of the neck/shoulder massage, stroking from the crown of the head or the base of the neck all the way down to the fingertips. Continue to stroke this area for about one minute.

2. *Round-the-bend:* If your husband is lying down on his stomach, you may follow Step 1 with this pattern. Otherwise, you will proceed directly to Step 3. Move around to the right side of your husband and pick up his right hand with your right hand, placing his hand in the crook of your right arm. With his right arm extended, use your left hand to stroke up along his upper arm, over his shoulder, around his shoulder blade, and back down the back part of his arm to the wrist. Stroke upwards lightly until you are back up at the top of the arm; then apply greater pressure so that you feel his arm pulling away from his body as your hand comes down around his shoulder blade and under his arm. Repeat this stroke four or five times. Then place his extended hand on your lap or shoulder, depending on how you're positioned. Follow with Step 3 in this position.

3. *Kneading dough:* Move up the arm with the same pattern as Step 2 of the neck/shoulder massage, using gentle kneading strokes

until you reach the fleshy, muscular portion of the upper arm. Concentrate the kneading pattern a little longer in this area. When you reach the top of his arm, place your hands on either side and use a long, smooth stroke to reach his wrist while pulling his arm toward you. Repeat this pattern—kneading up, pulling down—for several minutes.

4. *Hands-on:* Place your husband's right hand in your lap or on a nearby surface, palm up. Hold his hand in both of your own and place your fingers under his hand, as you'll be using your thumbs to rub the fleshy part of his hand. Rub in a circular pattern, moving your thumbs up the center of the palm, up and along the base of his fingers, then down across the edges of his hand. After rubbing this way for about a minute, use your right thumb to rub in a small circular motion at the base of his thumb and fingers. Spend about ten seconds on each one, then circle his thumb with your thumb and first two fingers and pull outwards while applying a firm grip, as if you were pulling a tight ring off his thumb. Repeat this pattern until you have done all five fingers.

5-8. *Repeat Steps 1-4* on the left shoulder, arm, and hand.

The Legs

Have your husband sit comfortably in a chair or assume a semi-reclining position. The leg massage discussed here is the least appreciated part of a body massage, but is very beneficial for someone who has a desk job and is unable to walk much during the day. Massaging the calves is particularly good for anyone on their feet a lot or after cardiovascular fitness activities that are weight-bearing, such as running, stair-climbing, rope-skipping, or racquetball. (Steps 3 and 4 may be done following a back rub with your husband lying on his stomach.)

1. *Up and over:* Begin by massaging up the center of the legs, using both hands, from along the inside of the knees to across the top of the thighs, and then back down along the outside of the thighs to the out-

side of the knees. In a large circular motion, press up, over, out, and down with a firm stroke. Repeat for two to three minutes; then cover the entire length of the legs in this fashion, from the ankles, to the top of the thighs, and back down to the ankles again. Be sure that your fingers point up toward the top of the legs on the way up and across the back of the legs on the way down. Repeat for one to three minutes.

2. *Knees up:* Place your husband's right knee over your left hand, wrist, or lower arm and lift it up slightly. Using the three middle fingers of your right hand, stroke clockwise around the kneecap for forty-five to sixty seconds. Be careful not to press on the bones too hard. Place your thumb to the left of his kneecap and your first two fingers to the right of it; then stroke up, lift, and repeat along the sides of the knee for thirty to forty-five seconds. Repeat these two patterns on the left knee, using a counterclockwise motion on the first stroke.

3. *Calves knead:* Reach around with your right hand to the back of your husband's left leg and begin to knead the muscles of the calf from the back of the top of the ankle to just below the knee. Avoid squeezing the Achilles tendon or the tendon behind the knee. Concentrate on the fleshy, muscular portion of the calf instead. Rub and squeeze in a circular motion with as much pressure as your husband finds comfortable. When you reach the top, stroke down along the back of the leg until you reach your starting point; then begin moving upwards again. You might find it helpful to hold his leg under the ankle with your left hand and lift it slightly. Repeat this pattern for one to two minutes; then follow with the opposite leg.

4. *Repeat Step 4* of the previous section *(Hands-on)* with each foot. If your husband is ticklish, adapt the massage so that it is relaxing, or skip this step altogether.

The Scalp and Face

These areas are important to massage if your husband carries tension in his jaw or forehead. This is one of the best helps to alleviating headaches I know of and can be done using a little bit of cornstarch rather than oil if you prefer. Have your husband sit in a chair, lay his head in your lap, or lie down with you facing the top of his head.

1. *Sleepy head:* Put your hands under your husband's head near the top of his neck. Lift his head up slightly and pull it a little bit toward you. Use your thumbs to hold his head in this position while you use your fingers to do a circular massage pattern along the back of his neck. Move your thumbs very slowly upwards as you continue to rub along the back part of the head until you are about one inch over the ridge that lies at the base of the skull. Slowly press in as you slide your fingers back over the area you just massaged. When you reach your starting point, move your hands about half an inch toward the ears and repeat the pattern. Continue until you have covered the entire back of the head. Ask your husband if he would like you to do some more of this. If he has chronic neck tension, he may never want you to stop!

2. *Chin pull:* Now reach down and put your hands along his jaw so that you are cupping his chin in your fingers. Using a smooth, continuous motion, pull your hands up along the jaw and under the chin, then over the ears to the crown of your husband's head. Lift your hands off and resume this pattern, repeating it several times.

3. *Shampoo:* Imagine you are shampooing your husband's hair, using the broad parts of your fingertips. If you have long fingernails, trim them before you begin any massage, but especially before this part. With circular patterns, rub his scalp rhythmically for about a minute, covering every square inch. Apply as much pressure as he indicates is comfortable.

4. *Tiny circles:* Use the three middle fingers of both hands and massage with gentle pressure from just above your husband's temples to the base of his jaw. The pattern is made up of circles about an inch in diameter that spiral slowly downwards over the temples, cheekbones, up into the hollow of the cheekbones, over the jawbone to the midline of the chin. When completed, slide your hands back up, using a slight pulling motion, and start over, with your hands about one quarter of an inch farther forward than they were the first time. Repeat the pattern four or five times.

5. *Facial stroke:* It may seem strange to you to be giving your husband a "facial," but he will probably find it soothing. With your hands placed lightly on the surface of his forehead, you will be stroking from the center of the face, outwards to the sides, and lifting your hands off the surface of the face after you go over each part of it to return to the middle: the forehead, eyebrows, eyelids (don't press!), nose/cheekbones, underneath the cheekbones, up along the front of the jaw and over the edge of the jaw, up across the temples to the top of his head. Repeat this pattern until you hear him snoring.

TAKE WHAT YOU NEED AND LEAVE THE REST

Not everyone enjoys being massaged. As with the rest of the information in *The Christian Woman's Guide to Sexuality,* take what you need from this chapter and leave the rest. Or you may find that you prefer hiring a certified massage therapist occasionally for your back rubs if your husband strongly dislikes giving them to you. Consider asking him to give you a gift certificate for a professional massage for your next birthday.

Most communities now have CMT's listed in the phone book for easy reference; many are Christian women. Getting a massage from a CMT is a terrific pampering treat for stressed-out moms and wives. Several grocery stores where we live now offer ten- to fifteen-minute mini-massages for customers, a less expensive alternative to the thirty- to sixty-minute treatments available elsewhere. And I recently noticed that even JC Penney at a nearby shopping mall provides professional massage services in their beauty salon.

This may seem a bit trendy for your taste, but it is actually a bona fide investment. By being careful about overdoing things and by taking care of yourself, you will have greater energy to carry you through stressful days.

> When money is tight, buy bread,
> but don't forget to purchase hyacinths for the soul. [2]
>
> BRENDA HUNTER

Chapter Review

Personal Reflections

1. Nurturing touch plays an important part in our marriage because it:

2. Getting a back rub usually/always/sometimes makes me feel:

3. When I applied some of the massage techniques in this chapter to my husband, we discovered:

4. The idea of hiring a certified massage therapist to give me a massage seems:

5. As I look at the scenes in the Bible where Jesus touched the people he was ministering to, I see:

Related Bible Passages for Further Study

- Psalm 16:5-11

- Psalm 143:5-8

- Isaiah 43:1-2

- Matthew 9:18-25; Luke 8:40-56

- Luke 7:36-50

- Luke 24:36-40

CHOOSING OUR ADVENTURE

Personal freedom demands that we choose the quality of our adventure. In fact, we must decide what our adventure will be. We cannot give ourselves to two adventures at the same time. We must decide what is worthwhile. Too many people live with divided hearts, and their lives are fragmented with a little bit of this and a little bit of that. None of it fits into a meaningful pattern, and the person, having made no decision and commitment to what is worthwhile, wastes years—or a lifetime. An ironic tragedy is to aim at nothing and hit it. Or perhaps still worse, to aim at the wrong thing and hit it.

Deciding what is worthwhile demands having a standard, a measure outside ourselves. On what basis will you judge what is worthwhile? What is worthwhile must have meaning in an ultimate sense, in God's sight, so that all the small pieces of each day, though they be trivial, will fit in with that meaning.[1]

GLADYS HUNT

Have you ever felt drained and empty after pouring yourself out on behalf of someone else or while trying to meet a deadline or in the middle of an important project? Have you ever become so stretched that you find yourself regularly weeping or yelling with little provocation— and no joy in sight?

As women, God has given us minds and bodies that are sensitive to the ebb and flow of life. We respond inwardly with a woman's nature to the changing currents of time. Though many sources of tension—a baby with colic, a demanding schedule, a limited budget—will not go away overnight, simply dreaming about "better days" to come does not help us cope constructively with what causes tension.

Each of us has a limit to the amount of stress we can deal with before our bodies and our minds react. And some of us cannot handle as much stress as the next person. We are *not* all created equal when it comes to the ability to withstand pressures and demands. Assessing our personal priorities; identifying what produces the greatest time, energy, and financial conflicts; developing a plan that helps us to resolve these conflicts, and promoting our health lowers our stress load.

MAKING A PERSONAL ASSESSMENT

What happens within your body when you confront conflict or tension? Do you notice your reaction immediately, or does your stress response tend to accumulate over a period of hours or days? What are your stress symptoms?

The symptoms listed in the chart below have been identified as possible stress reactions. They can also be caused by physical or psychological illnesses, but in the absence of a medical diagnosis following a thorough examination by a qualified physician, they usually indicate stress. You may use this list to help you identify the ways your body reacts to stress.

How Do You Handle Stress?
Monitoring Your Stress Responses
Figure 13-1

STRESS RESPONSE	TIME/DAY	REASON (*if known*)
Hot flashes or chills		
Neck pain or tenderness		
Rashes or hives not caused by allergies		
Frequent headaches		
Chest pain		

STRESS RESPONSE	TIME/DAY	REASON (if known)
Heart palpitations; irregular heartbeat		
Heart racing/pounding sensations		
Insomnia		
Irritable bowels		
Cold, clammy hands		
Upset stomach		
Heartburn or acid indigestion		
Teeth grinding		
Excessive sweating		
Twitching		
Trembling		
Inability to concentrate		
Constant daydreaming		
Frequent crying spells		
Tenderness under cheekbone		
Overwhelming urge to cry or run and hide		
Outbursts of anger		
Nightmares		
Overeating		
Lack of appetite		
Urge to smoke or drink alcoholic beverages more		
Forgetfulness		
Withdrawal from others		
Frequent sore throats		
Lowered resistance to infection		
Hyperventilation or breathlessness		

STRESS RESPONSE	TIME/DAY	REASON (*if known*)
Onset of new allergies		
Lack of energy		
Inability to relax		
Nervous laughter or giggling inappropriately		
Biting fingernails		
Dependence on caffeine for sense of vitality		
Constipation		
Diarrhea		
Nausea		
Dizziness		
Sense of feeling directionless		
Suicidal thoughts		
Self-criticism		
Other:		

When you experience stress-related signs and symptoms,
do you care about yourself enough to say:

STOP!

STOPPING THE COMPARISONS

So many pressures face us as women today. Stress is a continuing reality as we confront the demands upon us, whether we willingly choose them or have to accept them as the Lord brings them into our lives.

God's Word tells us: "Carry each other's burdens, and in this way you will fulfill the law of Christ," and "Each one should test his own actions. Then he can take pride in himself, without comparing himself to somebody else, for each one should carry his own load" (Galatians 6:2, 4-5). Within our churches, we need to depend upon the Lord's strength and sustenance to support and love one another without comparing ourselves to each other. Together we walk out the truth of what it means to be redeemed and forgiven as we respect one another's differences and celebrate our similarities.

We can do much to decrease the stressful aspects of our lives if we learn the skill of compassionately sharing one another's burdens while at the same time doing what we can to carry our own.

SIX STRATEGIES FOR STRESS RELIEF

As uniquely created individuals, we each need to determine what our "stress tolerance level" is and try not to exceed it on an everyday basis. The following strategies can help.

1. *Delegate responsibilities at home, at church, at work, and within your extended family.* This can be an invaluable stress management skill. In fact, this technique is the most widely used among top business executives today. By delegating responsibilities, you can decrease the load you carry and thereby reduce your stress level.

Take a long, hard look at your responsibilities. List everything you are responsible for in each dimension of your life. We are all managers at some level, just as we are all workers. Each of us is responsible for how we manage time, money, and other resources, and possibly for managing other people.

Now that you have made at least a broad category list, skim through it and put a check beside each item that could be delegated. Taking out the trash is an example; nursing the baby is not. Pick out a handful of tasks that would be the easiest to delegate and start there. Who else could do the task? How could it be done more simply? Could it be done less often? Are you a perfectionist who cannot bear the thought of someone else doing the task less capably? Delegate anyway. You can't do everything. Jesus knew this well. He trained his disciples to minister effectively and "delegated" much responsibility to them.

2. *Alter your work or home environment through learning to monitor your stress level and helping others to accommodate your needs for quiet times, rest, recreation, and relaxation.* Taking on a job outside the home that places unbearable pressure upon you will make you an unbearable person to live with. If your job places demands on you that prevent you from being a loving, sane, and spiritually centered person, why are you keeping that

job? If it is because there are no others available, could you alter your work environment to reduce the stress level? If you are in school, could you take fewer classes and delay graduation a semester or two?

When you are at home, do others recognize your need to unwind, or do you go right from the frenzied pace of an outside job to a similar pace at home? Do you have a tendency to keep giving out to others when you desperately need to be taking in something to nourish your mind, body, and spirit? Stop! Learn to monitor yourself and say that four-letter word that appears on red signs all over town. The best managers do, and so can you, whether the budget you are working with is $120 or $120 million.

Take your stress tolerance level into consideration when you add on new responsibilities, a new career, or a new position in women's ministry at your church. In discovering the price you pay for pushing yourself too hard, you may also find that you don't have to pay that price anymore.

3. *Change your lifestyle by using creative problem-solving and decision-making strategies that involve your ability to picture outcomes and honor your intuition.* Keeping in mind the benefits of a more relaxed approach to life will help motivate you. For example, good nutrition, exercise, and a sound night's sleep will provide you with more energy to face each day; acquiring stress management skills will help you to develop a lifestyle that enables you to be more vibrant and energetic.

The Lord has given us the Holy Spirit to guide us. As we pray for discernment, let us keep our ears open for that "still, small voice" that warns us before we pursue our latest idea of what will fulfill us. We don't become "more complete" in Christ through working to earn God's acceptance.

4. *Acquire time-management and goal-setting skills.* Setting up a series of steps helps us to reach our goals in an orderly fashion. In this way, amazing things can be accomplished. A major goal is normally achieved by setting up a sequence of smaller prior goals. On some days, setting just one or two goals for that day is all we can handle.

When we are ill, when we have several preschoolers running around the house needing attention, when we have guests staying in our home, or when any one of a number of situations finds us wondering how to cope, it may be that we have unrealistic expectations about what we can accomplish. Taking the time to begin our days with prayer and reflection on God's Word enables us to see what aspects of our lives are the most important to the Lord.

5. *Accept emotional and prayer support from a friend, small group, or trusted spiritual advisor.* Recent stress management research shows that emotional isolation can be a key factor in the kind of stress build-up that increases a person's risk of heart attack.[2] It is not just working less or simplifying our lives that lessens the impact of chronic stress in our lives; it is finding out what we are afraid of and facing our fears with God's help. Self-destructive thought patterns are harmful to our emotional well-being: all-or-nothing thinking (what I do must be perfect, or I really blew it); overgeneralizing (nothing ever works out for me); discounting the positive (acts of kindness, compliments, achievements, and positive events seem to have a negative undercurrent, no matter how nice someone or something appears to be); assuming the worst (I know what others are *really* thinking and the way things will turn out—and none of it is that good); and personalizing (I take responsibility for events that are actually outside my control, usually assuming that I am the cause when things go wrong).

If our fear is masquerading as a dark pessimism, we need to adjust our thinking to better fit the way things really are. We need the support of friends to do this—people to whom we can be accountable with our fears and worries, who will pray for us and speak the truth to us in love when we are not seeing things clearly. We can learn to walk confidently in the Lord's strength and use the good gifts He has given without worrying about possible failure. "For God did not give us a spirit of timidity, but a spirit of power, of love and of self-discipline" (2 Timothy 1:7).

6. *Adopt a healthful lifestyle to minimize the impact of stress.* Living a healthful lifestyle involves more than just being "whole" spiritually. It means doing our part in changing our habits and developing an awareness of how our lifestyle affects our bodies. We can form realistic expectations and reject the one-dimensional view of the perfect woman; we can take our eyes off of our failures, deficiencies, and shortcomings and say yes to living God's way; we can know that we stand complete in Christ. God will meet all our needs as we place our trust in Him.

PROMOTING OUR HEALTH

The belief that we are loved and accepted by God encourages us to develop lifestyle habits that conform to His design for our lives. Knowing that our bodies belong to God enables us to care for ourselves with thanksgiving rather than arrogance or pride.

With the Lord's help, we can choose not to abuse our bodies with alcohol, drugs, or tobacco. Learning to balance our need for exercise and rest teaches us to avoid the extremes of either a sedentary existence or a fitness-crazed mentality. The more we live in accordance with what's healthy for our bodies, the better we feel.

Have you ever noticed how just breathing clean, fresh air is an invigorating experience when there's a sense of appreciation for living? Health is a state of mental, emotional, physical, and spiritual well-being, not simply the absence of disease (Fig. 13-2). Within this model, well-being becomes the goal at the end of a long continuum. (By this definition, no one is perfectly healthy.) Each of us is at our own unique place along that line between total health on one end and premature death on the other:

Death/Health Continuum
Figure 13-2

	risks	*no risks*	
	symptoms	*education*	
	disease	*personal awareness*	
disability		*commitment to goals*	

PREMATURE DEATH	TOTAL HEALTH

According to this model, the most physically fit athletes can be unhealthy. Though someone may appear to be well, appearance is not an accurate indicator of our physical, emotional, and spiritual well-being (i.e., a person may become spiritually sick and yet still look fine). Current standards of fitness often ignore this key principle.

The central reality in our lives rests upon our acceptance of Jesus Christ as our Lord and Savior and the finished work of the Cross. Without this belief, living a healthful lifestyle is amazingly irrelevant. In a culture that clinically measures health by body fat percentages and oxygen uptake measurements, it is easy to overemphasize calories and workout schedules rather than the spiritual condition of our hearts.

Let us make no mistake—our Creator desires to change us from the inside out. The way we live is a reflection of our faith in every dimension of our existence. Day by day God is restoring us as we "put on the new self, which is being renewed in knowledge in the image of its Creator" (Colossians 3:10).

SELECTING AN EXERCISE PROGRAM

When we feel good because we are taking care of our bodies, we are more energetic in the sexual dimension of our lives as well. Our bodies were designed to function optimally when they are challenged by physical activity and given the opportunity to rest regularly. Thus, we gain multiple benefits from regular exercise that periodically places an appropriate amount of stress on our bodies.

The degree of effort we should expend will depend on our age, weight, current health status, and other related factors. Cardiovascular fitness comes through large muscle activity that is done rhythmically and continuously for a period of at least twenty to thirty minutes every other day or for a minimum of three days per week. By stimulating the heart to beat faster and the lungs to breathe more air, the body's ability to carry and use oxygen is enhanced.

If you are in an exercise class, how does your instructor measure up to accepted professional standards? The teacher's training should include information about proper posture, CPR (cardiopulmonary resuscitation), range of motion, basic anatomy, and other factors related to exercise physiology.

Look for these indicators of a program's quality. These same criteria also apply to exercise records, videos, and audio cassettes.

The program should have been developed by a physician, a registered physical therapist, or someone with a master's or doctoral degree in health or physical education. It should have a relatively injury-free track record. It should be sponsored or endorsed by a university, hospital, or professional medical organization and should have a good reputation within your community.

The class environment should be well-lit, have a wooden floor or protective covering such as gymnastics mats, provide good ventilation, be kept at a comfortable temperature, and have clearly posted charts so that participants may become familiar with their target heart rates.

The sessions should include five to ten minutes of warm-up and cool-down exercises, including numerous stretches held for ten to forty-five seconds each (no bouncing); stimulus periods combining fast and slow movements to maintain participants' heart rates within their target range for twenty to thirty minutes; heart-rate checks near the beginning and end of the workout; frequent monitoring of heart rates during the stimulus periods; and emphasis on using arm movements to maintain heart rates rather than excessive jumping and kicking.

Instruction on warning signs should be included so that participants learn how to monitor themselves both during and after the workout for signs of overexertion. These signs include nausea, vomiting, extreme breathlessness, side stitches, muscle cramps, prolonged fatigue lasting several hours after the session, pain in the calf muscles, pain in the front of the shins (shin splints), abnormal heart action, dizziness, loss of coordination, confusion, light-headedness, blurred vision, flare-ups of gout or arthritis, sudden inability to sleep at night, cold sweats, pallor, blueness of the lips or fingertips, joint or muscle pain, or pressure in the chest, arm, or throat due to exercise.

The ultimate proof of a program's quality lies in the satisfaction of its participants. Do they feel refreshed and invigorated after exercising, or are they too sore to move? Are injuries uncommon, or do many participants have to drop out due to strains and sprains? Do the majority of students keep coming back to the same program? Do they recommend it to others?

The individual's responsibility is to evaluate the level of personal involvement in a fitness program by answering these questions affirmatively:

1. Am I including adequate time for warm-up and cool-down periods?

2. Do I normally exercise at least three nonconsecutive days per week?

3. Do I spend at least twenty minutes in my target zone?

4. Do I have any warning signs?

5. Am I building up gradually to a pace that is right for me?

Choose an activity you enjoy and stay with it for at least six weeks before expecting to see a significant improvement in your fitness level. After two or three weeks, you will most likely notice improved physical fitness; you also may sleep more soundly, feel less tired, and start exercising more efficiently. As your fitness level improves, you can match your exertion with your heart rate to keep it in its target zone and may find that you will need to put more effort into exercising in order to challenge your heart and lungs.

THE ENJOYMENT OF WELLNESS

While a regular exercise program cannot be the answer for all of our problems, it can produce a number of remarkable benefits that make spending time on physical activity a worthwhile investment. Reported benefits of effective exercise programs include:

- increased mental alertness
- improved memory
- self-discipline leading to a healthier lifestyle
- increased self-confidence
- improved sense of well-being
- decreased or eliminated periods of depression or anxiety
- improved coordination
- increased stamina
- improved eating habits
- increased ability to cope with stress
- decreased ratio of body fat in relation to muscle mass
- decrease in the severity, duration, and frequency of illness
- increased appreciation for others
- alleviation of menstrual discomfort
- decrease in the severity and duration of PMS
- increased sexual responsiveness

To sum it up, physical activity in daily life can be divided into occupational, household, sports, conditioning, or other categories. As a subset of physical activity, exercise is planned, structured, and repetitive. Its specific goal is to improve or maintain one's level of physical fitness. When our lifestyles don't adequately challenge our bodies, cardiovascular endurance, strength, and flexibility are lost.

Incorporating the need for exercise into our lives plays a vital role in our ability to feel well. As wives and mothers, we can enjoy the benefits of wellness within our families as we model the importance of maintaining physical fitness to our husbands and our children.

DEVELOPING PELVIC STRENGTH

The muscles of the female body that are particularly vulnerable to the accumulated effects of aging, childbearing, and gravity lie in the pelvic region of our bodies. These muscles—located in the abdomen, lower back, and pelvic floor—are kept strong by doing exercises specifically targeting each area. The benefits to be gained through such exercise are:

- increased comfort during lovemaking
- reduction in the severity of premenstrual symptoms
- decreased discomfort during menstruation
- increased strength during childbirth
- partial alleviation of the effects of aging
- increased strength of sexual response

Strong abdominal muscles act like a natural corset by holding in the abdominal organs. They also prevent lower back pain by keeping the trunk of the body in proper alignment with the spine. Since muscles in this area put pressure on the intestines, constipation may be relieved by strengthening them. If surgery is ever necessary, these muscles will recover more quickly if they have been previously strengthened. The abdominal muscles also play an important role during childbirth by aiding the uterus in its expulsion of the baby through the birth canal.

The muscles of the lower back are responsible for our posture. By working in opposition to the muscles of the abdomen, they serve to stabilize the pelvis by keeping it in an upright position. Flexibility in the lower back helps to prevent stiffness and strain and promotes a woman's ability to relax during lovemaking.

The pelvic floor muscles are knit together to form a muscular sling that supports the contents of the pelvic cavity and withstands the pressures that occur within it. Because the poor condition of the pelvic muscles affects other parts of the body, it is not surprising that strengthening the pelvic floor can have dramatic results. The most distinctive part of this group is the pubococcygeus or PC muscle group (Fig. 13-3). This dynamic, highly specialized portion of the pelvic floor lies directly over the midline of the pelvic outlet and contains the openings to the bladder, uterus, and rectum. It is attached to the pubic bones in front and the tailbone in back. The PC group controls the shape of the vagina and contracts forcibly during orgasm. During intercourse, the PC group determines the amount of contact the vaginal wall has with the penis. Rich in nerve endings, the PC group can be consciously relaxed and tightened to increase

Pelvic Floor
Figure 13-3

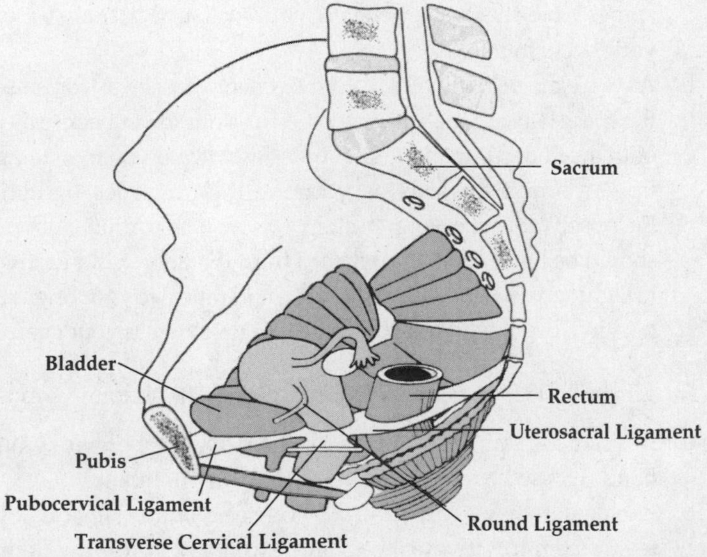

Sacrum

Bladder

Rectum

Uterosacral Ligament

Pubis

Pubocervical Ligament

Round Ligament

Transverse Cervical Ligament

sexual enjoyment for both partners during lovemaking. Because it tends to sag and stretch over time, strengthening the PC group through exercise enhances sexual responsiveness during intercourse by allowing a woman to become vaginally expressive toward her husband.

The following routine is designed to be done regularly unless you have a condition that prohibits this type of exercise. If your back is weak, begin with just the pelvic tilts, forward curls, stretches, and pelvic lifts. As your back and abdominal muscles become stronger, slowly add the other exercises, gradually building up the number of repetitions of each, until you are able to do all ten exercises at a comfortable level. The exercises outlined here may be incorporated into your regular fitness routine or may be done separately. They take about ten minutes and are easy to learn.

1. *Pelvic tilts:* This exercise improves posture, relieves lower back stiffness, and strengthens muscles in the abdomen, buttocks, groin, and pelvic floor.

    a. Lie on your back, knees bent, feet on the floor about hip distance apart, with your toes turned slightly inward and hands, palms down, at your sides. Keep your head down on the floor with your chin down and close to your chest to lengthen your spine. Note the curve beneath your waist near the base of your back. Inhale.
    b. As you exhale slowly, pull in your stomach muscles as you erase the space beneath the waist by pressing your lower back firmly onto the floor. Your abdominal muscles will aid you by pulling upwards and inwards as your buttock muscles tighten. Purposely squeeze your buttocks as you tilt. Your tailbone should be lifted one to two inches from the floor. Hold for five to eight seconds. Inhale as you relax, and return to your original position. Begin with five tilts, working up to ten as your goal.

2. *Forward curls:* This exercise tones and tightens the abdominal muscles.

    a. Begin in the same position as for the pelvic tilt but with your hands crossed over your chest, palms down. Inhale.
    b. Exhale slowly as you contract your abdominal muscles by using them to lift your head and shoulders up off the floor.

Hold for two to three seconds. Be sure to keep your lower back pressed onto the floor in a modified pelvic tilt. Keep your stomach muscles tightened.

c. Inhale as you lower your head and shoulders. By keeping them in an even line with your upper back, you need not lower your head all the way to the floor each time. Begin with eight curls, building up to between twelve and twenty as your goal.

3. *Knees to elbows:* You will strengthen lower back and abdominal muscles with this exercise.

a. Lie on your back with your hands behind your head, knees slightly apart, feet flexed and in the air. Press your lower back onto the floor. Inhale.

b. As you exhale, contract your stomach muscles, lift your head, elbows forward, reaching toward your knees as you move them slightly toward your elbows. Hold for two to three seconds. Inhale as you resume your original position. Begin with four and build up to between eight and twelve repetitions.

4. *Elbow lifts:* Abdominal and thigh muscles will be strengthened by this exercise.

a. Begin in the same position as for knees to elbows, but cross your feet at the ankles. Inhale as you raise your feet up higher, keeping your knees slightly bent.

b. Exhale, contract your abdominals, keeping your knees bent and ankles crossed while bringing your chin toward your chest, elbows close together and close to knees. Hold for two to three seconds. Inhale as you lower. Begin with four, building up to between eight and twelve as your goal.

5. *Crisscrosses:* This exercise strengthens the abdominal muscles with special attention to the oblique (side or waist) muscles.

a. Remain in the same position as for elbow lifts, but bend your knees and open them wide, keeping your feet crossed at the ankles. Inhale.

b. Exhale, contract stomach muscles, lift head, tucking chin forward as you reach your right elbow toward your left knee. You will feel the muscles on your right side aid you as you lift. Inhale and lower. Repeat by touching your left elbow to your right knee. Begin with four crosses on each side, working up to eight to twelve.

6. *Knee rolls:* This exercise also strengthens the oblique muscles as well as the lower back.

   a. After finishing the crisscrosses, bring your knees together, uncross your ankles, and stretch your arms out to your sides at shoulder level, palms down on the floor. Inhale as you bring both knees as close to your chest as you can.

   b. Keeping your arms and shoulders on the floor, exhale, rolling your knees as far to the right as possible. You may or may not be able to touch the floor. Inhale as you return your knees to the center; then repeat to the left side. Begin with four rolls to each side, working up to eight.

7. *Neck stretch:* The purpose of this stretch is to relieve stiffness in the neck and lower back.

   Finish the knee rolls by bringing both knees up to your chest and holding them with your arms. Slowly bring your head up to touch your knees, then lower. Repeat two more times.

8. *Back stretch:* To relieve lower back stiffness, do this stretch daily.

   Following the neck stretch, hold your left knee with both hands, pressing it toward your chest as you keep your right foot on the floor with knee bent. Hold for twenty to thirty seconds. Repeat with your right leg.

9. *Long stretch:* This stretch relieves tension in the back, neck, and shoulders.

   a. Now stretch both feet down by sliding your heels along the floor, feet flexed, arms stretched up over your head. Avoid arching your lower back. Inhale deeply as you stretch for six to eight seconds.

   b. Exhale, tighten buttocks, press back onto floor, count to four slowly. Repeat a. and b. two more times.

10. *Pelvic lifts (Kegels):* To strengthen the pelvic floor muscles, repeat this exercise four to eight times daily. No one will know you are doing pelvic lifts unless you raise and lower your eyebrows up and down! You can do them any time, anywhere, as long as your bladder is completely empty.

   a. You may remain on the floor after the long stretch to do this exercise. Simply relax your buttocks, abdomen, and thighs as you inhale.

   b. Now concentrate on lifting the sheet of muscles between your pubic bones and your tailbone as if it were an elevator moving up into your pelvis. You may place your hand over your pubic bone for a reference point as you try to lift the pelvic floor up to the level of your hand. Exhale as you lift— 2-3-4, hold for two counts, then lower—2-3-4 as you inhale. Do not tense any other place in your body. Repeat twelve times, building up to twenty-five, four to eight times daily. If your pelvic floor has poor muscle tone, doing 200 to 300 Kegels every day will greatly strengthen this vital area of your body.

> *The Lord your God is with you,*
> *he is mighty to save.*
> *He will take great delight in you,*
> *he will quiet you with his love,*
> *he will rejoice over you with singing.*
>
> ZEPHANIAH 3:17

Chapter Review

Personal Reflections

1. "Listening to my body" requires that I pay attention to:

2. Knowing that God is interested in every aspect of who I am—physically, emotionally, and spiritually—encourages me to:

3. Being a woman in today's society can be:

4. I see the connection between stress and self-destructive thought patterns most clearly if I:

5. When I take time out to enjoy the benefits of exercise, I realize:

6. God's strength is especially evident to me when:

Related Bible Passages for Further Study

- Psalm 84:1-7
- Psalm 91:9-14
- Isaiah 55:1-6
- John 6:35-40
- Ephesians 4:1-16
- Philippians 2:1-12

$\mathcal{L}$IVING WITH OUR FERTILITY

We need a revolutionary message in the midst of today's
relativistic thinking. By revolutionary or radical, I mean
standing against the all-pervasive form which the world spirit
has taken in our day. This is the real meaning of radical.
God has given his answers in the Bible—the Bible that is true
when it speaks of history and of the cosmos, as well as when it
speaks of religious things. And it therefore gives
truth concerning all reality.[1]

FRANCIS SCHAEFFER

Surely God is my salvation; I will trust and not be afraid.
The Lord, the Lord, is my strength and my song;
he has become my salvation.

ISAIAH 12:2

As we approach our sexuality from a biblical perspective, we will often find ourselves living our lives in striking contrast to current views of sex. Taking such a stand is radical, even revolutionary. But I believe that our bodies have become a battleground upon which a war of profoundly significant spiritual proportions is being waged.

By learning to view our fertility from an eternal perspective, we begin to hear the Spirit's gentle voice concerning this area of our lives. Simply asking the question, "Lord, what is Your will for us concerning children?" opens our hearts to hearing our Father's perfectly timed promptings.

Each and every child that is conceived possesses a life that Christ may enter into and live within throughout eternity. Bringing a child into the world affirms this truth. Throughout early biblical history, God's blessing was often associated with the desire that His people be fruitful, increase in number, and replenish the earth (Genesis 1:28; 9:1; 17:2, 20; 28:3). Even when the descendants of Abraham, Isaac, and Jacob had multiplied to the point that they were "as many as the stars in the sky," Moses replied to the apparent population explosion by saying, "May the Lord, the God of your fathers, increase you a thousand times and bless you as he has promised!" (Deuteronomy 1:10-11).

The Bible does not depict children as an unwanted or negative side effect of marital sexuality. When we sift through the Scriptures, this truth becomes wonderfully clear: Physical fruitfulness in marriage springs from God's hand as an integral expression of our sexuality. Though we play a key role in cooperating with God as we prayerfully consider the possibility of childbearing, it is our Creator who imparts life to each human being.[2] Our ability to bear children was established as part of God's original intent for marriage (Genesis 1:28).

When we welcome a child into our lives, a unique individual experiences what it means to be created in the image of God. Think of it: You and I are here today because our parents did not say no to childbearing. It is only through women's wombs that human life enters God's creation.

Our lives—each life—has significance beyond the grave because we are loved by God. He has shown us in His Word that human life is not disposable. One day we will be made new as we stand in His presence. Every tear will be wiped from our eyes (Revelation 7:17). Along with our children, we are moving through time toward the moment when we will stand together praising God as we finally see Jesus face to face. What a gift! What an opportunity—to experience what it means to be alive . . . to have become a part of the kingdom of God and share this experience with our children. This is what the Bible teaches us about the value of human life to the Lord: How we live out our sexuality before God with our bodies as we respond to our capacity to bear children matters, both now and in eternity.

AFFIRMING THE VALUE OF HUMAN LIFE

As we evaluate our responses to our Maker's design for our sexuality, we can also consider how our dependence on birth control methods has been shaped by the prevailing cultural view that conception depends on our personal decisions and actions alone.

A number of years ago, a missionary speaking at our church said, "There are only two things that we can do here on earth that we cannot do in eternity. The first is to evangelize. The second is to grow through adversity. Neither of these things will take place once we enter heaven."

Immediately, I thought to myself, *No, there is also a third thing, and that is parenthood. Since there will be no marriage in heaven, there will be no more conception, no more birthing, no more adoption, no more child rearing.* And that is when my eyes were opened to an amazing truth. Of all the things we do here on earth, few will matter more for eternity than opening our hearts to the bearing and raising of children.

It is easy to miss seeing or hearing this point of view today. Like the missionary in his sermon, many of us have learned to think about childbearing from the perspective of lifestyle preference and personal choice.

JONATHAN'S STORY

I will always remember 1980. It was to be the year that I graduated from college after ten years of part-time attendance, the year of launching out after spending eight and a half years of my life pregnant or breastfeeding without a single break. The youngest of our three children was finally weaned and toilet-trained, and we were celebrating the fact that there would be no more diapers to wash at our house.

I met with an adviser at the university to prepare my entrance into a graduate program in medical education, looking forward to a career in teaching health professionals how to become better educators. Suddenly I became ill with an infection and was unusually tired and irritable.

At the end of an office visit to my family physician, I asked him if he thought my period might be delayed as a result of the illness. As he wrote out a prescription, he told me we had better check to see if I was pregnant. "But I couldn't be," I replied to his preposterous proposal. "Don't even suggest it!"

I'll never forget the feeling in the pit of my stomach as he shared the results of the test with me. My head was reeling. I did *not* want to have another child, not then, not ever. I had had enough of nausea and heartburn and labor pain, thank you.

My previous pregnancies had been filled with joy and anticipation, but now I felt only guilt because I was angry. I read certain psalms repeatedly—especially Psalm 51. I wept off and on for nine months. When friends from the university would hear of my impending "bad fortune" (an unplanned pregnancy), they would ask me what I was going to do about "the situation." I told them that abortion was not a consideration for me. Silence inevitably followed, and they would look at me as if I had suddenly turned into a mindless reproduction machine.

During labor I still felt distant from the baby my body had nurtured for so long. As I propped myself up on my elbows to watch Jonathan's eight-and-a-half-pound body slip out into the world, I was amazed at my reaction. He was beautiful! Joanna and Katherine and David had a new brother! Here was our second son! I was meeting a new person only God had seen before, greeting a life that He had determined would join our family.

More tears began to flow, but they no longer tasted bitter because they sprang from a thankful heart. Over the following months, my heart opened up to Jonathan's presence. Soon I felt as strong a bond with him as I had with our previous children. Leaving the university was a small price to pay for the benefits we reaped from Jonathan's arrival. The long days of full-time mothering and breastfeeding enabled me to draw closer to the Lord than I ever had been before, causing me to reevaluate my roles as a wife and mother. "The steadfast love of the Lord never ceases."

When I look at sixteen-year-old Jonathan today, I can't believe that I initially couldn't see the beauty of his conception, that I ever considered him to be anything but a blessing. He has been such a gift to me. Had I felt differently about abortion, I would have missed one of the greatest opportunities for growth the Lord has ever provided us as a family. You see, God knew that Jonathan would enrich our lives even though we didn't plan his conception. Proverbs states, "In his heart a man plans his course, but the Lord determines his steps" (16:9). So it was for us. As we laid our plans aside, we were joyously broken through this experience for God's glory.

I share this story, not to judge others who might have reacted differently than I, but to show how we much we can grow when we respond to the will of God, even when it is hard or difficult or painful—and sometimes *especially* when it is so. Just when we think we have it all together, Jesus calls us to come closer to the Cross, to go further in our walk, to more deeply share with Him. The sacrifices of God really are a contrite heart and a broken spirit.

Becoming a mother in today's culture is a humbling experience. Praying about—and periodically lifting—the restrictions we place on our fertility is risky. But opening our hearts to God's will for our lives always involves risks. *Willingness to bring new life into the world enables us to respond in faith to a way of life in which we actively participate in expanding and caring for God's creation.* I urge you, in love and with deep respect for your understanding of God's will in this area of your life, to reflect on the significance of this.

THE MYTH OF THE NATURAL MOTHER

Most of us at one time or another have probably heard someone say, "Well, of course children are easy for *her* to have. She's naturally gifted to be a mother." Are there really two kinds of married women in the world— those who are natural mothers and those who are not? The truth is that the idea of the "natural mother" is a myth. There are no natural mothers.

The Bible does not teach us that God "calls" only a select group of married women into motherhood. Motherhood is not a peculiar talent, inborn trait, or special gift some women have and others don't. Being a mother is *a way of life, open and available to all married women.* It depends on one's willingness to make the necessary commitment and the sacrifices—to lay down one's life for one's children. Who in their "natural" minds would *want* to spend their time wiping dirty bottoms, preventing siblings from clobbering one another, doing tons of laundry, or sitting up all night with a hospitalized child? As we serve the little ones the Lord entrusts to our care, we know that what we do for them we also do for Christ our Savior.

If you seek examples of Jesus' love in action, look about you. Who are the mothers and fathers that exemplify Christ's love as they go about nurturing their children? Are they the parents who always seem to have it all together? Or are they the folks who usually sit at the back of the church near the aisle so they can make a fast exit for a bathroom emergency? You know, the ones who look tired yet somewhat amused as their kids take turns snuggling up to them, wriggling around, and sometimes slouching down as far as possible during the worship service.

As opposed to a natural call, the ability to be parents comes in the doing of the tasks and the opening of our hearts to these little ones. We are enabled to love our children as we surrender our time, resources, and energy to promote the growth and health of another human being. It doesn't take a college degree to learn how to do these things—just lots of prayer, patience, and calling out to God for help in times of need (like at least a hundred times a day). This requires no special talent—it requires brokenness, surrender, and service in obedience to Christ's calling.

Paul wrote that those who marry "will face many troubles in life" (1 Corinthians 7:28). He went on to say that an unmarried man or woman can be more fully concerned with the Lord's affairs than can those who are married (1 Corinthians 7:32-35). Was Paul right? Does marriage include a moral obligation to open our hearts to children—through childbirth and/or adoption—according to the Bible's teaching and the Holy Spirit's leading? Or, as our culture tells us, are children the optional products of marriage, designed to add meaning to our lives (or perhaps to pile on an unendurable burden)?

THE PATTERN OF THIS PRESENT WORLD

Nearly twenty years ago, an interview with Malcolm Muggeridge in *Christianity Today* presented his cogent thoughts on the subtle relationship of contraception to abortion. With a great deal of insight, he observed that the wide acceptance of birth control methods makes it "ridiculous to talk about abolishing abortion," adding, "if you have contraception, you will have abortion." Advocates of abortion essentially said the same thing when they later claimed that an increased acceptance of contraception in the sixties paved the way for abortion rights in the early seventies.

As Muggeridge also observed, if we "divorce eroticism from its purpose, [we] create the sort of conditions out of which come abortion and euthanasia. . . . If marriage is erotic satisfaction, then it is clear that monogamy won't meet that need. It only meets that need if it represents something more than that. . . .

"If you say, 'I demand sexual gratification, irrespective of any institution, and I demand the right to prevent its consequences,' then I know what will happen to man. Namely: unhappiness. The busting up of the Christian way of life will soon follow."[3]

Is this a far-fetched way of looking at birth control, or is there in fact a direct link between contraception and abortion, as Malcolm Muggeridge and abortion advocates believed? Considering the possible modes of action of current birth control methods, the boundary lines are increasingly difficult to distinguish.

Did you know that the world's experts do not fully understand how many of today's contraceptives work? Some methods of birth control, if conception takes place, interrupt pregnancy after it begins. Such drugs and devices are designed to induce abortion during the early weeks of pregnancy. A number of these medical technologies also act to prevent conception. Post-fertilization methods of preventing birth from taking place include the following:

Intrauterine devices, or IUDs, which in some way render the lining of the uterus incapable of receiving an egg.[4]

Oral contraceptives, which employ backup mechanisms that prevent implantation if an egg becomes fertilized. There is currently no way to estimate the number of abortions that oral contraceptives are responsible for each year, because there is no means of measuring the number of eggs that are actually fertilized among women taking oral contraceptives.[5]

Norplant, or progestin skin implants, which are believed to block [a viable] pregnancy in three ways, according to Dr. Philip Darncy, "by preventing the release of an egg in, on average, half of a woman's menstrual cycles, by causing a thickening of the cervical mucus that impedes sperm's ability to reach an egg and by preventing implantation within the uterine wall of any eggs that are fertilized."[6] Intramuscular injections of prostaglandins or progestogens (Depo-Provera), vaginal Silastic devices containing prostaglandins, and vaginal rings and implants containing progestin act against pregnancy in a similar fashion.

RU486, or mifepristone, also known as the "abortion pill," which directly acts against the establishment and continuation of pregnancy by blocking the body's natural secretion of progesterone, the vital hormone that prepares the uterus to receive a fertilized egg and helps to maintain pregnancy once implantation occurs.

The "morning-after" pill, which uses a high dosage of certain types of hormones to force menstruation to begin after an egg has possibly been fertilized. No statistics are kept as to how many women are prescribed this pill, which may induce abortion up to seventy-two hours following intercourse. The Food and Drug Administration recently granted its approval of this drug even though many health care providers have been prescribing it for years through what is termed "off-label use."

Prostaglandin suppositories, which stimulate uterine contractions in an effort to expel "the products of pregnancy."

Menstrual extraction, or "once a month" pills.

Vacuum aspiration.

These methods of birth control do not always prevent conception, but act in a variety of ways to prevent birth. *Birth control presupposes that births may be prevented through technology at any stage of prenatal development.*

Since the word *contraception* literally means "against conception," it is important to distinguish between what it means to *control birth* and to *prevent conception*. The moment of fertilization is a moral line of demarcation, the incredibly significant boundary between independent cellular life and the permanent fusion of genetic information that sets the life pattern of a person's existence in motion.

Those who value the lives of unborn children can better understand how contraceptives function—*and whether or not a particular method can be guaranteed to prevent conception as its sole function*—by seeking information from pharmacists on every possible mode of action associated with currently available methods of family planning. Simply asking, "Does it prevent conception 100 percent of the time, or does it prevent birth in some other ways?" can get the dialogue going. Be sure to ask your pharmacist the question as written; do not be distracted if it is not answered on your first try. Keep asking patiently until the question is answered clearly and directly to your satisfaction in terms you can understand. You can find out the mode of action of the birth control product you are considering by turning to footnote number 7 at the back of the book (product listings from the current *Physicians' Desk Reference Guide to Prescription Drugs*).[7]

Remember, there is no absolute clinical proof that oral contraceptives, minipills, Norplant, or IUDs prevent conception 100 percent of the time. If your physician, midwife, or nurse-practitioner informs you that it isn't possible for any of these methods to induce abortion, they are not accurately responding to your question. From a pharmaceutical standpoint, the only current conception control technologies that do not employ backup mechanisms that can abort a pregnancy following an egg's fertilization are barrier methods, including condoms, diaphragms, and cervical caps; spermicidal agents and cervical sponges; and surgical sterilization via vasectomy or tubal ligation.

RESPONDING WITH A BIBLICAL WORLDVIEW

As believers, we need to evaluate the ethic of conception control and its impact on creation in light of the Bible's normative picture of marriage, fertility, and the meaning of personhood. A possible way of approaching this is to compare our culture's view of reproductive rights to a clear, consistent ethic of marital fruitfulness based on a biblical worldview.

Toward a Christian Ethic of Family Planning
Figure 14-1

SOCIETY'S VIEW OF REPRODUCTIVE RIGHTS	BIBLICAL VIEW OF FRUITFULNESS
A. My body belongs to me; therefore: • I have the right to decide what to do with my body. • I am responsible to myself alone for my decisions and my actions. B. With regard to my sexuality: • I am free to express my sexuality in any way I choose. • I alone will decide how many children I will bear, if any, and when I will bear them. C. This in turn allows me to: • abandon any marriage contract that violates these rights. • refuse to bear children that I do not want to bear. • terminate any pregnancy I deem undesirable. • live my life according to what I think best suits my needs.	A. My body belongs to God;[9] therefore: • it is my responsibility to live in harmony with the Holy Spirit.[10] • I am responsible to God for my decisions and my actions.[11] B. With regard to my sexuality: • I am to present my body as a living and holy sacrifice to God and not be conformed to cultural patterns of sexual behavior.[12] • God will help me understand how to respond to my capacity for childbearing as I seek His will for my life and family.[13] C. This in turn constrains me to consider that God's Word: • views childbearing as a blessing, not as an unwanted burden.[14] • considers children to be an implicit part of family life and the expected fruit of the marriage union (see above references). • approaches human life as having eternal significance to a personal Creator and Savior.[15]
"WE RECOGNIZE THAT RIGHT OF THE INDIVIDUAL, MARRIED OR SINGLE, TO BE FREE FROM UNWARRANTED GOVERNMENTAL INTRUSION INTO MATTERS SO FUNDAMENTALLY AFFECTING A PERSON AS THE DECISION WHETHER TO BEAR OR BEGET A CHILD. THAT RIGHT NECESSARILY INCLUDES THE RIGHT OF A WOMAN TO DECIDE WHETHER OR NOT TO TERMINATE HER PREGNANCY" (U.S. SUPREME COURT).[8]	"CHILDREN ARE A GIFT FROM THE LORD; THEY ARE A REWARD FROM HIM" (PSALM 127:3 NLT).

From this model, I believe it is easier to understand how the assumption that "my body belongs to me" contradicts a biblical worldview. Given today's popular approach to personal choice and reproductive rights, it takes courage to say, "My body belongs to You, Lord. Help me to understand how to respond to my capacity for fruitfulness." As Christ's followers, let us give careful consideration to the question of conception control through studying the Scriptures, earnest prayer, and asking pastors and church leaders to provide a positive biblical basis for its practice.

FERTILITY AWARENESS AND FAMILY PLANNING

We now have the means to help us space our children as the Lord leads without drugs, surgery, or vaginal devices. Recent developments in reproductive biology have contributed a method of conception control to family planning that is effective and yet poses no medical risk for either partner. Couples who choose to be responsive to the Lord in this area can learn to share the responsibility of living with their fertility through using a family planning method based on fertility awareness.

The objective of using fertility awareness is to time lovemaking around the natural cycles of the wife's body and the signs of fertility that accompany them. The least invasive form of conception control, it is based upon recognizing the symptoms of ovulation.

Although many women ovulate about halfway through their menstrual cycle, this is not true for every woman. Timing intercourse by the calendar alone is ineffective in avoiding conception for this reason. The effectiveness of fertility awareness methods results from more specific observations. In natural family planning classes, now available around the world, trained instructors teach couples how to observe. Taking a series of classes and attending follow-up sessions is essential for couples who want to increase the effectiveness of this form of family planning.

A key principle of this approach is that a couple's relationship may be enhanced as each partner responds to the wife's patterns of fertility. It requires each partner to be committed to understanding the recurring rhythms of the menstrual cycle. Communication is essential. In living with an awareness rather than a denial of fertility, the possibility of conception is open-ended, granting the Holy Spirit room to prompt a couple from one month to the next. *This method is entirely compatible with the physical reality of our sexuality and acknowledges the value of ongoing responsiveness to the Lord as He leads each couple to affirm the dignity and worth of human life.*

Fertility awareness methods may be used to either prevent or achieve a pregnancy by helping couples to know the exact time of the month a woman is likely to conceive. Two methods are taught in natural family planning classes: the Ovulation Method, which involves observing the changes taking place in a woman's vaginal secretions; and the Sympto-Thermal Method, which combines mucus observation with temperature and cervical assessments. Both methods require recording observations on a chart and an initial cycle of abstinence so that secretions following lovemaking are not mistaken as a sign of fertility. Each method is highly effective when learned from a qualified instructor and followed conscientiously.

Within the neck of the uterus are hundreds of "crypts" that act as a storage area for sperm after ejaculation. Here the sperm are nourished and kept alive for up to five days. Over this period, the sperm are continuously circulating to promote the possibility of conception. This "time-release" action ensures that healthy sperm will be in the ovum's vicinity during the six- to eight-hour period following ovulation in which fertilization must occur.

Because sperm can travel very fast, they can make the trip up to the oviducts in less than an hour. They cannot, however, make this journey unless the woman's body has begun to secrete a special substance known as fertile mucus. Within this solution, the sperm are able to migrate to their destination in the oviducts where an egg may be waiting. Most eventually miss their mark and end up in the abdominal cavity. This incredible system is designed to promote conception through an interwoven set of biological mechanisms that attempt to link an egg cell and a sperm cell when they are at their peak. We often take this phenomenon for granted, and yet the process is absolutely mind-boggling.

THE OVULATION METHOD

Since the mucus manufactured by the crypts in the cervix varies in consistency, appearance, and chemical composition during the menstrual cycle, it is possible to know when fertilization would be most likely to occur. The mucus reflects the levels and types of hormones present in a woman's body at any given time, so becoming familiar with mucus patterns is a viable way of either planning or preventing pregnancy. Because sperm cannot live long in nonfertile mucus, fertility is just a temporary state that exists for only one phase of the menstrual cycle. *One of the best benefits of fertility awareness methods is that neither partner needs to use drugs or devices of any kind during the infertile phases of the cycle.*

After menstruation, cervical secretions tend to be thick and rather dry, appear opaque (yellow or white), and have the consistency of thick paste. Viewed under a microscope, it shows a maze of meshlike formations tightly woven together. This mucus acts as a plug within the cervical canal, a natural barrier to sperm, and is referred to as the "basic infertile pattern of mucus." Some women do not notice any mucus at all after a period. This is called the "basic infertile pattern of dryness."

The secretion of infertile mucus continues for several days. Then the pattern changes. A sticky, threadlike mucus appears after dry days, or a sensation of moistness remains after tacky mucus has been present. As the days go by, the cervix secretes a thinner, clearer mucus in increasing amounts. This is accompanied by a sensation of wetness in the vaginal area. The fertile mucus pattern that is smooth in consistency, watery, translucent (colorless or yellowish), and cloudy begins about six days prior to ovulation. When placed on the thumb and forefinger, it remains smooth on both fingers and can be stretched up to an inch between them.

The fertile pattern of mucus provides a woman with a signal that ovulation is approaching, giving her ample warning to either abstain from or engage in intercourse. Because sperm live three to five days in this type of secretion, intercourse must be avoided whenever a fertile pattern is observed unless a couple has chosen to conceive.

The last day of the fertile mucus pattern is the "peak day" of fertility during the menstrual cycle. Mucus on the peak day is shiny, slippery, and lubricative. This type of mucus resembles raw egg whites and may be stretched an inch or more in length. Under a microscope, it reveals long channels through which sperm may rapidly travel. The hormone estrogen is responsible for this change.

Menstruation taking place fourteen days after the peak day confirms that ovulation accompanied the "mucus peak." Once ovulation has taken place, the mucus once again becomes sticky, cloudy, and dry, resuming a basic infertile pattern. When the basic infertile pattern has continued for three days in a row, it may be assumed that ovulation has occurred and that the ovum has perished.

Fertility Awareness During the Menstrual Cycle
Figure 14-2

PHASE:	MENSTRUAL/ POSTMENSTRUAL	OVULATORY	POST OVULATORY
SECRETIONS	MENSTRUATION _____ DRY DAYS:	FERTILE MUCUS PATTERN	LATE DRY DAYS: INFERTILE MUCUS PATTERN
	INFERTILE MUCUS PATTERN Sensation of dryness in the vaginal area. Sperm cannot penetrate this type of mucus.	Dry sensation ends. Mucus begins—sensation of wetness in the vaginal area. Mucus now supports the life of sperm cells. Conception may occur from any genital-to-genital contact on mucus days prior to ovulation.	From the fourth day after mucus peak this cycle is infertile until the next cycle begins except under special circumstances
		PEAK _____ 1-2-3 Clear slippery mucus; highly stretchable and lubricative. Ovulation follows. Count 1-2-3 days of peak is fertile.	
TEMPERATURE	LOW ➡	RISING ➡	HIGH ➡
CERVIX	Low, firm, and closed.	High, soft and open.	Low, firm, and closed
DURATION	Highly variable, lasting from days to many weeks or even several months.	Somewhat variable, lasting from 7 to 11 days in most women.	Least variable, lasting about 10 to 15 days in 90 percent of all women.
ABILITY TO CONCEIVE	Woman is infertile. Genital contact will not cause pregnancy.	Woman is fertile. Genital contact makes conception likely.	Woman is infertile. Genital contact will not result in pregnancy.

Exceptions to these mucus signs are thoroughly covered in natural family planning texts and classes. Breastfeeding, vaginal infections, illness, medications, approaching menopause, and secretions related to sexual arousal and intercourse all affect mucus observation, but have been studied extensively so couples may learn how to respond to these conditions. Participating in a class and obtaining individualized counseling is essential to understanding how to apply this method to one's own circumstances.

Because few medical schools train students to understand and teach fertility awareness skills, many physicians are not equipped to teach this method and, therefore, do not recommend it to their patients. When asked about fertility awareness methods, some health-care providers assume that a woman is asking them about the calendar method of birth control, or "rhythm." Often they do not know of the benefits or effectiveness of this form of conception control. Frankly, it is less time-consuming and more profitable to prescribe oral contraceptives than to provide ongoing, inexpensive guidance in fertility awareness—a service not covered by many health insurance policies.

OVERVIEW OF THE SYMPTO-THERMAL METHOD

The Sympto-Thermal Method includes temperature observation as an additional means of determining fertility. After the ovum is released, the progesterone level in a woman's bloodstream rises, which in turn causes a rise in the temperature of the body when it is at rest. Progesterone also acts upon the reproductive system by suppressing further ovulation and drying up fertile mucus.

When the resting, or basal, body temperature rises, it confirms that ovulation has taken place. A woman cannot become pregnant once she has entered the high-temperature phase of her menstrual cycle.

The basal body temperature (BBT) changes slightly throughout the cycle and tends to be half a degree lower before ovulation occurs. Following ovulation, temperature recording confirms infertility until menstruation begins.

The BBT is taken upon waking after sleeping for at least three hours. Many women keep their thermometers by their beds and simply take their temperatures first thing in the morning before getting out of bed.

Most drugstores carry BBT thermometers, which have larger numbers and record a much smaller range in temperature than regular thermometers. For this reason, a BBT thermometer cannot be used when a fever is present and should be washed in only cool water to avoid breakage. Because a BBT thermometer is specially calibrated for accuracy and ease of reading, it is worth the extra expense.

The BBT may be taken orally, vaginally, or rectally. Because the oral temperature is generally lower than a vaginal or rectal reading, the same route should be used throughout an entire cycle to maintain consistency. Oral temperatures need to be taken for eight to ten minutes, while taking the temperature vaginally or rectally requires only five minutes. Falling asleep during the reading might incur breakage; so it is advisable to set a snooze alarm or timer for the required period and then go back to sleep. The thermometer should be stored away from heat sources such as radios, lights, radiators, and heat vents and should be shaken down after the temperature has been recorded.

Emotional stress, illness, restless sleep, medication, electric blankets, and alcohol consumption on the previous night can create higher than normal temperatures and are known as disturbances. These factors can be accommodated once a woman understands their significance in relationship to other signs of fertility.

The third way of determining fertility is by examining the cervix each day. This method has not been studied for its effectiveness and is of greatest benefit to those women whose mucus is very scanty or who experience a fairly continuous mucus discharge. It may also be useful when one's temperature has been affected by stress or illness.

When the cervix begins to rise, soften, and open, it may provide additional evidence that the ovulatory phase has started. Checking the cervix is no more difficult than inserting a diaphragm or cervical cap. As long as a woman's hands have been washed thoroughly and her fingernails have been trimmed, there is little risk of injury or infection. The cervix feels similar to the tip of one's nose when it is in a closed position. It may be checked by inserting one or two fingers upwards with the pads of the fingers aimed toward the pubic bone in front. Near the top of the vagina on the front wall lies a round protrusion with a dimple in it. This is the cervix. (After a vaginal birth, the dimple turns into a smile!) If the vagina is too dry to insert the fingers into comfortably, water may be used as a lubricant. Other substances should not be used because they may mask the presence of slippery mucus.

During infertile phases of the menstrual cycle, the cervix is easily reached when a woman is sitting on a toilet or standing with one foot on the edge of the tub or toilet stool. As fertility approaches, the cervix feels softer and recedes higher into the vagina, sometimes becoming nearly impossible to reach. Comparing the cervix as it changes from day to day provides additional proof of when ovulation occurs.

A SAFE, EFFECTIVE, AND LIFE-AFFIRMING FAMILY PLANNING METHOD

The theoretical effectiveness rate of fertility awareness methods when used as a means of child spacing is approximately 99.6 percent, or nearly as effective as oral contraceptives. Actual-use effectiveness, according to a leading authority in the field, Dr. Thomas Hilgers at Creighton University, is 94.8 percent.[16] The book *Contraceptive Technology* rated the effectiveness of the cervical mucus method at 98 percent when used consistently and well.[17]

In view of these statistics, why aren't more couples using these methods? When we consider the alternatives, *fertility awareness is an excellent means of family planning because it is safe, effective, and life-affirming*. Isn't it remarkable that a safe and effective method of conception control exists that is based upon symptoms—waking temperature, cervical fluid, and cervical position—that our Creator has built into our body's sexual design? Including information about fertility awareness in health education classes that teach about the menstrual cycle seems an ideal place to start. "When women learn that all this is happening inside their bodies on a regular basis, they are often amazed to think that all they were taught about their menstrual cycles in the sixth grade was whether to opt for tampons or sanitary napkins during their periods," health educator Toni Weschler observes poignantly in her book *Taking Charge of Your Fertility*.[18]

The three key reasons why fertility awareness methods make so much sense are:

- Ovulation occurs on only one day during each menstrual cycle in most cases.

- A healthy, nonsterilized male is always fertile, i.e., twenty-four hours a day, seven days a week, 365 days a year (366 in leap years); whereas a healthy, nonsterilized woman is only fertile for a brief time each month.

- A woman's egg dies after twelve to twenty-four hours unless it is fertilized.

And in case you need further convincing to consider using a fertility awareness method, think of the benefits you would reap:

- You would be free from all those messy and meddlesome contraceptives—and their significant side effects—that you have been struggling with for years.

- You would gain greater understanding of your menstrual cycle and how ovulation fits your own unique biological pattern.

- You would have a deepened awareness and appreciation for the privilege of fertility (and your potential children), based upon your ongoing openness to the Holy Spirit and God's creative design for your family.

- You would have mutual cooperation and enhanced communication within your marriage regarding lovemaking and sexuality.

Remember, we are living in a society that believes that oral contraceptives, Norplant, IUDs, sterilization—even RU486 and surgical abortion—are "better" than fertility awareness methods. As our dependence upon the Lord grows, as we hear the Holy Spirit's quiet voice concerning a creative, cooperative, Christ-centered approach to determining the size of our families and the spacing of our children, we will learn life-changing truths about trusting God in this eternally significant area of our marriages.

Suppose God tells you to do something that is an enormous test of your common sense, totally going against it. What will you do? Will you hold back? . . . In the spiritual realm, Jesus Christ demands that you risk everything you hold onto or believe through common sense, and leap by faith into what He says. Once you obey, you will immediately find that what He says is as solidly consistent as common sense. By the test of common sense, Jesus Christ's statements may seem mad, but when you test them by the trial of faith, your findings will fill your spirit with the awesome fact that they are the very words of God.[19]

OSWALD CHAMBERS

Chapter Review

Personal Reflections

1. As I read this chapter, I thought about:

2. From the Bible's point of view, every child that is conceived:

3. The relationship of contraception to abortion seems especially evident to me when I consider:

4. Becoming a mother, through childbirth or adoption, is:

5. Natural family planning teaches couples to be more aware of:

6. Opening my heart to children and responding to the Holy Spirit's direction in this area of my life is something I:

Related Bible Passages for Further Study

- Deuteronomy 30:15-20
- Psalm 28:6-9
- Psalm 71:1-6
- Psalm 145:3-7
- Ecclesiastes 7:29–8:5
- Hebrews 13:20-21

15

*E*MBRACING THE EXPERIENCE
OF CHILDBEARING

Instead of understanding ourselves by what was given

in our inheritance, we understand ourselves by what we become in

creating new life. . . . Love is detached from the cloying clutter

and therefore open to fertilization by the new, open to the ecstasy

of intercourse and the act of creation. Attachment is closed up and

walled in. Detachment opens out and grows up.[1]

EUGENE H. PETERSON

The test has confirmed it; a new life has begun! Within the womb a baby is growing. The news is staggering in its significance, yet it is something heard around the world every day. So incredible is this tiny miracle, yet so common. A most human event has entered into a man and a woman's relationship as God's creation is affirmed once again.

The nine months of pregnancy bring many changes to a marriage. As questions surface and new responsibilities are anticipated, the couple likely feels ambivalent as well as overjoyed. They may wonder: Who will this baby be? What kind of parents will we make? How will we manage to pay all the bills? Will our relationship be changed forever? Will we be able to give up our relative independence? How will it feel to be so tied down?

Getting married involved a step toward maturity and away from one's childhood; becoming parents is a more drastic move in the direction of growing up. Regardless of your ages, you two lovers are now expectant parents. Naturally, you will spend a great deal of time thinking about how the arrival of your baby will change what exists between you.

Before there is time to think about it, however, your baby will make his or her presence known. The moment the ovum is fertilized, a process is set into motion that alters a mother's body in significant ways. Although you cannot feel your baby moving yet, your body will quickly become aware that this cycle will be different. Your progesterone levels remain high after ovulation, signaling your uterine lining to remain ready for the embryo's arrival. While traveling through the fallopian tube, the rapidly dividing cluster of cells will issue a substance that begins to prepare your breasts for lactation. In this amazing way, your baby actually ensures his or her future supply of nutrients.

Once embedded in the uterus, the embryo sends another messenger into your bloodstream. Called HCG (human chorionic gonadotropin), this substance is capable of producing a feeling of queasiness for days on end. The nausea you may experience is a positive indication of the baby's secure attachment to the wall of the uterus. A connection has been established between vomiting, "morning sickness," and the extent of implantation. Nevertheless, it is difficult to appreciate this sign when an upset stomach lasts from dawn until dusk. Women who experience this discomfort find it discouraging and are not likely to be completely thrilled with being pregnant. Daily nausea definitely can have a negative effect on one's outlook on life.

All hope for a romantic maternity vanishes when fatigue sets in and you become ruthless about getting sleep. Even before the first missed period, napping, dozing off unexpectedly, and early bedtimes start to become a way of life. Though the transformations going on inside your uterus are neither seen nor felt, they are taking place at a brisk pace, demanding a high level of energy and nutrients.

Mood swings are commonplace as well. It would not be unusual for you to vary from one extreme to another as you reflect on your situation. Ambivalence—excitement mixed with apprehension—joy flipped over to reveal anxiety—a time of evaluating and sorting through many feelings. Pregnancy can provoke all of these things. The passage from being a couple to becoming parents is one of life's most meaningful and challenging events.

A SERIES OF GROWTH STEPS

It is only natural to wonder what the Lord had in mind when He designed this curious process. During pregnancy, a woman's body must undergo tremendous physiological changes as it carries a baby to term. For forty weeks this waiting period continues, producing opportunities for spiritual and emotional, as well as for physical, growth.

In responding to these changes in your own unique way as a couple, you can develop resources that bring you closer together before the baby comes. If you are willing to open your hearts up to one another, all sorts of interesting things may happen. Frustration can lead to the development of patience; fear can dissolve into the triumph of trust; fatigue can provoke the elimination of nonessential activities; and a fragmented lifestyle may be restructured on the basis of family-centered priorities.

Rather than being confused and surprised by the negative aspects of childbearing, you can creatively cope with the challenges you confront. Crisis can become a chance for teamwork and intimate sharing. In this way, your pregnancy can be a time marked by the deepening of the bond you share as your marriage reaps a harvest of spiritual dividends.

PREGNANT PAUSES

In addition to the obvious physical changes that will occur during your pregnancy, a more subtle change begins to take place. Up until now, your reproductive tract has been primarily receptive in its sexual function. But as the child within you grows, you will be faced with changing the way you view your sexuality.

Your previously empty womb is now occupied. Your breasts, formerly a source of mutual pleasure to you and your husband, will swell and change as glands develop that will eventually produce milk for the baby. Your vagina, the intimate area that has caressed your husband's penis in lovemaking, is preparing to take on its birth-giving role. In a culture that views the female body as a sexual object, these transformations can be strangely perplexing.

Our society has made the "38-22-34" figure into an icon. As a result, men and women alike are confused about how pregnancy, birth, and breastfeeding affect sexual activity. During pregnancy, you and your husband's feelings and attitudes about sexuality will converge with your feelings and attitudes about childbearing. In some relationships, the blending of these two dimensions of life will produce serious conflict. A husband might be unable to be aroused by his wife's enlarged body; a woman may find it difficult to mesh her maternal and sexual roles; both could find it discomforting to have a "third person" nearby during lovemaking.

On the other hand, many couples find that childbearing expands their ability to love and care for one another, both in bed and out of it. A mutual commitment to satisfy one another's sexual needs, express affection frequently, and share in numerous ways together will enrich your marriage bond, while a refusal to really listen to each other and spend time together can threaten to tear it apart.

A series of pauses affect virtually every couple's sex life during the nine months of pregnancy and the three-month adjustment period that follows it. For the span of a year, changes that are basically biological in nature will sweep into your relationship, greatly increasing your need for mutual understanding and communication.

Progesterone, the hormone that quiets smooth muscles during pregnancy, directly affects a woman's desire for sexual expression. It is nearly impossible to predict how any given woman will respond to the demands placed upon her mind and body. Each woman is unique and needs to be open to her own way of reacting to the experience of bearing a child. There are no clearly marked road maps to follow, even though countless women have traveled this road before.

The physiological changes brought about by childbearing and breast-feeding are, however, predictable for the most part in spite of the wide variety of possible individual responses. The personalities of the man and woman involved, along with their one-of-a-kind relationship, will influence how they meet the challenges. Becoming informed about what takes place during pregnancy, birth, and lactation reduces the mystery and provides a factual framework to base your decisions upon.

Unless you have experienced bleeding or have a history of miscarriage, lovemaking may continue as it did before pregnancy. Many couples find that freedom from using a family planning method enhances intercourse. There will need to be an ongoing revision of lovemaking positions throughout pregnancy and during recovery afterwards for the sake of comfort. Deep penetration and vigorous intercourse may be uncomfortable due to a greater amount of blood in the vessels within the pelvic area.

It is helpful to look at the common elements in each of the four trimesters or three-month periods of pregnancy and postpartum. Each is influenced by a characteristic set of body changes that influence sexual response and the desire for sexual activity (Fig. 15-1). Remember: no two women are exactly alike in which symptoms they exhibit or in the way they respond to what is happening within their bodies.

Sexual Response During Pregnancy
Figure 15-1

DESIRE

- Changes in body image and/or concern about the baby may significantly influence a woman's interest in sex.

- Desire for lovemaking fluctuates with moods, energy level, and discomfort experienced.

EXCITEMENT

- Time required for arousal may be shortened due to increased blood supply to pelvic area.

- Vaginal lubrication develops more rapidly and more extensively than when not pregnant.

- Breast enlargement may have a positive effect on women who had felt that their breasts were too small.

- Breast and nipple stimulation may relieve tension in breast tissue in some women; others may find contact painful or uncomfortable.

PLATEAU

- Marked enlargement of the outer third of the vagina may enhance sexual response.

- Increased sensation of pelvic fullness may accentuate pleasurable sensations prior to orgasm.

ORGASM

- Orgasmic frequency may result from heightened pelvic tension due to mother's increased blood volume.

- Spasms of the uterus, called Braxton-Hicks contractions, may replace or accompany orgasmic contractions in the pelvic floor muscles.

RESOLUTION

- Pelvic congestion is frequently not relieved by orgasm; feelings of fullness may remain.

- Length of this phase may be increased, resulting in a degree of discomfort in the pelvic area.

- Some women find it easier to become aroused again and may experience multiple orgasms.

- Braxton-Hicks contractions may not subside immediately.

THE FIRST TRIMESTER

For many women, an increased need for sleep, digestive changes, urination frequency, and breast tenderness are the trademarks of early pregnancy. Participating in lovemaking may take extra effort, but it is important to avoid neglecting the need for sexual sharing even though one's sex drive may seem to be at an all-time low.

Beginning a pregnancy with the commitment to remain sexually intimate with your husband is a key to avoiding problems later on. If you have concerns about sex during pregnancy, it may help to discuss specific questions with a health care professional trained in sexual counseling. For this reason, it is important to realize that one's choice of a birth attendant—whether it be an obstetrician, a family practice physician, or a midwife—plays a central role in the way a woman responds to her childbearing experience. Finding a person skilled in the art of counseling as well as in maternal-child health care is well worth the extra time and effort it may take.

It is not unusual if your pregnancy seems more real to you than to your husband initially. After all, none of these changes are apparent from the outside until the fourth or the fifth month. One of the best ways to deal with this is by keeping lines of communication open. If you take the time to share and express your reactions to your pregnancy, you can enable your husband to feel more included in the experience. An especially meaningful moment may be attending a prenatal visit together and hearing the baby's heartbeat for the first time. If your husband is not able to be there, the baby's heartbeat can be recorded on a cassette tape to share later on. If an ultrasound becomes medically necessary, he can also accompany you to the appointment and have the opportunity to see the baby's image displayed in full view.

Many wives feel an increased need for touch and receiving nurturing from others as pregnancy progresses. When the husband creatively responds to this need, it may be easier for the wife to relax and enjoy the sexual relationship during pregnancy. Helping with housework and cooking, encouraging the mother-to-be to eat well and get plenty of rest, finding many ways to express affection, and saying "I love you" go a long way in promoting sexual harmony. Through assuming an active spiritual role in home prayer times and shared Bible study, the husband can help his wife respond to the demands of childbearing. Also, learning the facts about a woman's sexuality during this time allows him to deal with any concerns he may have about the effects of lovemaking on pregnancy.

There are a number of things you can choose to do to enliven your marriage and enhance the quality of your pregnancy experience. Wearing support hose will lessen your chance of developing varicose veins, as will walking regularly. Taking one or two showers daily, with particular attention to rinsing off secretions around the genital area, will eliminate body odors that may make you feel self-conscious. Enhancing your appearance through selecting attractive, comfortable clothes can help you feel good about the way you look. Eating nutritious foods provides your body, and the baby's, with the necessary nutrients for the growth and maintenance of all of the cells that are working and developing at this time. Giving yourself permission to get the rest you need is also an important way of providing energy for the many different processes taking place.

Increasingly, women are finding that appropriate exercise reduces the lethargy that often sets in during pregnancy. Exercise can help the body adapt to gestation through strengthening the muscles affected by the baby's growth and by decreasing the discomforts related to carrying a baby. Choosing a type of fitness activity that is fun and contributes to your sense of vitality is worth the effort, as is checking with your health care provider prior to participating in an exercise program. Walking, swimming, and low-impact, low-intensity aerobic dancing are all excellent forms of exercise that promote cardiovascular endurance. Include a basic routine of stretching and conditioning exercises suited to pregnancy for a well-balanced program. Including your husband in regular walks is a way to stimulate sharing as well as to encourage a healthy attitude toward pregnancy. Being creative about structuring time together can be physically and emotionally beneficial.

THE SECOND TRIMESTER

By the fourth month of pregnancy, the initial adjustment period is over. Consequently, you may discover a renewed interest in lovemaking.

As your developing child grows, your abdomen will expand. By the sixth month, your breasts begin to make a substance called colostrum until breast milk begins to be produced about forty-eight hours after the baby is born. Tissue within your vagina will become increasingly more elastic, and a feeling of fullness in your pelvic area, resulting from the large amount of blood now circulating there, may become evident. Nausea may persist throughout your pregnancy, but the majority of expectant mothers have greater difficulty coping with indigestion, heartburn, and/or constipation at this point.

It is not unusual for sexual responsiveness to increase dramatically as the early discomforts of pregnancy subside. Many women continue to want reassurance of their partner's love and acceptance of their changing bodies through affectionate gestures like cuddling, hand holding, and back rubs. Making love with your husband benefits from an increased amount of lubrication in your vagina, but may be decidedly uncomfortable unless you are both willing to experiment with new positions for intercourse. Positions that avoid putting pressure on your abdomen and allow you to control the depth of penetration are preferable, such as lying side-to-side (either facing each other or with your husband behind you), your husband kneeling in front of you, or you sitting astride your husband.

Some women find that they begin to experience multiple orgasms during this phase of pregnancy due to the increased amount of vasocongestion present. This can be stimulating for one's husband, but can be somewhat surprising for you.

Being open to your body during pregnancy is just as important as at other times in life. Talking through some of the things that may be confusing to you will help prevent misunderstanding. There is no replacement for communicating your thoughts and feelings with one other if you desire lovemaking to be mutually enjoyable.

THE THIRD TRIMESTER

As the baby's due date approaches, a decrease in the frequency of intercourse is commonly reported. Medical advice ranges from warning parents to avoid intercourse for the last six or eight weeks to giving the go-ahead to participate in lovemaking until labor begins. Unless the amniotic sac has been broken, the baby is normally well protected within the uterus up until the time of delivery. Some health care providers even recommend making love as a way to stimulate the onset of labor. Research has shown that semen and nipple stimulation actually may help to "ripen" the cervix in preparation for birth; other studies have proven the effectiveness of nipple stimulation as a way of starting labor. Be sure to discuss with your health care provider any concerns or questions related to the effects of lovemaking on pregnancy and the onset of labor.

Many women notice that they have uterine spasms, called Braxton-Hicks contractions, following orgasm. This is particularly true of women who have given birth previously. These contractions vary in intensity, feel muscular rather than cramplike, and do not develop a regular pattern. They also become weaker over time rather than stronger, or closer together like true labor. Another difference in sexual response commonly reported is that the pelvic area continues to feel full and tense after orgasm during the resolution phase. Instead of a feeling of relief as blood leaves the area, the vessels stay congested as a normal consequence of late pregnancy. You may find it helpful to soak in a warm bath or gently massage the lower abdomen if this becomes a problem for you.

Toward the end of a first pregnancy, the fetus descends into the mother's bony pelvis any time from two to six weeks before delivery. This event is referred to as lightening or engagement. The cervix is pressed down when this happens, making the vagina less spacious. Rectal pressure may also be felt. If you and your husband wish to continue to make love up until the baby is born, you may find it challenging to find comfortable positions. Alternative expressions to intercourse, such as mutual touching and pleasuring, may be preferable. This is a time when your acceptance of the process of your body's preparation for birth will be particularly beneficial.

THE SEXUALITY OF GIVING BIRTH

Creating a child is a most intimate act. The birth of that child is no less intimate as a woman's total being becomes absorbed in the process of giving birth. Labor is not just something that happens to you; it is the fundamental effort required to bring new life into the world.

The Lord has designed this process to take place at the center of female sexuality as a baby emerges from the mother's body. The ability to actively participate in giving birth brings the act of marriage full circle and, when shared, becomes a landmark in the history of a marriage.

It is true that love has the power to cast out fear—even the fear of childbirth. Preparation for birth that allows two people to come to terms with the fruition of their sexual relationship can draw them together in profound ways. As a childbirth educator, I often have had the privilege of witnessing the admiration with which many men regard their wives. It is a beautiful thing to behold! A man and woman choosing to bring forth their child together are blessed in many ways. They may view the differences in their sexual natures with a greater appreciation than ever before.

Giving birth is a process involving hard work and, in most cases, a certain amount of physical discomfort or pain. Having realistic expectations can reduce feelings of anger afterwards. Looking to the Lord for strength is the most valuable birth technique that exists. Breathing and relaxation, prayer and listening to music, and strategically applied back rubs also contribute to the body's healthy adaptation to labor.

As the baby moves through your birth canal, your vagina will stretch to make room for your baby's passage. The muscles of your pelvic floor will separate as the baby presses through. You are likely to feel completely absorbed in what you are doing as you give birth, unable to do anything but push with your entire being as your baby prepares to leave your body for life outside your womb. Suddenly, the head will appear . . . then the ears, and whooshhh . . . there will be your baby's darling face! In one more contraction, his or her shoulders will fit through; then the body will quickly slip out in a rush of warm fluid. The umbilical cord will still be beating as you and your husband reach to touch your son or daughter for the very first time.

This is the result of that special moment shared nine months ago. It is nothing less than a stupendous accomplishment, and you will, understandably, be very proud. As tears of joy streak down your cheeks, you most likely will find yourselves praising God for the miracle of life you see before you. What an awesome thing this time together is!

Opening up to birthing a baby requires a willingness to trust God for the way He has designed the sexual function of our bodies. Labor is a powerful physical, emotional, and spiritual experience as the uterus works to accomplish the task of opening the cervix and pressing the baby out of the womb. There is little in today's world to prepare us for such a task. But the Lord has given something that will teach us much about what is required of us: His love. Our Father's love is the underlying theme upon which His creation is founded. Thanking God for the wonder of our bodies enables us to appreciate the amazing tasks they are capable of. Trusting Him to lead us *because He loves us* helps us to cast off fear and put on acceptance. We are not here by accident. The way our bodies function is an integral part of His pattern for our lives.

THE FOURTH TRIMESTER

The six weeks following your baby's arrival are a continuation of childbirth as the uterus shrinks to its previous size and breastfeeding begins. Within minutes after the baby's arrival, the placenta detaches from the wall of the uterus, and the blood levels of progesterone and estrogen plummet. As your baby is placed at your breast and begins to suckle, a hormone called oxytocin is released that causes muscle cells in the uterus and breasts to contract. This in turn encourages your uterus to reduce the amount of bleeding from the place where the placenta was attached and will signal the glands within your breasts to begin the initial phase of lactation.

Another hormone, prolactin, begins to be secreted by the pituitary gland, triggering tissue in your breasts' gland cells to begin milk production. Although your breast milk will not appear until some time between thirty-six and seventy-two hours after your baby's birth, colostrum will be secreted in the meantime. It is the perfect substance for your baby's early feedings, consisting mainly of proteins, antibodies, water-soluble vitamins, and minerals.

This highly select blend of nutrients also contributes to the health of your baby's intestinal tract, protecting him or her from the bacteria and viruses present in your birth canal and associated with other human contact. It is now clear that breast milk is the ideal food for human infants and breastfeeding also speeds the recovery of the mother. This wonderful diet for newborns is actually a liquid tissue alive with many beneficial organisms. It is also species-specific and cannot be duplicated. Appreciating the qualities of breast milk will enable you to get through the early adjustment period more easily because you'll know that you are giving something to your baby that no one else can provide.

THE TRANSITION PERIOD

During the first few weeks after giving birth, both you and your husband will be faced with interrupted sleep, a need for time spent alone together, and a transition period that involves the adjustment of your family relationships and sexual roles. At times, you may feel overwhelmed by the changes taking place. This period is actually quite similar to a honeymoon in that you will be spending time "falling in love" with your new baby during what has been called the "babymoon."

Just as pregnancy may be compared to courtship and giving birth to the wedding ceremony, the postpartum period is similar to the intensity of the days following one's marriage celebration. A great deal of emotional energy is spent on forming a bond with your baby that will serve as a foundation for a lifetime of parenting. It is often an exhausting effort.

In the midst of this upheaval, your body is healing from the process of childbirth. A discharge from the uterus, called lochia, continues until the womb has returned to its normal state. Your breasts will swell and fill with milk and may leak periodically for several weeks. Your pelvic floor will gradually regain its strength. Your abdominal muscles will initially feel soft and saggy until they resume their regular tone. Stretch marks may be apparent at various places where your skin has stretched to accommodate your baby's growth. If an incision was made in your perineum during delivery, it will gradually heal, leaving scar tissue that may initially produce a feeling of tightness in your vagina.

Considering this challenge to a woman's body image, is it any wonder that you may find yourself becoming concerned about getting pregnant again? Having intercourse with your husband may be the *last* thing on your mind! It is common to temporarily think that you will never be sexually desirable or responsive again.

It is difficult for a man to understand what is going on within his wife's mind and body at this time. After all, his body has experienced none of the feelings of pregnancy or the birth, and he can never know what it is like to have milk secreted from his body. The only way for him to understand is for you to verbalize your feelings to him. In his mind, the experience of sex will always be associated with the release and excitement of ejaculation. But in your mind, sex produced an emotional and physical upheaval in addition to joy. It may take you some time to sort through your feelings about what has taken place within your body. Resuming intercourse may be delayed for several weeks to several months as your body and mind begin to feel comfortable with making love again.

During this time, you will benefit from hearing that you are loved and appreciated just for who you are. It is easy to think that things will never return to normal, to wonder how all the pieces will ever fit together in the future. Taking time out to rest, nap, get out for brief periods of time, and spend time in leisure activities (such as taking a long bath or listening to music with headphones on) can restore your appreciation for life if you are emotionally down, fatigued, or suffering from feelings of isolation.

Sexual expression can become a natural outcome of taking the time to touch and talk. If intercourse is painful or seems to be temporarily undesirable, employ alternative forms of lovemaking. Lying naked together by candlelight may help you feel less self-conscious about how your body looks. Agreeing to mutually satisfy one another without the expectation of intercourse may relieve your anxiety, if present, about making love. It may be that you just want to be held or touched affectionately for the time being. If so, let your husband know this. If your husband desires sexual release, use pleasurable touching techniques that allow both of you to share in his experience of orgasm. This is a perfectly natural way for you to to meet each other's physical needs.

PROMOTING SEXUAL HARMONY DURING TIMES OF STRESS

Most husbands and wives find that any crisis or stressful event affects all aspects of their relationship, including sexual sharing. Intercourse, when undesirable during pregnancy or recovery after birth, may be missed less if alternative forms of lovemaking are employed. Kissing, hugging, massage, and pleasurable touch are ways a couple can bolster sexual harmony.

Being open to each other's feelings and understanding the need for *love, time, and patience* will enable a couple to weather the changes in their lives more easily. Remember the reasons underlying the desire for sexual expression. It was created to be:

A means of conveying and sharing love. Many women feel isolated and emotionally vulnerable during pregnancy and after giving birth. Sexual sharing can be an important way of reassuring one that she is still sexually attractive even though her body looks and feels different.

An affirmation of one's sexual identity. It is not unusual for a woman to have conflicting feelings about her body's sexual functions. Sharing these reactions with her husband can enable her to accept her capacities for giving birth and breastfeeding while at the same time recognizing her need for sexual expression through lovemaking.

A relief from the stressful aspects of marriage. Most men and women feel refreshed and relaxed after they experience orgasm. The stresses of childbearing and parenting place taxing demands on the marital relationship. Intimate contact can help a couple to be a source of pleasure to one another in the midst of these responsibilities.

An exclusive part of the marriage relationship. Sexual sharing is an important means of reestablishing and maintaining this exclusive aspect of the relationship. It can remind them of the special attraction they have toward one another. While sex does not solve marital problems, it can be an important means of saying, "I love you. You are still the most important person in my life."

MORE HELPFUL HINTS

When you feel that you want to begin having intercourse again, you will benefit from taking a warm, relaxing bath beforehand. Starting the second week after giving birth, you can help your vagina and perineum to heal by doing up to 100 Kegels (pelvic lifts) daily in sets of twenty-five and applying a small amount of uncontaminated vitamin E oil to this area. Put a few drops of the oil on your first two fingers and gently rub it into the walls of your vagina after it has healed. Additional oil may be massaged into the perineum, the area lying just behind the vaginal outlet toward the anus. Do not rub from the rear forward, as this may contaminate your vagina with germs from your rectum. Vitamin E oil promotes healing and will help the skin to be more resilient and stretchy. It may take about six to twelve weeks of doing both of these things regularly before your vagina is sufficiently recovered from childbirth to resume lovemaking.

It is important to be sure that your husband's penis is slippery before guiding it into your vagina. Your vaginal lining may be dry and tender initially, and the application of a sterile lubricant will make intercourse more enjoyable.

You may prefer to be the one to place your husband within your body, making sure to expand your pelvic floor muscles by bulging them outwards as you do so. This will widen your vaginal opening and relax your PC muscles, which may become constricted if you feel anxious or fearful about lovemaking. If intercourse is still uncomfortable, you may also find it helpful to ask your husband to gently insert two clean, well-lubricated fingers into your vagina and rotate them to help you identify possible areas of discomfort and encourage relaxation of your pelvic floor muscles. Tender, delicate stimulation of the clitoris may also be especially desirable. Guide your husband's hands to indicate what pleases and arouses you.

If there are areas of tenderness within your vagina, assume a different position for intercourse that allows you to control the depth of penetration when you're ready to make love. Guiding your husband's penis away from irritated areas may be achieved through your use of positions that change the angle of intercourse. The woman-astride position, with you either facing toward or away from your husband's torso, may be comfortable. If this position makes you feel too exposed, lying in a semi-sitting position propped up on pillows, with your husband either sitting or kneeling in front of you, may help. A rear-entry position with you leaning over a chair or dresser covered with a pillow while standing up is preferable to the use of this position while kneeling because penetration will be considerably less deep.

Making sure to include adequate time for pleasuring before intercourse will enable your mind and body to be aroused enough to feel receptive to making love. Also your husband will require less time to ejaculate after entering you so that excessive rubbing of the vaginal tissue may be avoided. If lovemaking proves to be painful in spite of trying a variety of things to relieve discomfort, you and your husband may want to resume touching without intercourse as a way of fulfilling your desire to be sexually close to one another.

Women vary in the length of time it takes to recover from giving birth, with some feeling ready to resume lovemaking two to three weeks following delivery and others still feeling pain a year or more afterwards. A consultation with a health care provider skilled in providing counseling and diagnosis for a long-term difficulty is recommended if pain is still present after four to six months, providing you have been doing Kegels and applying vitamin E oil on a regular basis.

BREASTFEEDING AND SEXUALITY

When a woman is breastfeeding a baby, her body secretes prolactin in large amounts, which produces a feeling of tranquillity. Many women report that this sense of peacefulness is not conducive to promoting a desire for sexual expression, since the sexual response cycle is based on a feeling of tension. Because prolactin levels are highest during a feeding and for the period immediately following it, nursing a baby two to three hours before lovemaking may help. This is precisely the opposite of what some books and articles recommend, however. Several sources suggest nursing just prior to going to bed so the mother's breasts will be fairly empty and less likely to leak. It all depends on one's point of view: would you rather feel more responsive and leak milk occasionally during lovemaking or feel unresponsive and experience less leaking? Lactation consultants jokingly suggest that the husband should bring some cookies to bed with him as a way of taking a lighter look at this phenomenon!

You may also wear a bra with cotton nursing pads to absorb leaking if you feel self-conscious about your milk supply. A waterproof mattress pad under the sheets with an absorbent towel to lay on will keep bedding clean. The leaking of breast milk does not usually continue past the first six weeks, and in those women who continue to experience it, most have become accustomed to it by this time.

· If you are using fertility awareness as your method of family planning, you will need to receive special instructions about how breastfeeding affects the mucus sign. Frequent nursing hinders ovulation and menstruation for an average of fourteen months following a baby's birth if the mother refrains from using bottles and pacifiers, continues to nurse at least every four hours around the clock, and avoids starting solids until the baby is six to eight months old.

If a natural pattern of breastfeeding is not practiced, your fertility is likely to return much earlier. In either case, if you wish to avoid pregnancy, you will need to know how to check for fertility while you are lactating.

Mothering an infant can be a tremendously satisfying experience. Babies benefit from having frequent, regular contact with their mothers, and breastfeeding is an ideal way to provide for this need. It is not unusual for mothers to notice that they have ministered to their baby and other children all day out of their emotional energy reserve. Having a husband who is sensitive to the physical and emotional demands placed on you enables him to minister to you in a mature way through praying for you, accepting the way you feel, meeting your need for adult companionship, and being committed to sharing himself with you in love.

CHILDBEARING: A SEXUAL PASSAGE

Bearing one's first child involves a sexual passage in all women's lives. It is safe to assume that most couples are challenged by the events they face during this unique time.

Moving through the phases of pregnancy, childbirth, and breastfeeding can draw a husband and wife closer together, or it can drive them further apart. Much depends on their ability to listen, to care, and to understand one another's needs and desires (Fig. 15-2).

No one passes through this time without experiencing difficult moments. With the Lord's help and a commitment to love each other, the bond a man and woman share can become stronger, offering a couple the opportunity for a fresh discovery of one another and the chance to explore new dimensions of their sexuality.

Factors Affecting Sexual Expression
During the Childbearing Year
Figure 15-2

THE FIRST TRIMESTER

Every woman's pregnancy is unique and presents an opportunity for emotional growth as new experiences are encountered. Before the pregnancy is even confirmed, hormonal changes alter the mother's physiology in many ways. Sexual expression is influenced by these changes in the reproductive system, and most couples face unexpected challenges and significant surprises.

PHYSICAL:

- Fatigue, increased need for sleep
- Nausea, indigestion, vomiting
- Breast tenderness
- Feeling of fullness in pelvic area
- Possible spotting—frequent urination, possible leaking

EMOTIONAL:

- Bond created by baby's conception
- Ambivalent feelings about the experience of pregnancy
- Feelings of self-protectiveness
- Concern about weight gain, body image
- Pregnancy may seem more real to the mother than the father.

WHAT TO EXPECT:

- Change in lovemaking frequency
- Revision of lovemaking habits to avoid discomfort
- Increased vaginal lubrication
- Less abandonment with greater degree of gentleness

- Increased tension in pelvic area during sexual arousal due to increased blood supply to that area

WIFE'S RESPONSE:

- "Touch and talk" before sexual sharing

- Commitment to understanding husband's spiritual, emotional, and physical needs

- Discount what friends may say about their experiences, when necessary.

- Discuss specific concerns with health care provider.

- Avoid using pregnancy as an excuse to refrain from lovemaking if there are other reasons why sexual sharing is bothering you.

- Express affection in a variety of ways.

HUSBAND'S RESPONSE:

- Willingness to accommodate pregnancy through creative problem-solving

- Help with housework, encourage wife to rest.

- Lots of "tender pats," fewer passionate caresses if wife is less responsive

- Commitment to understanding wife's spiritual, emotional, and physical needs

- Develop a factual view of lovemaking during pregnancy; deal with fears regarding harming the baby during intercourse.

- Find many ways to say "I love you."

- Spiritual leadership, shared prayer, and Bible study

THE SECOND TRIMESTER

During this trimester, the initial adjustment to pregnancy has been made. Nausea and fatigue may be greatly diminished, and the chance of having a miscarriage is greatly reduced. Until the sixth month, the baby and the mother's abdomen are not yet large enough to present much of an obstacle to lovemaking, but a woman may feel awkward and unattractive to her husband due to her changing shape.

PHYSICAL:

- Possible vaginal and nipple tenderness
- Swelling of the vagina and labia
- Less relief following orgasm due to pelvic fullness
- Nausea may persist
- Indigestion, heartburn, and constipation are common throughout the remainder of pregnancy.
- Increased vaginal lubrication

EMOTIONAL:

- Fear of harming baby or provoking a miscarriage may persist.
- Feeling of fetal movements may be a distraction or an impediment to lovemaking.
- Feeling of well-being may be a boon to sexual expression.
- Sexual response may increase dramatically due to pelvic congestion, nipple sensitivity.

WHAT TO EXPECT:

- Increased energy reserve
- Fluctuations in desire for lovemaking
- Desire for reassurance through cuddling, hand holding
- Greater sense of stability
- Need to revise positions for lovemaking as baby grows
- Increased feelings of femininity

- Increased feelings of dependency on husband

WIFE'S RESPONSE:

- Acceptance of maternal role

- Increased bonding with baby as movements are felt and interpreted

- Willingness to feel comfortable with expanding waistline and breast changes

- Commitment to improve nutrition and promote fitness through appropriate exercise

- Continued commitment to include husband in pregnancy

- Acceptance of changes in sexual response

HUSBAND'S RESPONSE:

- Create opportunities for courtship activities.

- Support necessary lifestyle changes through involvement in wife's activities.

- Pray for wife and baby often.

- Offer continued patience, love, practical help, and understanding.

THE THIRD TRIMESTER

Sexual activity declines for many couples as the baby's due date approaches. Discomfort during lovemaking is commonly given as a reason for this decline, especially during the ninth month. Unless a couple is told that lovemaking is contraindicated, intercourse may continue during this period and may even be beneficial, preparing the cervix for birth.

PHYSICAL:

- Fatigue, insomnia, restlessness

- Increased pressure within pelvis

- Lower back discomfort

- Braxton-Hicks contractions

- Enlarged abdomen

- Frequent urination

- Colostrum secretion

- Increased vaginal discharge

EMOTIONAL:

- Anxiety about labor and birth, becoming parents, baby's health

- Excitement about receiving a new person into the family

- Need for recognition of baby, self

- Changes in body image

- Worry about husband's opinion of weight gain, decreased ability to be active, productive

- Increased feelings of vulnerability, need for protection

- Need for nonsexual nurturing

WHAT TO EXPECT:

- Established patterns of lovemaking are challenged and subsequently modified.

- Decreased vaginal space after baby engages in pelvis

- If interested in lovemaking, creative positions and gentle movement may be preferable.

- Intercourse may be too tiring or uncomfortable to be enjoyable.

- Rate of orgasm often declines.

- Uterus may stay very firm for several minutes after orgasm.

- Husband may be attracted to (or perplexed by) elasticity of vaginal tissue and amount of lubrication present.

WIFE'S RESPONSE:

- Discuss concerns with husband.

- Share openly with the Lord; pour your heart out to Him.

- Trust in the Lord's ability to strengthen and uphold you.

- Prepare for giving birth, breastfeeding.

- Avoid comparing yourself to others; accept your own uniqueness.

- Satisfy each other's sexual needs without intercourse if lovemaking becomes painful.

- Be thankful for the life within you, for your body's amazing ability to care for your baby.

- Pray often and avoid worrying.

HUSBAND'S RESPONSE:

- "Get in touch" with your wife every day through back rubs, hand holding, putting your arms around her, and cherishing her.

- Accept her decreased sex drive, if present.

- Realize that this is a temporary state of affairs.

- Participate in birth preparation together.

- Find new ways of expressing your appreciation.

- Encourage communication.

- Welcome the opportunities for growth God gives you.

THE FOURTH TRIMESTER

Adjustments in lovemaking habits accompany a baby's arrival as part of a larger transition period that includes many changes in social and family roles. With each child's birth, relationships shift to include a new family member. The mother's fatigue and time-consuming involvement with the baby challenge others to support and understand her during the time her body returns to its normal state. There is no replacement for communicating each other's needs through talking and taking time out to openly share concerns, fears, and the emotional responses following the end of pregnancy.

PHYSICAL:

- Fatigue
- Healing of the uterus, pelvic floor, and perineum
- Adjustment of the breasts to lactation
- Vaginal dryness and tenderness
- Vaginal tightness
- Leaking of milk
- Fluctuations in desire for sexual interaction
- Stretch marks, change in measurements from pre-pregnancy

EMOTIONAL:

- Fear of pain during intercourse
- Feeling that episiotomy site may be damaged during intercourse
- Postpartum "blues"
- Engrossment with baby as bonding takes place
- Possible fear of pregnancy
- Distracted during lovemaking by baby's presence in house
- Disappointment in lack of muscle tone or amount/rate of weight loss
- Frustration at not being able to get more things done

- Possible jealousy and resentment of baby taking up so much of wife's time

WHAT TO EXPECT:

- A temporary period of transition and readjustment
- Decreased vaginal lubrication and elasticity
- Mood swings
- Need for patience while healing is completed
- Restructuring of social life and responsibilities to allow for rest, time alone as a family
- "Babymoon" that differs from the everyday routines

WIFE'S RESPONSE:

- Accept help, allow others to nurture you.
- Encouragement to eat well and get plenty of rest
- Pelvic floor exercises and pure vitamin E oil to promote healing
- Be sensitive to husband's needs and concerns.
- View the transition period as a unique, temporary time in your life.
- Come to terms with changes in size and body image.

HUSBAND'S RESPONSE:

- Gain satisfaction through providing and caring for wife and child(ren).
- View fatherhood as a full-time commitment.
- Plan to take time off for the "babymoon."
- Do not pressure wife to resume intercourse when pain is present; employ alternative expressions of lovemaking, if desired.

LACTATION

The process of breastfeeding produces a unique relationship between a mother and her baby. This bond enables a woman to nurture her infant physically as well as emotionally. The love poured out into the mother-child relationship through the giving of one's milk is a significant gift and one that is not without its costs. The baby's father can express his love for his child best by loving the mother and helping her to feel that what she is contributing to the family is valuable.

PHYSICAL:

- Fatigue, an increased need to rest and take naps

- Full, possibly leaking breasts

- Probable lack of ovulation and menstruation for a significant period of time if fully breastfeeding

- Vaginal dryness due to decreased estrogen levels

- Frequent stimulation of the breasts through nursing

EMOTIONAL:

- Increased feelings of femininity

- Appreciation for the process of nursing, especially after the initial adjustment period

- Pleasurable sensations produced during feedings may cause concern if not understood and accepted as normal.

- May feel emotionally and physically drained at times

WHAT TO EXPECT:

- Sexual stimulation causes release of milk.

- Return of desire for lovemaking will occur earlier in women experiencing a high degree of sexual tension, later in those struggling to cope with new demands and investing a large amount of energy in forming an attachment to the baby.

- Most women find nursing to be a pleasurable experience.

WIFE'S RESPONSE:

- Acceptance of pleasant maternal feelings produced by baby's sucking

- Commitment to meet own needs for nutrients and rest

- Share feelings with husband

- Avoid feeding the baby in the late evening before going to bed, or make love earlier in the evening to coincide with baby's schedule.

- Keep a sense of humor about leaking and take measures to make it less bothersome.

HUSBAND'S RESPONSE:

- Encourage wife to have some time to herself each day: warm baths, time to do something creative, go for walks, etc.

- Affirm wife's sense of dignity by recognizing that she is nurturing and caring for your child.

- Express your love in practical *and* romantic ways.

Love is not a possession but a growth. The heart is a lamp with just enough oil to burn for an hour, and if there be no oil to put in again, its light will go out. God's grace is the oil that fills the lamp of love.[2]

HENRY WARD BEECHER

Chapter Review

Personal Reflections

1. The experience of pregnancy has been especially interesting when I:

2. As I consider the emotional, physical, and spiritual dimensions of my sexuality during pregnancy, I realize:

3. Giving birth requires:

4. Breastfeeding affects a woman's sexuality in several ways, including:

5. Making time to make love once the baby arrives is:

6. After looking at the overview of how the different phases of child-bearing affect a couple's sexuality, I think God intends for us to:

Related Bible Passages for Further Study

- Psalm 8:1-2
- Psalm 18:1-2
- Psalm 37:39-40
- Psalm 71:1-3
- Ecclesiastes 4:9-12
- Isaiah 40:10-11

ℰNTERING INTO
THE FULLNESS OF LIFE

Let patience have her perfect work. Statue under the chisel
of the sculptor, stand steady under the blows of his mallet. Clay
on the wheel, let the fingers of the divine porter model you at
their will. Obey the Father's lightest word: hear the Brother
who knows you and died for you. . . . We die daily.
Happy are those who daily come to life as well.[1]

GEORGE MACDONALD

Through each day the Lord pours his unfailing love upon me,
and through each night I sing his songs, praying
to the God who gives me life.

PSALM 42:8 NLT

Aging, menopause, wrinkles, and gray hair? Or wisdom, maturity, and—a wealth of life experiences? When we think of growing older, which do we think of first?

What does it mean to be marble in the hands of a Master Sculptor over one's entire lifetime? Can we trust Him to chisel His life within us as we seek to conform to His image? How do we become clay that responds smoothly to the firm hands of the Potter as He molds and shapes us over the years?

As we love Jesus, we give Him the freedom to carve His ways into our minds and hearts. Through surrendering control of our lives to God, dedicating each day to the Lord on a moment-to-moment basis, we enter into fullness of life. None of us can do this perfectly, but with God's grace we remain headed in the right direction. Learning to trust Jesus through *all* of the seasons of our lives allows Him to teach us about the extent of His love for us. And what is His love like?

As we walk with Him from day to day, we will find His love to be the bread sustaining us when we are tired and weak. It will come as living water rushing into our souls to cleanse away sin and satisfy our soul-thirst. At times, it will be as our gentle Shepherd's voice, reminding us not to worry, as we trust God to provide for every need. When we look at a waterfall or gaze at the stars on a clear summer night, we will joyfully feel the majestic nature of our Creator's love manifested in His handiwork. Our response will be to whisper: "Jesus, we love You! Thank You for bringing Your life to us!"

We believe in Jesus not only because of what He did 2,000 years ago, but because of who He is today and because of what He continues to do in our lives. His miraculous source of life—the same life that turned water into wine, fed 5,000 people with five loaves of bread and two fish, healed people of incurable diseases, raised the dead, and rose victorious from the grave—is now represented in us through the Holy Spirit. For active followers of Jesus, aging is not so much the loss of youth as it is the opportunity to discover new dimensions of our walk with the Lord.

We each have something to offer to the body of Christ. *What we do with our time matters.* Do you believe that? Whether we are younger or older, physically impaired or healthy, introverted or outgoing, high school graduates or professors with Ph.D.s, we can serve our Lord wherever we are, in whatever we do, whether we lead a choir, write letters to prisoners, serve on a church staff, organize a food bank, work in a women's clinic, lead a Bible study, serve on the mission field, argue legal cases, or care for children. Each day brings us unique, one-of-a-kind opportunities to express our love to Christ.

Since the turn of this century, the average life expectancy for women has gone from forty-five to close to eighty years. Until recently, few women had the luxury to contemplate how to spend "the rest of their lives," as women today do. From all directions we are pressured to live for the future: to invest, achieve, accumulate, insure, and predict. In contrast, Jesus asks that we trust Him with our future, whatever it might be, and get on with the matter of living for Him in the present, right where we are, regardless of our age.

BUILDING FOR THE FUTURE BY DEPENDING ON GOD

The life patterns and habits we acquire during the early years of adulthood lay a foundation for the way we live during the later years of our earthly existence. No demarcation lines divide "youth" from "middle age" or "middle age" from "old age." Our histories develop on a day-to-day basis, with each event we encounter added to our experience of what it means to be alive.

We cannot say, until we look back, that this or that day will be any more significant than any other. We also do not feel ourselves pass from being young to being old. *Aging is a natural process that is merely a continuation of who we already are.* You and I will not be different people ten or thirty years from now. We will just be *more* of who we are today.

Expecting to look and feel the same way at sixty-five as we did at twenty-five denies the honor and dignity that can come with a lifetime of learning. If we do not fully acknowledge our mortality or the probability that we will live to be at least seventy years old, we will find it difficult to head into the future gracefully.

But if we begin early to build for the future through adjusting the way we view aging, and learning to depend daily upon God, we will be more likely to have positive things to contribute to the world around us as we grow older. Our perspective significantly differs from cultural views on aging when we shape our identity in conformity with God's will for our lives.

Growing older in the years allotted to us permits us to mature in faith and hope. The accumulation of time spent in Bible study, prayer, ministry, and Christian service builds up a treasure that can never be taken away from us. We will never lose the time and resources we invest on behalf of the Gospel. The kingdom of God Jesus talked about teaches us to use our gifts and talents wisely rather than for the sake of material gain alone.

When we meet older people who drain our energy through their bitterness and dissatisfaction, we are seeing a harvest reaped from seeds sown over the span of a lifetime. What a joy it is to meet people radiant with Christ's love in the later years of life! In contrast, they continue to minister God's strength to others even though their natural strength is waning. It is a privilege to be with a man or a woman whose faith has become deeply rooted in his or her heart after weathering the trials of life.

A SHINING EXAMPLE

When my husband and I first became Christians, we went to a church pastored by a man in his late sixties. Ted and Myrna Mosies were godly people to those of us who flocked to the services conducted in the cinderblock building Ted constructed. We became an active part of the body of Christ through this loving couple's acceptance of our countercultural lifestyle. No other church in our county would have been comfortable having us walk in their front door.

On Sunday mornings during the early seventies, hundreds of youth from miles around would come to hear Pastor Mosies teach. He never seemed to notice the beards, long hair, blue jeans, and sandals that most of the congregation wore. On the other hand, few of us thought of Ted as "old." We loved to hear him teach in his Dutch accent and listen to him sing "In the Garden." In a world where there seemed to be an abundance of bigotry, Leach Road Community Church offered us a taste of paradise.

It was comforting to be around our pastor and his wife. They lived in a simple one-bedroom house in a working-class neighborhood. They always had something to give to others, yet never seemed to be lacking in any way. Ted *always* picked up hitchhikers. The Mosieses were constantly feeding people, helping people, and ministering to people—all in Jesus' name. How they let their lights shine—and all at an age when they should have been slowing down and retiring.

Over the years, Ted's health deteriorated. He developed diabetes and lost his teeth due to a massive infection. As his body became weaker, he continued to trust the Lord to sustain him. At about the same time, each of us stopped going to the church as we moved away, either in an actual or a symbolic way, as Ted took a break from active pastoring. Not too long afterward, he went to be with the Lord when his body ceased functioning. It was as if he realized that he finally could "retire" once his ministry to us was over.

Soon afterward Myrna had a devastating stroke, leaving her partially paralyzed and unable to speak. When I greeted her at my sister's wedding in 1986, I wasn't surprised to see the beauty of the Lord resting on Myrna's face. With pure white hair and eyes that sparkled with Christ's love, Myrna's physical debilitation wasn't what caught my attention. It was the rare, incredible sweetness resting upon her face. I simply could not look at her without feeling touched in a powerful way by the joy of the Holy Spirit.

When I think of what it means to grow older, I will always think of Ted and Myrna Mosies. I will remember the things they taught me about God. Like Mary of Bethany, these two precious people were not content to store up treasure for themselves when they could share it with Jesus.

Paul wrote that "the mind controlled by the Spirit is life and peace" and that "if the Spirit of him who raised Jesus from the dead is living in you, he who raised Christ from the dead will also give life to your mortal bodies through his Spirit, who lives in you" (Romans 8:6, 11). These words apply to all believers, regardless of how young or old they are. We can reject the current cultural mind-set that makes women afraid of growing older. With God's grace, each of us can become a light that shines forth God's love as we set our minds upon Him.

THE DIGNITY OF MATURITY

She is clothed with strength and dignity;
*   she can laugh at the days to come.*
She speaks with wisdom,
*   and faithful instruction is on her tongue.*
She watches over the affairs of her household
*   and does not eat the bread of idleness.*
Her children arise and call her blessed;
*   her husband also, and he praises her:*
"Many women do noble things,
*   but you surpass them all."*
Charm is deceptive, and beauty is fleeting,
*   but a woman who fears the Lord is to be praised.*

PROVERBS 31:25-30

Menopause is not a disease.
Growing older is not an illness.
"Crow's feet" are not caused by a lack of moisturizer.

Believe it or not, we *can* laugh at the days to come when we realize where we're heading! Myths about aging are rampant in our society. Here are a few of the prevalent beliefs that influence the way women view the effects of aging on their sexuality:

FICTION: *No matter what happens to a woman in midlife, menopause is the culprit.*

FACT: Just as getting married and childbearing involve sexual passages, menopause involves changes that have an impact on a woman's life. It's the other changes taking place in most women's lives at or around the time of menopause that have a much greater effect on our everyday activities and priorities.

A number of events between the ages of forty-five and sixty bring changes in a woman's role and status as well as in her body. These are:

- Life patterns shift as children grow up, leave home, get married, and possibly start a family of their own.

- A number of family members and friends become chronically ill; loved ones close to the family die.

- Working adults prepare for retirement; many women make career changes or return to school for a first or second degree.

- The issue of death is faced more realistically from a personal standpoint.

- Minor changes occur in sexual function that involve a readjustment in attitudes and practices related to lovemaking.

- A change in the metabolic rate reduces one's caloric requirements by about 200-300 calories per day.

Did you know that the concept of the "midlife crisis" is relatively new to the field of mental health? *Crises can occur at* any *time in life when a person assumes new roles and moves from one phase of life to the next.* Each of us responds in a unique manner to cope with life changes during adolescence, college graduation, getting married, childbearing, or the loss of a loved one. *Any event that rearranges our lives can precipitate such a crisis.* A life crisis occurs when the coping response to a particular situation is not helpful, such as bouts of sadness, withdrawal from others, or outbursts of anger. Understanding this allows us to respond to these symptoms on an individual basis, if and when they occur.

When a woman realistically prepares ahead for midlife by anticipating the changes, long-term disruption in her life is less likely—with the exception of becoming a widow. For instance, if a woman expects to fall apart when she stops menstruating, then that will be a real possibility. Much depends on our outlook and ability to recognize stressful times that require special attention to our diet, rest, recreational activities, and time spent drawing near to God through prayer, fellowship, and Bible study.

FICTION: *A woman is not the same person after she goes through her "change of life."*

FACT: Menopause is part of God's design for our lives. It is the time when a woman's ovaries no longer produce changes in the uterine lining that cause monthly bleeding in the absence of conception. For most women, the process of the *climacteric* begins between the ages of forty-five and fifty. Menopause, or the stopping of menstruation, is just one part of this process.

During the climacteric, the production of estrogen recedes, and progesterone secretion is phased out almost entirely. Most women notice they tend to gain weight more easily. The majority of women, however, do *not* experience the distressing symptoms commonly associated with menopause such as depression, insomnia, headaches, and skin changes. Of those that do, it is unclear which of these are associated with factors other than a reduction in hormone levels.

It has been estimated that as few as one in ten women experience "hot flashes" or the sensation of heat spreading over various places on the body. The exact cause of hot flashes is unknown; some women seem to have a similar sensation in the week following childbirth. This is a physically harmless experience that varies in frequency, strength, and duration in the women who report it.

Viewing this symptom as if it is a sign of a disease may actually inhibit our ability to respond in an accepting manner. It is usually a temporary irritation best handled by using stress management techniques such as relaxation and slow breathing, and by reminding oneself that it will not harm the body.

Instead of becoming a different person after menopause, a woman is likely to feel that she is passing into a phase of her life that will allow her to express *more* of who she is. The care and nurture of children and teenagers excludes participation in activities that demand large amounts of time and energy away from the family. During the years when a woman concentrates on raising her children, she develops valuable skills that later lend themselves to ministry within the wider community she lives in. Child-rearing, for example, is a fantastic training ground for the development of time-management skills, creative approaches to getting jobs done, learning to be patient in the midst of multiple demands, and finding ways to express one's gifts in a multitude of situations.

For example, I have learned to have my "quiet time" with the Lord in prayer while washing dishes, making beds, doing the laundry, and vacuuming the rug. It seems the more I concentrate on Jesus, the less aware I am of the routineness of my tasks. This habit has helped me to avoid becoming resentful on many occasions and, at the same time, has made it easier to carry the Lord's presence with me wherever I go, into whatever I am doing. Other women have shared that they have also developed a rich prayer life under similar circumstances. I wonder where the church would be today without the countless women who devote hours of prayer to its mission while doing mundane things like fixing sack lunches or scrubbing out bathtubs.

The point to remember is this: the things you are doing today will follow you into the future. We will reap what we sow. Our early adult years can be a time of learning disciplines that will be put to good use in the years ahead. Our youth will never be "taken" from us if we spend it on the Lord's behalf.

FICTION: *A woman's desire for sex is greatly reduced after menopause.*

FACT: Some women desire sexual sharing less after menopause, but the majority find their love lives relatively unaffected. Hormone levels vary from woman to woman, and it is not known to what extent a decrease in desire may be related to biological (as opposed to psychological) factors.

What *is* known is that one-half of all menopausal and postmenopausal women report no change in their desire for sexual activity, and one-quarter say that they experienced an increase after menstruation stopped.[2] Since most men find that their sexual response becomes slower with age, an interesting thing takes place in many marriages: the husband is likely to require a longer time to become erect, which means that the time spent during the excitement and plateau phases of lovemaking must be significantly longer.

It is as if the Lord designed these changes into our bodies to enliven the sexual dimension of our lives at a time when communication and mutual understanding are more important than ever. Changes in physical responses to sexual arousal can become an opportunity for a couple to discover new ways to approach this aspect of their relationship.

The primary change that a woman must learn to cope with is the reduction of cervical mucus, causing the vaginal lining to become thinner and drier. This reduction is similar to what happens while a woman is breastfeeding, but will be more pronounced and involves gradual changes in the entire reproductive tract. After weighing the risks and benefits of hormone replacement therapy, many women decide that a primary advantage is the positive effect it has on keeping the vaginal tissue moist. Spending a longer time arousing one another, using positions that enhance comfort, and stroking a lubricant onto the husband's penis will also make intercourse easier. Frequent lovemaking actually "exercises" vaginal tissue, making it healthier than when regular intercourse is avoided.

FICTION: *Mental instability is a natural part of menopause.*

FACT: The belief that emotional instability is the cornerstone of menopause is inappropriate because it focuses on a single facet of a woman's life, causing her to view a normal process as an abnormality. Rather than attempting to understand the underlying causes for emotional expressions, blaming "The Change" becomes an easy way to explain every nuance of her behavior. Considering the other changes likely to be going on in her life, it is easy to see that a woman will encounter feelings she may find difficult to deal with.

Living in a society that places a premium on leanness, supple skin, and a youthful appearance can threaten our self-esteem as we grow older. If we build our sense of worth around our external appearance rather than on the eternal bedrock of Christ's love for us, we may find our identities based on sinking sand. Actively following Christ does not produce this type of neurosis. As celebrities parade their face lifts and tummy tucks before us, we can view the quest for endless youth with compassion instead of envy.

At any time in life, imbalances can occur in the level of chemicals in the brain, producing depression, erratic behavior, or outbursts of anger in stressful situations. A thorough physical examination should be conducted whenever a woman feels she has lost joy in living, experiences memory loss, or cannot control her anger. There may be physical causes for these symptoms that can be treated with medication. As followers of Christ, we sometimes forget this well-known fact. We may fall into a way of thinking that values medical treatment for our bodies but devalues treatment for the mind.

In light of current research this is unwise. There are now medications that can correct imbalances in the brain. These treatments for depression and anger can bring entire families out from under the oppression of one member's struggle to cope. It is unwise to refuse to seek professional help and try to "go it alone" when certain emotional states become overwhelming. It is not normal to be suicidal, listless, or out of control. Blaming menopause for these mental health concerns prevents a woman from getting the help she needs and deserves.

FICTION: *Menopause is an experience that fills most women with dread.*

FACT: Are you kidding? Most women are through with being fertile *long* before their bodies are. Many women have had hysterectomies in their thirties and forties, experiencing the loss of menstruation far in advance of their biologically determined date for this event. For the rest of us, can any of us claim to have been particularly fond of menstruating? I doubt it! Having one's period simply is not the highlight of the month for any woman.

Because of the mystery and folklore surrounding menopause, many women are unclear about what it actually involves. The last period in a woman's life usually occurs between forty and fifty-five, but it can happen as late as sixty. In the years preceding menopause, a woman's menstrual cycle is disrupted. Her periods are likely to become irregular as a result.

None of the troublesome symptoms commonly associated with menopause—hot flashes, vaginal dryness, disruption in the menstrual cycles during the climacteric—pose a threat to a woman's health *unless they are associated with other causes.* Because disease unrelated to menopause can occur, it is essential to discuss any health-related concerns with one's primary physician. *Menstrual changes that warrant immediate medical attention are bleeding between periods, prolonged or excessive menstrual bleeding, or having a period six months or more after the period that seemed to be the last.* These symptoms could indicate a life-threatening malignancy, such as cancer of the uterus, and must be evaluated by a physician.

The most common treatment for unpleasant symptoms associated with menopause is hormone replacement therapy, or HRT. Because estrogen therapy is associated with an increased risk of breast and uterine cancers, its long-term use should be thoroughly evaluated by a woman and her husband along with the woman's health care provider. The hormones used may be a combination of progesterone and estrogen, or estrogen alone in the form of vaginal cream or oral tablets. There are a number of things associated with menopause and aging that HRT cannot prevent or treat, including weight gain, wrinkled skin, and depression. HRT does relieve hot flashes and vaginal dryness, however; it also aids in maintaining the vagina's acid-base balance, thus making it more infection resistant. In addition, HRT appears to prevent osteoporosis and may contribute to a decreased risk of heart disease. Various remedies besides hormones also act to decrease the severity of symptoms associated with menopause. Alternative treatments consist mainly of herbal therapies, vitamin and mineral supplements, and stress management techniques.

For many women, a healthy diet and vigorous exercise are an additional aid in easing the effects of aging. Exercise keeps bones strong and reduces or eliminates depression if participated in on a regular basis (three or four times per week), while calcium supplements and sound eating habits provide the body with nutrients needed by the body at this time.

FICTION: *Life becomes less interesting for women after menopause.*

FACT: Entering these later years of one's life can be highly fulfilling and meaningful. Many Christian women find themselves feeling more aware of God's love than ever before as they learn to grow in their ability to trust Christ to lead them through life's changing seasons.

Although a mother's responsibility to her children changes when they leave home, she does not cease to be a mother. Her children will never outgrow their need for encouragement, reassurance, affirmation, and love. If she is blessed with grandchildren, she will have numerous ways to contribute to their lives. For a woman adjusting to living alone after losing her husband through death or divorce, new avenues of ministry may suddenly open up, allowing the unexpected opportunity of serving God in a way she had never dreamed of before.[3]

Most importantly, the church never loses its need for those who are willing to serve Jesus. One of my favorite stories in the New Testament is about a disciple named Dorcas, who "was always doing good and helping the poor" (Acts 9:36). She was beloved by many.

When Dorcas became ill and died, Peter was called to her bedside, where he found many women weeping over her body. Dorcas had made robes and other clothing for the widows who were there, which they showed to Peter as he entered the room. After sending them out, he got down on his knees and prayed, and then he turned toward the figure lying on the bed. After he spoke her name and told her to rise, Dorcas opened her eyes and sat up. Imagine the joy that broke forth in her town that day as her many friends praised God for sending this precious woman back to them! Who claims that life is less interesting after menopause?

> *Trust in the Lord with all your heart*
> *And lean not on your own understanding;*
> *in all your ways acknowledge him,*
> *And he will make your paths straight.*
> *Do not be wise in your own eyes;*
> *fear the Lord and shun evil.*
> *This will bring health to your body*
> *and nourishment to your bones.*
>
> PROVERBS 3:5-8

Chapter Review

Personal Reflections

1. Growing older isn't:

2. As more women in the public eye cope with the effects of aging through plastic surgery, it increases people's expectations of:

3. I grew up to view menopause as:

4. From a biblical viewpoint, aging is:

5. Promoting a healthy lifestyle later in life will benefit my:

6. When I look to the Lord as the source of my identity, growing older seems:

Related Bible Passages for Further Study

- Job 12:10-12
- Psalm 33:20-22
- Psalm 86:1-7
- Psalm 119:169-175
- Psalm 143:8-11
- Philippians 4:4-8

17

*Q*UESTIONS

Let nothing perturb you,

nothing frighten you.

All things pass;

God does not change.

Patience achieves everything.

Whoever has God lacks nothing.

God alone suffices.[1]

TERESA OF AVILA

This book was born out of the many conversations I have had with women about sexuality—this chapter out of counseling with women who have sought my support, advice, and care. Although each person's experiences are unique, I have found many women's concerns to be remarkably similar.

Little has been written by women from a Christian perspective on this area of our lives, leaving a limited number of resources that give a biblical view of female sexuality. Although a one-question/single-answer format is not usually encountered in reality, I hope the ideas and suggestions generated here will encourage you to seek solutions to any concerns you have about your sexuality.

Why do some women have greater sexual satisfaction than others?

The ability to respond to the God-given design of our sexuality depends primarily on our willingness to accept and enjoy the strong feelings and sensations our bodies are capable of producing. We are more likely to value the sexual relationship we share with our husbands when we view our sexuality as God's good gift. When we are freed from the fear, shame, or guilt we may associate with lovemaking, it helps us to become more comfortable with our bodies. Orgasmic response is especially dependent on our conscious decision to stop controlling our body's reactions to sexual pleasuring.

Why is it so easy for my husband to become sexually stimulated? It often seems to take me forever.

To a certain degree, the ability to become sexually aroused is learned. Although women usually require a longer period of caressing and skin contact before becoming aroused enough to experience orgasm, this need not always be the case. Mental preparation beforehand can reduce the amount of time it takes to become sexually excited.

Thinking of sex as separate from the context of one's daily life can be a setup for disappointment. God has created us to be whole persons in body, mind, and spirit. Satisfying sexual sharing is the result of weaving the physical dimension of our sexuality into the fabric of our everyday lives.

Sexual fulfillment is much more than what we see charted on a graph of the four phases of sexual response. It starts with a time of embracing before getting up in the morning, in riding to work together, or sharing conversation over breakfast. It continues later in the day when an "I love you" is expressed over the phone or during a prayer as one's spouse is remembered in the afternoon. A warm hug in the kitchen before dinner, a time of hand holding while reading the newspaper, and a walk alone around the block together while discussing one another's impressions of the day can all be part of a prelude to physical sharing later in the evening.

Marital relationships are enlivened in countless ways outside the bedroom. Nurturing expressions of intimacy and learning to cherish our husbands plays a big part in keeping the sexual excitement of marriage alive. Sexual arousal is not something we can create artificially.

When two people are courting and anticipating getting married, do they normally require a lot of skillful maneuvering to produce sexual desire for one another? Not at all. Over time, it can be easy to lose this sense of urgency and begin taking one another for granted. Some of that change is a relief. But we never truly outgrow the things that sustain and empower our marriage bond.

Evaluate your level of intimacy; then determine whether you have been neglecting meeting one another's needs for affection. Find ways to share what is on your mind, and daily communicate your experiences to one another. Think about the times when your arousal was totally unplanned and spontaneous—what made the difference? What are your expectations concerning your sexual relationship with your husband? Is making love with him disappointing? Why?

After thinking about these questions, you may find it helpful to discuss your concerns with your husband. On the other hand, you may also be ready to make some changes without much preliminary discussion. If so, why not take some positive steps to enrich this aspect of your marriage, starting today?

Have you had a night away from your children in the past year? What about the possibility of setting up regularly scheduled dates so you can spend time giving one another your undivided attention? By planning ways of building your anticipation of lovemaking into your day, your desire to be sexually responsive may become a natural expression of the closeness you feel with your husband.

It really bothers me when the first thing that happens after I get into bed is that my husband starts initiating lovemaking and expects me to feel the same way. I don't know how to deal with the negative reaction I have toward his attitude.

Instead of viewing your husband's arousal as an instinctive drive for sexual satisfaction, stop and think for a moment about your body from your husband's point of view. Lying next to you is likely to make your husband yearn to be physically close to you. The closer he gets, the more his body will likely respond. Sexual sharing is one of the ways he feels closest to you.

If you have not discussed your feelings before going to bed, he may automatically assume you want the same thing he wants—the union of your two bodies, followed by the pleasant release of sexual tension and a sound night's sleep. Unless you share your feelings in a more neutral setting, you may both end up feeling frustrated.

What is it that makes you feel uncomfortable? What could you both do differently? How might the two of you work out a way to communicate your desire for lovemaking? Do you feel that your husband is neglecting your need for hugging and kissing without intercourse? For emotional intimacy? Does he touch you in ways that irritate you rather than excite you? What might he do differently?

Frequently, resentment is the result of mixed communication about sexual sharing. The solution is to identify what is bothering you and find ways to alleviate the source of your anxiety or frustration through talking with your husband about how you feel. Using "I" messages will help you to emphasize your point of view and may help you to avoid having your statements viewed as an attack or a criticism: "I would really like it if you would touch me like this rather than being so direct. There . . . that's great! That's much better." "I get pretty tense when you do that. Let's try this instead." "I can see that you're ready to make love right now, but I'm feeling really tense. I think a quick back rub would help me to unwind from the crazy day I've had."

There will be times when your husband will desire to make love, and you won't want to. At other times you may want to be sexually expressive, and *he* will be too tired. Meeting one another's sexual needs will necessitate an ongoing dialogue throughout your marriage. Valuing your sexual relationship and recognizing the importance of regularly nurturing the physical bond between you will help keep you from neglecting this vital area even when difficulties—or differences of opinion—arise.

Before we got married, my husband and I had quite a bit of sexual contact. Now that we are husband and wife, we seem to be too busy for lovemaking during the week. On the weekends, all my husband seems interested in is sex. It really bothers me. What can I do?

First of all, it is important for you to think about how you used to view sex before you were married. In the back of your mind, you may still be associating sex with sneaking behind your parents' backs or parking along a deserted road. Sexual activity that takes place outside the covering of marriage may be exciting physically, but it produces a separation between our bodies and our spiritual identities.

What you are feeling is something many women say they encounter after getting married. Since the wedding ceremony took place, everyone knows you are a sexual person. Perhaps your parents warned you that having sex before marriage could result in pregnancy or sexually transmitted diseases. You may not have heard an authentically biblical view of sexuality before. In your mind, you may still see sex as dirty or dangerous or disgusting.

Under these circumstances, it is not surprising that it would feel unnatural for a woman to respond to her husband with her body. God's view of sexuality, as you have seen in this book, is quite the opposite of what it is often interpreted to be. Knowing this, you can ask the Lord to help you transfer your "head knowledge" into your heart. Because your body responds to your deepest feelings and inner emotions, you can also ask God to enable you to view your husband's sexual desire as a healthy aspect of his sexual design.

Through lovemaking, your husband's feelings of attachment toward you are nurtured. God has created him to want to be physically united with you. When you open your heart up to tenderly accept the way your husband's sexuality was designed to be expressed, you may find yourself welcoming and encouraging his touches in a new way.

Now that you are married, sex *will* seem different. The tingling excitement that you used to feel is gone because your husband's body has become familiar to you. Now your love has a chance to deepen as you learn to give yourself to your husband *because you love him*. Not because you want to win him, entrap him, get him to love you. Not even to prove that you are attractive. But because the love you are able to express to him through your body strengthens the bond that brings unity to your marriage.

Making love is not a frivolous act disconnected from the rest of your lives. As your husband's wife, your invitation to share sexually signifies far more because you embrace him for who he is. It is just the two of you now, with all of your strengths *and* all of your weaknesses.

Sexual expression, after all, is not meant to be the fitting together of two identical halves into a neat package marked "one flesh." It is the union of two entirely different personalities as they learn how to say, "I love you even though I am not like you. You have become a part of me. I accept you as you are. I love you." This involves giving one's body out of joy for our beloved. It means that my body is no longer my own, but my husband's, and that my husband's body belongs to me. This is a radical departure from our society's prevailing belief system. I urge you to consider the beauty of your sexuality from a biblical point of view rather than from a cultural perspective.

The practical side of this is that you may want to begin making love more often. Why wait for weekends to express your love to one another? Try cutting back on outside activities. For the time being, think of your bed as the most important place for the two of you to spend time together. Learn to speak with your body. Use it to comfort your husband as well as to arouse him. Plan your time together creatively.

Perhaps it is time for you to invest in a tape player for your bedroom and get some tapes that you would enjoy listening to together. Or you could get some massage oil and spend an hour caressing your husband in a way you would like to be caressed. Maybe this weekend would be a great time to just stay at home and turn the phone off. Let down the walls you have placed between yourself and the powerful sensations your body is capable of feeling. Accept the pleasure of your husband's touch and the peaceful feeling between the two of you that comes in the afterglow of lovemaking. Talk about what's on your mind and heart.

You have nothing to hide. God has covered your past in Jesus and now invites you to celebrate your marriage by affirming the beauty of your sexuality as you freely share yourself with your husband.

Before our baby was born, my husband and I made love practically every day, but now we're lucky if it's once a week. It has been six months since our daughter was born, and I still don't feel back to normal. Is something the matter with me?

It sounds as if you and your husband have enjoyed an intimate relationship that provided a strong bond to see you through this period of transition. But now that you are parents, your focus cannot be on just the two of you. Your love is expanding to include a new person who has a personality and temperament unique and different from each of your own. Your daughter has many needs that can be exhausting at times to meet. What you are experiencing is a normal reaction to learning how to balance your personal needs with the needs of your husband and child. All of this takes time. In a society that expects instant relief from distressing symptoms, we often wish God could grant us instant maturity as well.

Even though your baby is almost completely dependent on you, it is important to remember that she is growing less so each day. The goal of all of your efforts as her mother is to raise her to eventually be able to leave your home and have a full, productive life of her own. On the other hand, the bond that you and your husband share will need to be nurtured and closely tended for life.

I once had a couple in one of the childbirth classes I teach who were in their forties and expecting their eighth child. Out of the thousands of men and women I have had the privilege to work with, this particular couple stands out as a memorable example of devotion and caring for one another. They were like a couple of teenagers. They would laugh and tickle one another during the exercises, hold hands during breaks, and acted just as interested in learning about giving birth for the eighth time as they probably were for the first. Here was this couple old enough to be grandparents, with a daughter in her sophomore year in college; yet they acted as if the entire process of childbearing were completely brand-new.

Finally, on the fourth night of class, I asked them what their secret was. The wife smiled as she glanced over at her husband, and they both began to give me the same answer simultaneously. It turned out that ever since they had dated before getting married, they had spent Friday nights out together. "Even if it's just to go for a half-hour walk, Bob and I make sure we have time alone. He's made me feel just like I used to before I married him by *always* taking that time out for me."

You see, this couple had learned an important lesson early in their marriage: Marriage is the most important human relationship a man and woman voluntarily commit themselves to in love. It was designed to survive raising kids to adulthood and all of the stresses and strains involved in family life. Obviously, this relationship does not just automatically outlast all of these things. It must be carefully and lovingly nourished if it is to handle the demands placed upon it.

I think that if you talk to your husband and encourage him to plan times for just the two of you, that would be a good start. Cultivate the art of dating. I have included a list here that my husband and I compiled from an assignment we gave to participants in a marriage enrichment class we have often taught. Your own community probably has a wide variety of things unique to your own locale that you could add to the list.

Whether it is a special night out that involves dressing up and making reservations at an exclusive restaurant or an evening of fishing in a canoe, it's spending time alone together that counts. Getting away together from the dishes, the laundry, and the baby—even for a brief time—will do each of you good.

The other thing I would like to encourage you to do is to pay attention to what you are eating, how much rest you are getting, and whether you are getting the exercise you need. (Review the chapters on stress management for specific information on these topics.) Caring for an infant is a demanding job. *Every child deserves to have parents who love each other enough to value the importance of promoting one another's physical, emotional, and spiritual health.*

The following ideas will give you a place to start. It may seem like a big effort at first, but you will begin to reap the benefits immediately. As your bond is renewed and enlivened by your commitment to spend time together and promote one another's health, your sexual relationship will most likely be refreshed as well.

100 ACTIVITIES FOR ROMANCING YOUR MARRIAGE

1. Go for a ride and a talk in the country.

2. Bathe together by candlelight.

3. Sit outside in the moonlight, sharing goals and dreams, concluding with thanksgiving for the blessings given to you by God.

4. Work together outdoors, planting trees or gardening.

5. Offer to give your spouse a body massage with scented oil.

6. Get up early together and have coffee or tea out on the patio.

7. Go for a walk in the woods.

8. Go horseback riding and picnic on the trail.

9. Build sand castles at the beach.

10. Go out for dessert.

11. Rent a VCR and a good movie and eat popcorn together.

12. Take a bicycle ride. For improving your teamwork, rent a tandem bike.

13. Share a meal at a nice restaurant and go to a play afterwards.

14. Visit a planetarium.

15. Take a dinner train ride.

16. Go sledding or ice skating. (Take hot cocoa along.)

17. Go for a walk and a talk in a small town with lots of history.

18. Try a water slide or go to a pool for a swim.

19. Get up and watch the sunrise together. (Someone suggested that playing golf at this time of day can be fun, too.)

20. Take a buggy ride together at Christmastime.

21. Take dancing lessons and learn something new about "partnering."

22. Go to the state capitol building for a tour, but get lost in a deserted hallway.

23. Attend a high school or college football game (or volleyball, basketball . . .).

24. Enroll in an adult education class together.

25. Go to a hospital nursery and reflect on the wonder of your child(ren)'s birth(s).

26. Go miniature golfing.

27. Go to a motel for the evening, but return home by midnight.

28. Meet one another for lunch to discuss recent scriptural insights.

29. Rent a sailboat and go out together at a nearby lake.

30. Sit on a blanket at the park, fly a kite, read.

31. Arrange for a hot air balloon ride.

32. Rent a manual paddle boat and go for a short cruise if you live near a lake or a river.

33. Go to an art gallery and browse.

34. Attend a concert, especially one held outdoors so you can curl up and look at the stars while listening to the music.

35. Go bowling.

36. Go on a walk through an area of town with old, interesting homes.

37. Get your hair cut at the same time and place.

38. Get all dressed up and go to an exotic restaurant.

39. Go shopping together—groceries, gifts, or plants.

40. Spend time at a mountain cabin together, reflecting on the majesty of God.

41. Plan and work on a creative project building something.

42. Attend a wedding and reminisce.

43. Take a day trip to an interesting town within an hour's driving distance of your home. Have lunch at the local diner; browse the stores; learn about a little community history.

44. Go to an auction and purchase something funny.

45. Visit antique shops and learn about old furniture.

46. Go for a drive and look at Christmas decorations while sharing memories.

47. Go to the drive-in.

48. Plan a surprise date. Blindfold your spouse and take her (him) to someplace unusual.

49. Shoot an entire roll of film of one another outdoors.

50. Go on a hay ride.

51. Take a walk in the rain under an umbrella.

52. Go to a department store and buy each other some sexy underwear. (No peeking until you get home!)

53. Rent a canoe and go canoeing. Find a quiet spot to read your current favorite book on marriage aloud to one another.

54. Share a plate of nachos at your favorite Mexican restaurant.

55. Set aside an evening for making photo albums or looking at slides.

56. Meet each other for coffee on a workday morning once a month or more, if schedules allow.

57. Go to the library and find a new subject to explore together.

58. Get season tickets for the symphony (or travel series or theater . . .).

59. Play tennis at a local park.

60. Go Christmas caroling with other couples.

61. Drive out to the country and spot satellites.

62. Go for a hike along trails in a nearby park. Take a Bible and a blanket along, curl up together, and read Song of Songs.

63. Browse in a Christian bookstore and listen to demo tapes.

64. Go to a park and swing on the swings while holding hands.

65. Share a sundae or a soda at a local ice-cream parlor.

66. Stroll along the main street in your town and go window shopping after all the stores have closed (assuming the streets are safe at night).

67. Take a ride to see the colors change in the autumn or spring.

68. Have someone baby-sit your child at *their* house. Then go back home and spend the evening in bed.

69. Attend an art, antique, recreation, or craft show.

70. Listen to a favorite mystery on tape while sipping your favorite beverage and sharing a plate of cheese and crackers.

71. Tuck the kids in bed; wait until they're asleep; then have a water gun fight. In your bathing suits.

72. Plan a romantic rendezvous six weeks in advance and keep it a secret between just the two of you.

73. Play board games for the evening: Scrabble, Careers, Chinese Checkers—whatever! Order a carry-out pizza.

74. Spend an hour serenading one another with silly and/or serious love songs.

75. Go fishing by moonlight. Forget about the fish. Gaze at the moon and stars instead.

76. Make a scrapbook or put together a photo album about your marriage based on a humorous theme.

77. Go roller skating.

78. Take a trip to town; buy some penny candy or caramel corn. Share it while relaxing at a park.

79. Set up a pup tent in the back yard and zip two sleeping bags together for an after-dark encounter.

80. Slow dance to your favorite music in the living room with your best nightgown on.

81. Order Chinese egg rolls takeout to eat while snuggled up in bed listening to your favorite music.

81. Construct a family tree containing as many relatives as you can remember, listing any interesting, distinctive, or peculiar characteristics for each.

82. Take turns reading George MacDonald and C. S. Lewis fairy tales aloud together, such as *The Princess and the Goblin, The Golden Key, The Light Princess,* and the Chronicles of Narnia.

83. Study a foreign language together; plan to take a trip to a locale where the language is spoken.

84. Enroll in a noncompetitive fitness program together.

85. Go to an arboretum or an aviary for a stroll.

86. Browse through a bookstore; then go out for some tea or coffee.

87. Buy a planisphere, which shows "the principal stars visible for every hour of the year." Carry an old afghan to a hilly spot away from city lights and locate the major constellations.

88. Go wading along a beach.

89. Visit the city fountain and just sit and talk for a while.

90. Cuddle up and watch a thunderstorm from a covered porch or through a large picture window.

91. Do some photography together at a local nature center or zoo.

92. Buy some *Archie* comic books and read them aloud together.

93. Go out for a late breakfast on Saturday morning.

94. Write a family history book as a late-evening project, instead of watching TV.

95. Audit an art or music appreciation class together at a nearby college or university.

96. Park along a safe deserted road and see what happens.

97. Go to a nice restaurant, but just order an appetizer or dessert.

98. Read poetry together by candlelight—perhaps Elizabeth Barrett Browning and Robert Browning—and conclude with a special prayer for the strengthening of your love for one another.

99. Take an international cuisine cooking class together.

100. Go for a walk in freshly fallen snow. Then take a hot shower together after returning home.

My husband often seems more interested in watching adult-oriented late night movies on cable by himself than he is in making love to me. When we do make love, several times he has been too rough with me. Is this normal?

If your husband has spent or is currently spending time in looking at erotic or pornographic magazines, cable movies, Internet sites, or videos, he has developed a view of female sexuality that does not line up with a biblical perspective. All too often, sexually explicit materials depict violent themes, creating a desire to dominate or exploit one's sexual partner in an effort to gain a sense of power through sex. The view of women presented in such materials promotes lust and destroys the purity that is to be maintained within marriage: "Honor marriage, and guard the sacredness of sexual intimacy between wife and husband. God draws a firm line against casual and illicit sex" (Hebrews 13:4, THE MESSAGE).

We live in a society that uses sex to sell everything from deodorant soap to vodka. From an early age, males are confronted with visual images of women paid large sums of money to seduce the photographer's camera. Hoping to sell more of their products, companies hire advertisers who attempt to create an association between what they are selling and the physical and emotional reactions induced by their ads. These images seduce men in subtle ways, not the least of which is to imply that there is nothing wrong with "admiring" a woman's ample-sized breasts displayed before the camera in the latest diet soda commercial.

Gradually, our sensitivity to nudity and sexual themes has been eroded through our constant exposure to sexual images. An era of unprecedented acceptance of pornography has resulted. Noting this heartbreaking trend, a weekly newsmagazine perceptively pointed out that "virtually any adult American has a license that the Lord never allowed Sodom and Gomorrah."[2]

Your husband's behavior is not unusual. His private involvement in sexual fantasy is constantly nurtured by a culture that has devalued the sanctity of sexuality and the human body. Jesus clearly spoke to the issue of sexual fantasy and its effects on marriage when He said, "You have heard that it was said, 'Do not commit adultery.' But I tell you that anyone who looks at a woman lustfully has already committed adultery with her in his heart" (Matthew 5:27-28).

Adultery—in any form—is the ultimate betrayal of the marriage bond. When Jesus compared visually oriented lust to extramarital intercourse, He was teaching about the spiritual and emotional impact of one's thought life upon one's beliefs and attitudes about sexuality. Looking at another woman's breasts and genitalia violates her privacy and constructs a way of seeing her as an object rather than as a person. This attitude denies women their dignity as created in the image of God. Whether the women themselves give their consent to be used in this way is irrelevant. As Christians, we recognize the importance of each individual to God. To look at another person's body and deny this truth violates the basic principles that underlie the meaning of our Creator's design for human sexuality.

Erotica and pornography depersonalize sex by removing it from the purpose for which it was created, treating people as sexual objects and emphasizing parts of the body over the person's intrinsic worth and value. Women and men who display their bodies for profit are *real* people, with feelings of emptiness, alienation, and guilt before a holy and righteous God.

We are called to reject the treatment of other human beings as objects and to love them compassionately. We are also to wage spiritual warfare upon the powers of darkness that debase and dehumanize sexuality through sexual sin.

You are not in *any* way obligated to act out sexual situations with your husband derived from a fantasy life fed by pornography. Period. By saying no to such behavior, you can encourage him toward repentance as you pray for healing in this area of his life. You are not merely a body for your husband to have sex with in whatever way he pleases. Your husband is called by God to love your body as he loves his own (Ephesians 5:28). *When your husband forcefully dominates you during intercourse without considering how it is affecting you, he is not loving you according to God's plan for your marriage.*

You may or may not feel comfortable confronting him about this. There may be no one with whom you feel you can discuss this situation. Begin by praying. With a loving attitude, encourage your husband to talk to your pastor or to a Christian counselor. If you attend a church that defends erotica as an acceptable means of enhancing sexual pleasure, look elsewhere for help. Until he is willing to accept his share of the responsibility for damaging the sanctity of your bond, your husband is preventing both of you from living in sexual harmony with one another.

More than anything else, your husband needs you to love him enough to refuse to downplay the significance of his sexual behavior. While you are not to act the part of the Holy Spirit in his life, you are called to sexual purity. Demonstrate your love for your husband through setting and keeping boundaries in your sexual relationship and invite the Holy Spirit to do the rest.

I know that this is not an easy time for you. But as you seek to honor Christ through prayer and study of the Word, God will give you wisdom and direction. I recommend that you consider obtaining the advice of a godly counselor. The Lord knows your heart. He will meet your needs. He will never forsake you.

After divorcing my first husband, I became a Christian and am now married to a man I dearly love. I find myself at times, however, remembering what it was like in bed with Brad and feel terrible about having ever been with anyone but Mike.

We have already discussed the spiritual reality of the bond created between a man and a woman during sexual intercourse. However much we would like things to be different at times, we cannot change the past. The truth is that you and Brad were husband and wife. Your marriage did take place. You had a relationship that included intimate sexual sharing. You have experienced the shattering of that bond through the breakup of your marriage. It is a part of your history—part of who you are today.

Divorce is a tragic event in the lives of two people. Sexual sharing was created by God to produce emotional, physical, and spiritual intimacy within marriage. Memories related to earlier sexual intimacy remind us of the destruction of a relationship that exposed the deepest parts of us to another person.

Remembering the things you shared with your first husband reminds you that sexual openness is not something that can be taken back once it has been shared. Wishing that you had not had sexual experiences with anyone but Mike is a natural response to the love you feel for him. As memories from your past surface, try to view this recall as part of a cleansing process. Through your faith in Jesus Christ, God has forgiven you for "missing the mark" when you were living in ignorance of His design for your life.

Do not let the Devil accuse you of sin that has been covered by the blood of Christ. Commit passages of Scripture to memory, such as John 1:9, to use against the enemy whenever you feel burdened with sin from the past. When you think of something painful, use it to remind you to grow closer to Jesus. You need not pretend it did not happen or that you do not have feelings related to your first husband. With the passing of time and the commitment you have made to making your marriage to Mike succeed, you are walking away from the wounds left by your first marriage. The Lord has made you a new creation (2 Corinthians 5:17).

It is now your responsibility to see to it that no one robs you of the reality of your reconciliation to God and the joy of your salvation. Stand firm in the knowledge that your debts are canceled. You no longer have to keep paying interest on debts you no longer owe through fearing memories of your first marriage or regretting your past. We have been called to "live a new life" as we glorify God for enabling us to make peace with the past through the free gift of life He has bestowed upon us through Jesus Christ (Romans 6:4). I pray that this truth will bring peace to your mind and heart as love and care for your new husband increase.

My sixteen-year-old daughter has asked me to help her obtain a prescription for birth control pills. She knows that I am against her having intercourse outside marriage, but I am convinced that she will be sexually active whether I like it or not. I don't want her to get pregnant.

It sounds as if you have already made it clear to your daughter that you do not want her engaging in premarital sex, but have you shared why? Simply saying that it is wrong is not enough. Expressing the reasons extramarital sex is not in your daughter's best interest is essential. Avoid using STDs and pregnancy as scare tactics and stick to the heart of this issue: sexual openness produces emotional as well as physical vulnerability, joining two people together in such a way that a unique bond is produced between the two of them. In serial relationships, this bond is repeatedly fractured and lessens the possibility that a lifelong commitment to one person can be sustained. God has designed marriage to protect our hearts and minds and bodies. When His design is ignored, deep wounds result.

In asking for your help, your daughter is seeking your approval for something you believe would injure her emotionally and spiritually. As her mother, you have always wanted to keep her from harm. An unwanted pregnancy would be a difficult situation to have to face. But what about having to deal with the fruit of a relationship that will produce lifelong memories and deeply affect how your daughter views her sexuality?

You have always sought your daughter's best interest and are trying to do so now. Consider the responsibility you have in showing your daughter God's truth in a loving way. Know that you have a right to act according to your values even though other moms may think you're outdated.

Until your daughter is an adult and on her own, your values and decisions will continue to influence and guide her life. Sit down and explain how you feel about sexuality and the role it has played in your own life. Pray for the Lord's help and wisdom in knowing what to say. Even though your daughter is sixteen, she is still watching you as she learns what it means to be a woman. If you humbly represent God's love to her in a way she can understand, she cannot help but be touched by your example.

I haven't been interested in sex at all lately. It seems like whenever we finally get the chance to be alone at the end of the day, there is something going on that prevents me from becoming aroused.

The most common excuses for avoiding lovemaking have deeper reasons behind them. If a woman repeatedly tells her husband that it's too cold, too hot, too late, or too early, something more important must be going on. Look at the list on page 266 and check off any of the real reasons you may have had for not making love during the past few months:

___ I felt neglected by my husband.

___ I felt resentful that he expected sex but had not related to me in a loving way.

___ I felt unattractive.

___ I have had difficulty feeling sexually fulfilled during lovemaking.

___ I just wanted to be held or have a back rub without my husband expecting sex afterwards.

___ I was sick and had no interest in sex.

___ I feel that my husband just takes me for granted.

___ My sex drive was low so I couldn't get excited about lovemaking.

___ I resent his enjoying sex while ignoring my needs.

___ I don't know how to tell him how to "pleasure" me or touch me.

___ I have difficulty expressing my needs and end up feeling depressed or resentful.

___ I expect my husband to take responsibility for my sexual pleasure instead of taking responsibility for myself.

___ Sex just isn't fun anymore.

___ I expect my husband to take the lead in lovemaking. I am unable to be the "aggressive partner" in our relationship.

___ I often feel bored or disinterested in lovemaking and participate only to please my husband.

Once you have completed this list, look back over your replies and think about the times lovemaking has been satisfying to you. What do you think made the difference? Have you seen any connection between your active participation in sexual sharing and your husband's ability to enjoy it?

The Lord has designed a reciprocal principle into this dimension of your life so that as you give pleasure, you open up your ability to receive pleasure. Have you structured your lives together to fully accommodate this principle and to nourish this part of your relationship? In several chapters of this book, I have outlined many ideas for cultivating sexual intimacy with your husband. A summary of some of the most important are listed below. Check off any steps you think would be helpful to you.

___ Talk with your husband about your reasons for not wanting to make love with him.

___ Bathe or shower before going to bed in order to relax.

___ Read the Psalms to gain a fresh perspective on life.

___ Take a nap before dinner to have more energy later in the evening.

___ Obtain help with household and child-rearing responsibilities to lessen the daily load you are carrying.

___ Have more alone time for quietly reading, writing, praying, thinking, dreaming, etc.

___ Ask your husband to plan interesting dates for you to enjoy together.

___ Try something new: Be open to enjoying your body and being more expressive with it during lovemaking. Ask your husband what would please him and try it.

___ Suggest to your husband that you both read a book on the differences between the way men and women communicate.

___ Assess how you feel about your body *just as it is*. Take steps to enhance your ability to feel attractive *just as you are* without resorting to drastic diets, an exhausting fitness program, complete beauty makeover, plastic surgery, or expensive clothes.

___ Reduce daily stress by taking two concrete steps to manage it (time by yourself for at least thirty minutes daily, a long bath, listening to music, etc.).

___ Spend time praying about your lack of sexual interest. Ask the Lord to give you insight, wisdom, and direction concerning your current situation.

___ Verbalize your feelings with your husband about your joys and frustrations concerning your relationship.

___ Buy a basket and fill it with pampering treats: facial mask, herbal soaps, foot lotion, bath gel, body cream, etc. Soak in the tub as you use your purchases.

___ On Saturday morning, lie naked with your husband as you quietly hold each other before the day's activities start.

___ Sign up for an exercise class appropriate for your fitness level, or start a walking program to increase your energy.

___ Consider temporarily (or permanently) cutting back on outside obligations.

___ Tell yourself the truth about why you are avoiding lovemaking. Commit yourself to working toward resolving your reluctance.

___ Start a new routine that recognizes your need for middle-of-the-day refreshment: quiet time in the afternoon with tea and a good book; resting with your feet up for thirty minutes or longer; a "silence break" at work with the door closed for twenty minutes.

___ Schedule a spiritual retreat away from home for a few days with your sister or a friend—or by yourself.

___ Keep a journal. Express your feelings about lovemaking in writing.

___ Take more time out to do the things you enjoy.

___ Give each other a massage.

___ Read several good books on sexuality written by Christian authors.

___ Go away for the weekend alone together. Use room service for meals. Take along your favorite music, an audio player, and scented candles.

Do you have any advice about sexual etiquette in the bedroom?

The art of making love can benefit from a set of etiquette rules similar to those that govern any polite conversation. Keeping in mind that I offer you these simple, time-tested, rigorously researched suggestions with more than an ample dose of humor, these rules are:

1. *Do not interrupt once the excitement begins.* You will have time to talk about it later! Speaking without words is just that—words spoken about

an important piece of news have nothing to do with the matter at hand. Bringing up something you forgot to tell him earlier will distract both of you from what your bodies are trying to say to each other. If you're ambivalent about making love with your husband, take time to talk about your feelings before you give him the thumbs-up signal.

2. *Do remember to say please and thank you.* Courtesy between lovers is a powerful sign of their mutual respect. Expressions of appreciation are always welcome, and neither partner ever has the right to demand something without asking! Forceful activity that takes place without one's consent is unkind, unloving, and illegal. There are many nice ways to ask and just as many ways to say thanks as you show your love to one another: flowers, special dates, a surprise note tucked into a sack lunch.

3. *Do not make fun of one another.* Each of us feels vulnerable about our bodies. When someone jests about an area we are already sensitive about, we feel a sense of exposure that causes us to become defensive and protective. Even casual remarks made in passing can hurt our feelings and close us off from being sexually open. Be careful about the words you use about your husband's body. Being blatantly honest about his "spare tire" or latest acne outbreak will not help either of you to be more open with one another.

4. *Do give compliments and affirmations freely.* Lovers never tire of hearing the words "I love you." Neither do they refuse to accept genuine compliments, no matter how frequently they are given. Affirmations are positive verbal strokes that people give to one another to validate each other's special qualities and lovableness. They do not have to be earned.

An affirmation boosts our self-esteem in healthy ways and better enables us to appreciate the unique things about ourselves that the Lord has given to us: our bodies, our minds, our talents, our abilities, and our histories. Affirmations invite us to grow. Solomon's book, the Song of Songs, is chock-full of affirmations between himself and his lover as they share their appreciation and love for each other. What deep physical love they had for one another! Here are a few examples of the kinds of affirmations you can use during lovemaking:

"I really like to hold you."

"You look great tonight!"

"I am so thankful for you."

"Your body feels really good to me."

"I like the way you do that."

"You are the perfect lover for me."

"I am so glad I am here with you."

"You don't have to rush. . . . I enjoy that!"

"I love touching you there."

5. *Do say "excuse me" when its appropriate to do so.* No matter how long a couple has been married, it is polite to say "excuse me" when digestive upset causes gas and burps or when one of you needs to make a trip to the bathroom in the middle of lovemaking. Showing this small courtesy is so simple to do that the habit need never be dropped.

6. *Do respect one another's need for privacy.* This can be amazingly difficult if you have only one toilet in your house or apartment. Barging in on one another during moments that are meant to be private goes beyond the boundaries of marital intimacy. We all need at least a *few* moments to ourselves every day.

7. *Do not laugh at the wrong times.* During lovemaking, humorous events can and do happen. Laughing right out loud is an appropriate expression *some* of the time. Be sensitive about not using laughter at times when it will be interpreted as making fun of something that your husband actually feels quite badly about.

8. *Do come dressed for the occasion, or undressed, if you prefer.* Become familiar with what kinds of clothing your husband likes seeing you in, and don't be afraid to experiment. Clothing says a lot about who we are, and bedclothes aren't any different. Before lovemaking, put as much thought in dressing for your husband's eyes alone as you do for going to work, going to church, or going out for dinner.

9. *Do make the atmosphere conducive to lovemaking.* Having a toddler snuggled up to you when your husband comes to bed or trying to get together in the middle of a messy bedroom are two examples of creating the wrong type of environment for lovemaking. Fresh flowers, sheets dried out on a sunny day on the clothesline, a cool fan, a blazing fire in the fireplace—these kinds of things add real comfort to sexual sharing. Invest in a tape player for your bedroom, and play instrumental music such as that recorded for the purpose of promoting relaxation. Some couples prefer Bach while others enjoy listening to the smooth jazz sounds of a guitarist like Larry Carlton. One couple wrote in their book that they light a candle as a signal that they want to make love. What are your

unique signals? What things can you do to make your bedroom secure, soundproof, inviting, and attractive?

10. *Do pay attention.* Attentiveness is always appreciated by those who are engaged in a dialogue. If you have to work at paying attention, it's a pretty sure bet that you are finding it difficult to become sexually aroused. Rather than frustrate your husband with your lack of interest, why not take time out for a moment to talk about what you're feeling and whether or not you feel up to lovemaking? You may have other needs that haven't been met (food, rest, touch, affection) that are preventing you from enjoying sex. Remember—ignoring your needs won't make them go away.

There it is—the top ten list for courteous lovers! Some couples never lose their ability to be polite to one another, witnessed by the fact that some men still open the car door for their wives (seen any lately?) and women may be found who wait up at night for their husbands. Developing one's own sense of style in courteous ways of expressing love is up to each of us as individuals.

In closing, my prayer is that we may never neglect this area of our lives or simply take it for granted. Our sexual relationship with our husbands is worth nurturing, paying attention to, protecting, improving, upholding, praying for, celebrating, encouraging, appreciating, reflecting on—and *enjoying*.

> God's grace is sufficient for our weakness. Christ's worth does cover our unworthiness, and the Holy Spirit does make us effective in spite of our inadequacy. This is the glorious paradox of living by grace. When we discover we are weak in ourselves, we find we are strong in Christ. When we regard ourselves as less than the least of all God's people, we are given some immense privilege of serving in the Kingdom. When we most despair over our inadequacy, we find the Holy Spirit giving us unusual ability. We shake our heads in amazement and say with Isaiah, "Lord . . . all that we have accomplished you have done for us." (Isaiah 26:12)[3]

JERRY BRIDGES

*C*LOSING THOUGHTS

The bed is the heart of the home, the arena of love,
the seedbed of life, and the one constant point of meeting. It
is the place where, night by night, forgiveness and fair speech
return that the sun may not go down on our wrath; where the
perfunctory kiss and the entirely ceremonial pat on the backside
become unction and grace. It is the oldest, friendliest thing
in anybody's marriage, the first used and the last left,
and no one can praise it enough.[1]

ROBERT FARRAR CAPON

The willingness to share one's body in marriage is developed, nurtured, and encouraged over the span of a lifetime. Each day brings its own unique challenges and opportunities for us to learn about the wonder of God's plan for our lives.

In this book a personal, biblical perspective of female sexuality has been presented. It is my hope that *The Christian Woman's Guide to Sexuality* has been an encouragement to you. You may not have agreed with everything I've said, but if you embraced the fullness of your sexual design with a new insight as a result of considering its many facets and expressions, that is what is most important. It has been my intent to share a truly Christ-centered view of women's sexuality. The rest is up to you.

It is customary to close in prayer at the end of a class or a time of fellowship. As you reflect on what you have read in this book, I would like to offer a prayer just as if we were sitting in the same room, having talked

about its contents together. Let us thank God for what He is teaching us
and for the bond we share through Jesus as sisters in the Lord:

> *Dear Heavenly Father,*
>
> *Thank You for creating us in Your image. We praise You that
> we are fearfully and wonderfully made. We also praise You for the
> many diverse dimensions of our sexuality as women. We pray that
> You will enable us to glorify You through our marriages as we open
> up our hearts to receive the gift of our sexuality in all of its fullness.
> We thank You for joining us together with our husbands as one in
> You, Lord God. In Your strength, we ask that You would help us love
> our husbands with gentleness and humility. Through the power of
> Your Holy Spirit, grant us wisdom.*
>
> *Lead us, dear Lord, with Your strong, steady hand in a world
> that we often find confusing and frustrating, so that we may abide
> in You more completely. Make Your truth clear to us as we follow
> You, so that we may live our lives in a way pleasing in Your sight.
> We ask these things in the name of Your precious Son, Jesus Christ.*
> *Amen.*

As the time we share with our husbands unfolds, our ability to care
for and about them is refreshed and renewed on a continuing basis when
we commit ourselves to loving God. When we find the true source of our
identity in our Creator, as well as the strength to follow Him in this present age, we find our attitudes and outlooks transformed. *In Christ we are
complete.* The love we share with our husbands springs from the rich
reservoir of God's unfailing faithfulness, mercy, and grace toward us—
the source of our present joy and future hope.

> *I will praise the LORD at all times.*
> *I will constantly speak his praises.*
> *I will boast only in the LORD;*
> *Let all who are discouraged take heart.*
> *Come, let us tell of the LORD's greatness;*
> *Let us exalt his name together.*
> *I prayed to the LORD,*
> *and he answered me,*
> *freeing me from all my fears.*

Those who look to him for help
  will be radiant with joy;
    no shadow of shame will darken their faces.
I cried out to the LORD in my suffering,
  and he heard me.
He set me free from all my fears.
For the angel of the LORD guards all who fear him,
  and he rescues them.
Taste and see that the LORD is good.
Oh, the joys of those who trust in him!

PSALM 34:1-8 NLT

Appendix A

$\mathscr{A}$ COMPARISON OF THREE VIEWS OF HUMAN SEXUALITY

I. HUMANISTIC

Origin of human life:

Humans evolved from apes and "lower" life forms; humans are characterized by higher brain functions.

Purpose of sex:

Sex is viewed as a means to an end:

1. Attainment of mutual satisfaction.

2. A way to give and receive love.

3. Erotic pleasure seen as a symbol of achievement.

Acceptable forms of sexual expression:

Any form of sexual activity is okay if it occurs between consenting partners.

View of sex as it relates to the family:

Sex may be unrelated to producing children, to marriage, or to an absolute value system.

Individual rights:

An individual has the right to choose how to express his or her sexuality based upon considering one's self and the dignity of one's sex partner(s).

Belief in an afterlife:

Beyond death lies endless peace, bright white light—or nothing at all.

Accountability:

An individual is accountable to the rest of humanity for his or her actions.

Summary of goals:

1. Mutual satisfaction.

2. Self-determination.

3. The "best for the most" or for the collective good.

Consequences:

Serial relationships leading to:

1. Fragmentation of self.

2. Divided allegiances.

3. Adulteration of pair-bonding through the formation of multiple bonds.

Social results:

Unwanted children disposed of through abortion.

Cohabitation viewed as normal.

Divorce viewed as normal.

Pornography widely distributed.

Prostitution common.

Greater acceptance of alternative lifestyles: group marriage, homosexuality, "swinging sex."

Sexually transmitted diseases now epidemic.

Greater tolerance for the sexual victimization of others.

Increase in the incidence of sexual assault and abuse.

II. HEDONISTIC

Origin of human life:

Not concerned with own origin; humans viewed as sophisticated animals.

Purpose of sex:

Sex is viewed as an end in itself:

1. Pleasure for pleasure's sake.

2. Anything goes.

3. Focus on self-gratification.

Acceptable forms of sexual expression:

Any form of sexual activity is okay if it occurs between consenting persons.

View of sex as it relates to the family:

Sex is unrelated to producing children, to marriage, or to an absolute value system.

Individual rights:

An individual has the right to choose how to express his or her sexuality based upon one's physical desires.

Belief in an afterlife:

What may happen after death makes no difference—live for today.

Accountability:

An individual is accountable to no one for his or her actions.

Summary of goals:

1. Satisfaction of one's sex drive.

2. Sex as an expression of self.

3. Seeking one's own good above that of others.

Consequences:

Sexual addiction leading to:

1. Enslavement to physical desires.

2. Diffusion of identity.

3. Fornication; approaching others as sexual objects.

Social results:

Unwanted children disposed of through abortion.

Cohabitation viewed as normal.

Divorce viewed as normal.

Pornography widely distributed.

Prostitution common.

Greater acceptance of alternative lifestyles: group marriage, homosexuality, "swinging sex."

Sexually transmitted diseases now epidemic.

Greater tolerance for the sexual victimization of others.

Increase in the incidence of sexual assault and abuse.

III. JUDEO-CHRISTIAN

Origin of human life:

Humans were created in the image of their Creator God (Genesis 2:18, 23–25).

Purpose of sex:

Sex is viewed as a means to an end:

1. The means through which "two become one flesh."
2. To make the earth fruitful for God.
3. An end to "aloneness" and emotional isolation.

Acceptable forms of sexual expression:

Sexual activity between a man and a woman within marriage only.

View of sex as it relates to the family:

Sex is a gift of God that strengthens the marriage bond; children are viewed as a blessing, and certain forms of sexuality are viewed as destructive to sexual identity in *all* situations: adultery, prostitution, rape, promiscuity, incest, bestiality, homosexuality, pornography, exhibitionism.

Individual rights:

An individual expresses his or her sexuality in accordance with the will of God as laid out in the Bible; he or she belongs to God. Each spouse's body belongs to the other.

Belief in an afterlife:

Beyond death lies heaven or hell, eternal life or eternal damnation.

Accountability:

Each individual is accountable to a personal Creator for his or her life choices, words, and actions.

Summary of goals:

1. Mutual belonging.
2. Self-control.
3. Seeking the good of one's partner above oneself.

Consequences:

Lifetime bonding leading to:

1. Liberation from sin.
2. Living in harmony with self and others.
3. Living in harmony with God.

Social results:

The continuation of family heritage: children, grandchildren, and great-grandchildren.

Respect for the dignity and worth of each person created in the image of God.

Rejection of sexual sin in all forms—contributing to the health and stability of one's culture.

Appendix B

*P*RAYERS AND BLESSINGS

When we start to get worried, feel frustrated, or become anxious regarding our husbands' attitudes and behavior, it is easy to suddenly slip into a reaction regime or control mode. We may begin dealing with our concerns by attempting to manage our husbands' lives—in a multitude of different ways—instead of taking our hands off the situation while single-mindedly seeking God's wisdom and relying on His unwavering grace and goodness. (Sound familiar?)

The next time you're faced with this particular temptation, why not first try taking time out to ask God directly for the Spirit's strength, protection, and sustenance?

Through praying for and blessing our husbands, we can choose to let go of our attempts at controlling their lives, thereby releasing our husbands more fully to the Lord's loving care—and trusting Him with the consequences. To do this, you might keep a journal, use a prayer book, read the Psalms, spend quiet time with God, or develop your own unique approach. The following prayers and blessings are examples to encourage your future endeavors. Simply add or substitute your husband's name wherever you wish.

> *In times of trouble, may the Lord respond to your cry.*
> *May the God of Israel keep you safe from all harm.*
> *May he send you help from his sanctuary*
> *and strengthen you from Jerusalem.*
> *May he remember all your gifts*
> *and look favorably on your burnt offerings.*
> *May he grant your heart's desire*
> *and fulfill all your plans.*

> May we shout for joy when we hear of your victory,
>> flying banners to honor our God.
> May the Lord answer all your prayers.
>
> ———————————— PSALM 20:1–5 NLT

I never cease to give thanks for you when I mention you in my prayers. I pray that the God of our Lord Jesus Christ, the all-glorious Father, may give you the spiritual powers of wisdom and vision, by which there comes the knowledge of him.

I pray that your inward eyes may be illumined, so that you may know what is the hope to which he calls you, what the wealth and glory of the share he offers you among his people in their heritage, and how vast the resources of his power open to us who trust in him.

EPHESIANS 1:16–19 NEB

May God himself, the God of peace, make you holy in every part, and keep you sound in spirit, soul, and body, without fault when our Lord Jesus Christ comes. He who calls you is to be trusted; he will do it.

1 THESSALONIANS 5:23 NEB

> The LORD watches over you—
>> the LORD is your shade at your right hand;
> the sun will not harm you by day,
>> nor the moon by night.
> The LORD will keep you from all harm—
>> he will watch over your life;
>> the LORD will watch over your coming and going
>> both now and forevermore.
>
> PSALM 121:5–8

We ask God that you may receive from him all wisdom and spiritual understanding for full insight into his will, so that your manner of life may be worthy of the Lord and entirely pleasing to him.

We pray that you may bear fruit in active goodness of every kind, and grow in the knowledge of God. May he strengthen you, in his glorious might, with ample power to meet whatever comes with for-

titude, patience, and joy; and to give thanks to the Father who has made you fit to share the heritage of God's people in the realm of light.

COLOSSIANS 1:9–12 NEB

May the God of hope fill you with all joy and peace as you trust in him, so that you may overflow with hope by the power of the Holy Spirit.

ROMANS 15:13

Give ear to my words, O Lord,
consider my sighing.
Listen to my cry for help, my King and my God,
for to you I pray.
In the morning, O Lord,
you hear my voice;
in the morning I lay my requests before you
and wait in expectation.

PSALM 5:1–3

To him who is able to keep you from falling and to present you before his glorious presence without fault and with great joy—to the only God our Savior be glory, majesty, power and authority, through Jesus Christ our Lord, before all ages, now and forevermore! Amen.

JUDE 24, 25

OTES

PREFACE TO THE REVISED EDITION

1. Dietrich Bonhoeffer, *Life Together*, trans. John W. Doberstein (New York: Harper, 1954), 58.

CHAPTER 1

1. Augustine, quoted in *The Joy of the Saints*, ed. Robert Llewelyn (Springfield, Ill.: Templegate, 1989), 1.
2. Lewis B. Smedes, *Sex for Christians* (Grand Rapids, Mich.: Eerdmans, 1976), 29.
3. Dick Keyes, *Beyond Identity: Finding Yourself in the Character and Image of God* (Ann Arbor, Mich.: Servant Books, 1984), 102, 135.
4. Ibid., 106-7.
5. George MacDonald, *Unspoken Sermons*, second series, "Self-denial," 1885, in C. S. Lewis, *George MacDonald: An Anthology* (New York: Macmillan, 1947), 68.

CHAPTER 2

1. Hannah More, "Self-Love," in *Spiritual Awakening*, ed. Sherwood Eliot Wirt (Wheaton, Ill.: Crossway, 1986).
2. Alan Wheelis, *The Quest for Identity* (New York: Norton, 1958), 174.
3. John Stott, *Involvement, Vol. II: Social and Sexual Relationships in the Modern World* (Old Tappan, N.J.: Revell, 1985), 140.
4. Dick Keyes, *Beyond Identity; Finding Yourself in the Character and Image of God* (Ann Arbor, Mich.: Servant, 1984), 216, 217.
5. Edith Schaeffer, *The Art of Life* (Wheaton, Ill.: Crossway, 1987), 42.

CHAPTER 3

1. George Appleton, ed., *The Oxford Book of Prayer* (Oxford: Oxford University, 1985), 171.
2. For a detailed discussion on the far-reaching impact of today's beauty culture and what the Bible says about beauty, see: Debra Evans, *Beauty and the Best: A Christian Woman's Guide to True Beauty* (Colorado Springs, Colo.: Focus on the Family, 1993).
3. David Garner et al., "Cultural Expectation of Thinness in Women," *Psychological Reports*, 47 (1980): 483-91.
4. Irene Daria, "Truth in Fashion," *Glamour*, February 1993, 149; Roberta Pollack Seid, *Never Too Thin: Why Women Are at War with Their Bodies* (New York: Prentice Hall, 1989), 15.

5. Isaac Newton, quoted in *Fearfully & Wonderfully Made: A Surgeon Looks at the Human & Spiritual Body*, by Paul Brand and Philip Yancey (Grand Rapids, Mich.: Zondervan, 1980), 161.

6. Jean Banyolak and Ingrid Trobisch, *Better Is Your Love Than Wine* (Downers Grove, Ill.: InterVarsity, 1971), 21.

7. Oswald Chambers, *Daily Thoughts for Disciples* (Grand Rapids, Mich.: Discovery House, 1994), 226.

CHAPTER 4

1. Ingrid Trobisch, *The Joy of Being a Woman* (New York: Harper & Row, 1975), 3-4.

CHAPTER 5

1. Lewis B. Smedes, *Sex for Christians: The Limits and Liberties of Sexual Living* (Grand Rapids, Mich.: Eerdmans, 1976), 186-87.

2. H. Norman Wright, *Understanding the Man in Your Life* (Waco, Tex.: Word, 1987), 196.

3. Mike Mason, *The Mystery of Marriage* (Portland, Ore.: Multnomah, 1985), 126-27.

4. Randy C. Alcorn, *Christians in the Wake of the Sexual Revolution* (Portland, Ore.: Multnomah, 1985), 186-87.

CHAPTER 6

1. Richard J. Foster, *Money, Sex & Power: The Challenge of the Disciplined Life* (San Francisco: Harper & Row, 1985), 92.

2. Eugene Peterson, *Praying with Jesus: A Year of Daily Prayer and Reflections on the Words and Actions of Jesus* (San Francisco: HarperSanFrancisco, 1993), November 23.

CHAPTER 7

1. Clifford and Joyce Penner, *The Gift of Sex: A Christian Guide to Sexual Fulfillment* (Waco, Tex.: Word, 1981), 53-54.

2. John White, *Flirting with the World* (Wheaton, Ill.: Harold Shaw, 1982), 80-81.

3. John Sandford, quoted in *Promises to Keep: Daily Devotions for Men Seeking Integrity*, ed. Nick Harrison (San Francisco: HarperSanFrancisco, 1997), 203.

CHAPTER 8

1. Dante Gabriel Rossetti, *The House of Life: A Sonnet-Sequence by Dante Gabriel Rossetti* (Portland, Maine: Thomas B. Mosher, 1898), 20.

2. Frank S. Mead, *12,000 Religious Quotations* (Grand Rapids, Mich.: Baker, 1989), 244.

3. Anne Morrow Lindbergh, *Gift from the Sea* (New York: Vintage, 1978), 104-5.

CHAPTER 9

1. Joyce Huggett, *Two into One: Relating in Christian Marriage* (Downers Grove, Ill.: InterVarsity, 1981), 74.

2. Ibid., 49.

3. Matthew Henry, *Matthew Henry's Commentary* (Grand Rapids, Mich.: Regency/Zondervan, 1961), 7.

4. Walter Wangerin, Jr., *As for Me and My House: Crafting Your Marriage to Last* (Nashville, Tenn.: Thomas Nelson, 1987), 251.

CHAPTER 10

1. Frederick Buechner, *Listening to Your Life* (San Francisco: HarperSanFrancisco, 1992), 4.
2. Katherine W. Pettis and R. Dave Hughes, "Sexual Victimization of Children: A Current Perspective," *Behavioral Disorders,* February 1985, 137; Marianne Neifert, *Dr. Mom: A Guide to Baby and Child Care* (New York: Signet, 1986), 438-39; Dan B. Allender, *The Wounded Heart* (Colorado Springs, Colo.: NavPress, 1990), back cover.
3. Phillips Brooks, quoted in *12,000 Religious Quotations,* ed. Frank S. Mead (Grand Rapids, Mich.: Baker, 1989), 320.
4. Peter Damian, quoted in *The Wisdom of the Saints,* ed. Jill Haak Adels (Oxford: Oxford University Press, 1987), 60.

CHAPTER 11

1. Anne Morrow Lindbergh, *Gift from the Sea* (New York: Vintage, 1978), 45.
2. Ibid., 52.
3. Ibid., 57.

CHAPTER 12

1. Paul Brand and Philip Yancey, *Fearfully and Wonderfully Made: A Surgeon Looks at the Human & Spiritual Body* (Grand Rapids, Mich.: Zondervan, 1980), 139.
2. Brenda Hunter, *What Every Mother Needs to Know* (Sisters, Ore.: Multnomah, 1993), 210.

CHAPTER 13

1. Gladys Hunt, *Ms. Means Myself* (Grand Rapids, Mich.: Zondervan, 1972), 44-45.
2. Benedict Carey, "The Talking Cure for Stress," *Health,* November/December 1996, 68-74.

CHAPTER 14

1. Francis A. Schaeffer, *The Great Evangelical Disaster* (Wheaton, Ill.: Crossway, 1984), 149, 150.
2. Genesis 17:16; 20:18; 30:22; Ruth 4:13; 1 Samuel 1:5, 19-20; Job 10:8-9; 33:4; Psalm 139:13-16; Isaiah 44:2; 66:9.
3. M. Gibling et al., "From Fantasy to Reality—An Interview with Malcolm Muggeridge," *Christianity Today,* April 21, 1978, 10.
4. GynoPharma Inc., "Is an IUD the Right Birth Control for You?" (Somerville, N.J.: GynoPharma Inc., 1988); T. W. Hilgers, "The Intrauterine Device: Contraceptive or Abortifacient?" *Minnesota Medicine,* June 1974, 493-501; Searle Laboratories, "For the Patient: Cu-7" (Chicago: Searle Laboratories, 1977); *The Medical Letter,* Vol. 22, No. 20, October 3, 1980; "Mechanism of Action of IUDs in Women," *American Journal of Obstetrics and Gynecology,* Vol. 36, No. 3, September 1970.
5. B. M. Kahar, "Pharmaceutical Companies: The New Abortionists," *ALL About Issues,* February 1989; Ortho Pharmaceutical Corporation, *A Guide to Methods of Contraception* (Raritan N.J.: Ortho, 1979), 8; R. Killich, "Ovarian Follicles During Oral Contraceptive Cycles: Their Potential for Ovulation," *Fertility and Sterility,* 52 (1989): 580; *Nursing '85 Drug Handbook* (Spring House Corporation, 1985), 470; Department of Health and

Human Services, *Facts About Oral Contraceptives* (Washington, D.C.: U.S. Government Printing Office, 1984); and R. A. Hatcher, F. Guest, F. Stewart, et al., *Contraceptive Technology*, 16th rev. ed. (New York: Irvington, 1994); *The Random House College Dictionary*, rev. ed. (New York: Random House, 1982), defines birth control pill as "an oral contraceptive for women that inhibits ovulation, fertilization, *or implantation of a fertilized ovum,* causing temporary infertility" (emphasis added).

6. "Birth Control Breakthrough Almost Here," *Self*, August 1989, 172.

7. The *Physician's Desk Reference*, 50th ed., 1996 (Montvale, N.J.: Medical Economics Co., 1996) clearly explains the way *all* combination oral contraceptives work to prevent births. In each product's "mechanism of action" description, the same explanation simply says: "Combination oral contraceptives act by suppression of gonadotropins [e.g., sex hormones]. Although the primary mechanism is inhibition of ovulation, other alterations include changes in the cervical mucus, which increases the difficulty of sperm entry into the uterus and the endometrium [uterine lining], which reduce the likelihood of implantation."

The term "implantation" here refers to the embedding of an early embryo in the womb, because only a fertilized egg can implant in the uterine lining, not an unfertilized ovum. In other words, *since combination oral contraceptives do not stop a woman's ovaries from releasing eggs 100 percent of the time, they are also designed to work to prevent birth in two other important ways:* 1) by changing the cervical mucus to discourage the movement of sperm toward an egg that may be traveling through the fallopian tube; and 2) by making the uterine lining (endometrium) incapable of supporting a new life if an egg *is* fertilized and the early embryo—a developing person in the first week of his or her development—then seeks shelter and sustenance after reaching the inside of the womb.

Normally, the uterine lining significantly thickens and develops a rich blood supply by the time a woman ovulates. Oral contraceptives dramatically alter this natural physiological feature by acting to make the endometrium too thin and blood-deprived to be capable of nourishing life. *Thus, the pregnancy will be aborted by chemically-induced means if an egg is fertilized following the failure of an O.C's other mechanisms of action* (hormonal suppression of ovulation and interference with sperm mobility).

For your information, here is a list of combination oral contraceptives that contain the "mechanism of action" statement given above, as indicated by brand name and manufacturer. Also included are all of the applicable page numbers from *PDR '96* so that you may check out the specific details for yourself:

TRI-LEVELEN® (Berlex), p. 652;

OVCON® (Bristol-Meyers Squibb), p. 760;

DESOGEN® (Organon), p. 1817;

MODLICON® (Ortho), p. 1872;

ORTHO-CEPT® (Ortho), p. 1851;

ORTHO-CYCLEN® (Ortho), p. 1858;

ORTHO TRI-CYCLEN® (Ortho), p. 1858;

ORTHO-NOVUM 1/35® (Ortho), p. 1872;

ORTHO-NOVUM 1/50® (Ortho), p. 1872;

ORTHO-NOVUM 10/11® (Ortho) p. 1872;

ORTHO-NOVUM 7/7/7® (Ortho), p. 1872;

BREVICON® (Roche), p. 2134;

NORINYL 1+35® (Roche), p. 2134;

NORINYL 1+50® (Roche), p. 2134;

TRI-NORINYL® (Roche), p. 2164;

NOR-QD® (Roche), p. 2135;

LO/OVRAL® (Wyeth-Ayerst), p. 2746;

LO/OVRAL 28® (Wyeth-Ayerst), p. 2751;

NORDETTE 21® (Wyeth-Ayerst), p. 2755;

NORDETTE 28® (Wyeth-Ayerst), p. 2758;

TRIPHASIL-21® (Wyeth-Ayerst), p. 2814;

TRIPHASIL-28® (Wyeth-Ayerst), p. 2819.

For MICRONOR® (Ortho), a progestogen-only O.C., the mechanism of action statement reads: "The primary mechanism of action through which MICRONOR prevents conception is not known, but progestogen-only contraceptives are known to alter the cervical mucus, exert a progestational effect on the endometrium, and, in some patients, suppress ovulation" (*PDR '96*, p. 1872). Again, *the uterine lining is not capable of supporting human life after conception takes place if a woman uses a progestogen-only birth control method.* This is due to hormonally caused irregularities in the endometrium. Any woman using a progestogen-only birth control product should also be informed that *ovulation has been shown to take place as much as 80 percent of the time in women using this method, potentially increasing the likelihood that the product's abortive back-up mechanisms will prevent birth from taking place.*

NOTE: the progestogen-only birth control product category includes the NOR-PLANT® skin implant system and DEPO-PROVERA®, a long-lasting, injectable form of a progesterone-like drug, as well as other progestogen-only products currently in development or new on the market since this book is written.

If you would like more information, here are a couple of questions you might ask your pharmacist as you start discussing today's birth control products: "Is there an oral contraceptive on the market that does *not* change the lining of the uterus—or do all available O.C.s include this as a mechanism of action? What available birth control products would you recommend that act to prevent conception by completely stopping ovulation or without altering the uterine lining?"

8. Quote from *Roe v. Wade,* the U.S. Supreme Court decision on abortion, January 22, 1973.

9. Psalm 100:3; 139:13-16; Isaiah 64:8; Romans 12:1; 1 Corinthians 6:19-20.

10. Romans 8; Galatians 5:16-26; Ephesians 5:15-21; Philippians 2:1-11; Colossians 3:1-17.

11. Psalm 51, 139; Matthew 16:27; Romans 14:8; Galatians 6:4-5.

12. Romans 12:1-2; 1 Corinthians 12:20; Ephesians 5:1-5.

13. Psalm 128; Proverbs 31; 1 Timothy 5:14; Titus 2:3-5.

14. Genesis 1:28; 9:1; 17:6, 20; 28:3, Exodus 1:7; Deuteronomy 1:10-11; Psalm 107:37-43; 127:3.

15. Psalm 145:10-13; 2 Corinthians 5:1-10; Ephesians 1:3-10; 1 Timothy 6:11-16; 1 Peter 5:10; 1 John 1:1-2; 5:11; Jude 20-21.

16. T. W. Hilgers, *Fertility Appreciation: The Ovulation Method of Natural Family Planning* (Omaha, Neb.: Creighton University Natural Family Planning Education and Research Center, 1983), 45.

17. R. A. Hatcher et al., *Contraceptive Technology.*

18. Toni Weschler, *Taking Charge of Your Fertility* (New York: HarperCollins, 1995), 66.

19. Oswald Chambers, *My Utmost for His Highest: An Updated Edition in Today's Language*, ed. James Reimann (Grand Rapids, Mich.: Discovery House, 1992), May 30.

CHAPTER 15

1. Eugene H. Peterson, *Earth and Altar* (Downers Grove, Ill.: InterVarsity Press, 1985), 163.
2. Henry Ward Beecher, quoted in *12,000 Religious Quotations*, ed. Frank S. Mead (Grand Rapids, Mich.: Baker, 1989), 275-276.

CHAPTER 16

1. C. S. Lewis, *George MacDonald: An Anthology* (New York: Macmillan, 1947), 100, 121.
2. American Medical Association, *Health and Well-Being After 50* (New York: Random House, 1984), 74.
3. Biblical examples of this encouraging phenomenon can be found in Ruth 1:1–4:22; 1 Samuel 25:2-42; 1 Kings 17:7-24; Luke 2:36-38; Acts 16:13-15, 40. (Lydia does not appear to have had a husband, given the references to her as the person exclusively in charge of her household.) See also: Debra Evans, *Women of Character: Life-Changing Examples of Godly Women* (Grand Rapids, Mich.: Zondervan, 1995).

CHAPTER 17

1. Teresa of Avila, *A Life of Prayer*, ed. James M. Houston (Portland, Ore.: Multnomah, 1983), xxv.
2. Aric Press, "The War Against Pornography," *Newsweek*, March 18, 1985, 58.
3. Jerry Bridges, *Transforming Grace: Living Confidently in God's Unfailing Love* (Colorado Springs, Colo.: NavPress, 1991), 162-63.

CHAPTER 18

1. Robert Farrar Capon, *Bed and Board: Plain Talk About Marriage* (New York: Fireside, 1965), 70-71.

LOSSARY

Abdomen: The portion of the body containing the stomach, intestines, bowels, bladder, and reproductive organs.

Abdominal wall: The muscles that form a corsetlike structure between the pubic bone and the ribs and from side to side across the abdomen.

Abortifacient: Any drug or substance capable of inducing abortion.

Abortion: The spontaneous or deliberate ending of a pregnancy before an unborn child can survive independently of the mother.

Adultery: Sexual intercourse in which at least one partner is married to another person.

Acquired immune deficiency syndrome (AIDS): A disease affecting the system of the body that fights infection; has a 100 percent mortality rate.

Adrenaline: A naturally secreted substance that stimulates the adrenal glands and narrows blood vessels. Also called epinephrine.

Aerobic exercise: Any type of physical exercise that causes the heart and lungs to work harder through the repetitive movement of large muscle groups for a sufficient length of time.

Amenorrhea: The absence of menstruation. Primary amenorrhea is the term meaning that menstruation has never begun; secondary amenorrhea refers to cases in which the menstrual cycle has either temporarily or permanently stopped.

Amniocentesis: The removal of a small amount of amniotic fluid for diagnostic or therapeutic purposes.

Androgens: Any steroid hormone that produces the growth of male features.

Androgynous: Bearing both anthers and pollen (plants) or having both male and female qualities.

Anemia: A reduction of the number of red blood cells resulting in reduced ability of the blood to carry oxygen.

Anorexia nervosa: A potentially fatal psychological disorder resulting in severe weight loss, amenorrhea, and emaciation.

Anovulation: The absence of ovulation.

Antepartum: Around the time of birth.

Anus: The opening of the rectum between the buttocks.

Areola: The pigmented ring of skin around the nipple.

Autonomic nervous system: The division of the nervous system that regulates vital functions of the body that are not consciously controlled, including the activity of the heart, smooth muscles, and glands.

Bartholin's glands: Two small glands found at either side of the vaginal entrance; they secrete a lubricative substance during sexual arousal.

Basal body temperature: Temperature of the body taken orally, rectally, or vaginally after at least three hours of sleep. It is taken before doing anything else.

Basal body temperature method of family planning: A method of family planning that relies on identifying the fertile period of a woman's menstrual cycle by taking and observing the basal body temperature each morning.

Bidet: A plumbing fixture designed to cleanse the female genitals and rectal area.

Billings method: See *Ovulation Method of Family Planning.*

Biopsy: The surgical removal of body tissue for diagnostic purposes.

Birth: The process by which a new human being enters the world and begins life outside the mother.

Birth canal: Passage formed by the vagina and the uterus when the cervix has completely opened up during labor.

Birth control: The prevention of birth.

Birth rate: The number of births during a specific period of time in relation to the total population of a certain area.

Blastocyst: The fertilized ovum during its second week of development when it is a hollow ball of cells.

Bulbourethral glands: Two small glands located on each side of the prostate that secrete into the male urethra.

Breast self-examination: A method in which a woman may routinely check her breasts and surrounding areas for signs of change that could indicate cancer.

Cardiovascular fitness: Well-being of the heart and circulatory system promoted through diet, weight management, and aerobic exercise; enhances the oxygen level in the blood.

Celibacy: A way of life that involves commitment to sexual abstinence.

Central nervous system: One of two main divisions of the nervous system made up of the brain and spinal cord, the main network of control and coordination for the body.

Cervical canal: The opening within the uterine cervix that protrudes into the vagina.

Cervical crypts: Indentations within the lining of the cervical canal that act as storage compartments for sperm.

Cervix: The lower necklike segment of the uterus that forms the passageway into the vagina.

Chromosomes: Threadlike bodies within the nucleus of a cell that make up strands of DNA (deoxyribonucleic acid). Chromosomes contain the genetic material that is passed on from parents to their children. Each normal cell in humans contains forty-six chromosomes arranged in twenty-three pairs from the time of conception.

Cilia: Small hairlike projections lining the surface of the fallopian tubes; they create motion to direct the ova to the uterus.

Clitoris: The female organ devoted entirely to increasing sexual tension and providing pleasurable sensations when stimulated. It is the structure that corresponds to the glans penis in males and plays a key role in sexual response.

Coccyx: The tailbone or small bone located at the tip of the spine.

Coitus: The sexual union of two people of the opposite sex during which the penis is inserted into the vagina.

Coitus interruptus: See *Withdrawal Method.*

Colostrum: The substance that precedes the production of breast milk; it is rich in protein and high in antibodies.

Conception: The physiological union of a sperm and an egg that initiates the growth of a new person and triggers the onset of pregnancy.

Conception control: The prevention of fertilization.

Condom: A soft, flexible sheath worn over an erect penis during lovemaking to prevent sperm from entering the vagina.

Contraception: Any drug, device, surgery, or method of family planning that prevents conception.

Contraction: A unit of work performed by a muscle over a period of time, including the rhythmic tightening of muscles during orgasm and the uterine muscles during childbirth.

Copulation: Sexual intercourse.

Corpus luteum: A term meaning "yellow body" that describes a small secretory structure that develops within an ovarian follicle after an egg is released.

Cystitis: Inflammation of the bladder and urinary tract. See *Urinary Tract Infection.*

Cystocele: The bulging of the bladder and the front wall into the vagina as the result of giving birth, advanced age, or surgery.

Deoxyribonucleic acid (DNA): A large molecule carrying the genetic information within the chromosomes of a cell.

DES (diethylstilbestrol): A synthetic estrogen used during the 1950s and 1960s to prevent miscarriage. In 1971 it was found to cause a rare form of vaginal cancer, and vaginal changes were discovered in a significant number of the daughters born to women who had taken DES during pregnancy.

Diaphragm: A dome-shaped latex device worn over the cervix during sexual intercourse to prevent sperm from entering the uterus.

Dilation: The normal increase in the size of a tube, blood vessel, or body opening.

Dilation and curettage (D & C): A surgical procedure in which the cervix is opened and the uterus is scraped with a small spoonlike instrument called a curette. Used to remove polyps or an overgrowth of uterine tissue, as a way of diagnosing cancer, and after childbirth to remove tissue retained by the uterus. Also a method of abortion involving the crushing of the unborn child and its extraction from the uterus.

Diuretic: Any drug that increases the passage of urine from the body. Used to prevent the excessive accumulation of fluid and commonly used as a treatment for high blood pressure.

Divorce: The separation of a married couple through legal means.

Douche: The cleansing of the vagina with fluid.

Dysmenorrhea: Painful menstruation resulting from the shape of the uterus and/or the process of menstruation. Prostaglandins have been linked to menstrual pain and antiprostaglandin medication such as ibuprofen often greatly relieves the pelvic discomfort associated with menstrual cramps.

Dyspareunia: Painful or difficult sexual intercourse.

Ectopic pregnancy: A pregnancy occurring outside the uterus, usually in an oviduct.

Edema: The presence of an excessive amount of fluid in body tissues. Also referred to as fluid retention.

Ejaculation: The sudden release of semen from the male urethra. The feeling of ejaculation is called orgasm. It is a reflex action that occurs in two phases. First, sperm fluid and secretions from the prostate and bulbourethral gland are moved into the urethra. Second, strong muscular contractions force ejaculation. The average number of male sex cells contained in a single ejaculation may be between 200-300 million.

Ejaculatory duct: The passage through which semen enters the urethra.

Embryo: In humans, an unborn child between the second and eighth week of pregnancy, a period that involves rapid growth, initial development of the major organ systems, and early formation of the main external features.

Emotion: The feeling part of human awareness. Physical changes often come with changes in emotion, whether the feelings are conscious or not.

Emotional response: A response to a specific feeling, occurring with physical changes that may or may not be obvious.

Empathy: The ability to know and share the emotions of another person and to understand the meaning of that person's behavior.

Endocervix: The membrane that lines the inner canal of the cervix.

Endocrine system: A system of ductless glands that secrete hormones into the bloodstream. These glands are the adrenals, ovaries, pancreas, pituitary, parathyroid, testicles, thymus, and thyroid.

Endometriosis: A growth of endometrial tissue outside of the uterus, thought to occur in about 15 percent of women. Women who do not get pregnant until later in life are more likely to get this disease, with the average age at diagnosis being thirty-seven. The most common symptoms are severe menstrual cramps and painful intercourse, painful bowel movements, and soreness above the pubic bones. Pregnancy seems to prevent or correct this problem in some women.

Endometrium: The lining of the inner surface of the uterus, consisting of three layers, with two of the layers being shed during each menstrual flow. The third layer provides the surface that the placenta attaches to during pregnancy.

Endorphin: Any one of the substances of the nervous system made by the pituitary gland, producing effects like that of morphine as a way of reducing pain within the body.

Engagement: The descent of the fetus into the pelvic cavity, occurring during late pregnancy or at some point in labor.

Engorgement: Swelling of the breasts with milk.

Epidemic: A disease that spreads rapidly through a part of the population.

Epididymis: A long, tightly coiled tube that carries sperm from the testicles to the vas deferens. Each testes has an epididymis attached to it that is approximately twenty feet in length.

Episiotomy: A surgical procedure performed during the second stage of childbirth in which the opening of the vagina is enlarged with a cut.

Erectile: A term used to describe tissue capable of being raised to an erect position as it fills with blood.

Erection: The condition of hardness, swelling, and raising of the penis or clitoris.

Estrogen: A hormone secreted by the ovaries that regulates the development of secondary sexual characteristics in women. Estrogen is also produced by the adrenal glands, testicles, and both the fetus and the placenta.

Fallopian tube: One of a pair of funnel-shaped tubes opening at one end into the uterus and at the other end into the pelvic cavity over the ovary. Ova pass through these tubes and are carried to the uterus by muscular contractions and the beating of hairlike structures called cilia. Fertilization of an egg usually takes place at the far end of the tube. These tubes are also called oviducts.

Female sexual dysfunction: The inability of a woman to enjoy participating in lovemaking or the inability to have an orgasm. Characteristics include pain, vaginal spasms, lack of sexual arousal, anxiety, fear, and negative feelings about sexual response.

Fertile: Having the ability to reproduce offspring; fruitful; not sterile.

Fertile mucus: Cervical mucus capable of facilitating the transport of sperm through the female reproductive tract.

Fertile period: The time of the menstrual cycle during which fertilization may take place, beginning three to six days before ovulation and lasting for two to three days afterward.

Fetus: An unborn child after the eighth week of pregnancy.

Fibroid: A noncancerous tumor of the uterus, usually occurring in women between thirty and fifty years of age.

Fimbria: The fringelike borders of the open ends of the fallopian tubes.

Folic acid: A form of vitamin B that is water soluble and is vital to the production of blood cells and hemoglobin, especially during pregnancy.

Follicle: A pouchlike recessed spot in the ovary, the place in which the ovum matures.

Follicle stimulating hormone (FSH): A pituitary gland hormone that stimulates the growth of graafian follicles in females and the production and maturation of sperm in males.

Foreskin: The loose fold of skin covering the end of the penis or clitoris.

Freudian: Referring to the concepts of Sigmund Freud (1856-1939), who stressed that the early years of childhood form the basis for later neurotic disorders.

Frigidity: The inability to respond to sexual stimulation.

FSH: The abbreviation for follicle stimulating hormone.

Fundus: The rounded portion of the uterus from which contractions originate during labor.

Gender: The specific sex of a person; male or female.

Gene: The basic unit of heredity in a chromosome that carries characteristics from parents to their child.

Generation: The act or process of reproduction; procreation.

Genesis: Origin; generation; the act of producing or procreating.

Genetic code: A code that fixes patterns of amino acids that are the building-blocks of body tissue proteins, determining the physical traits of an offspring.

Genetic engineering: The process of creating new DNA molecules.

Genitals: External sex organs.

Gestation: The period between conception and birth.

Gland: An organ of highly specialized cells capable of releasing material not related to its normal metabolism.

Glans: The sensitive tissue lying on the end of the penis and clitoris that is capable of swelling and hardening when filled with blood during sexual arousal.

Gonad: A primary sex organ; an ovary or a testis.

Gonadotropin: A gonad-stimulating hormone.

Gonorrhea: A common sexually transmitted disease that has few early symptoms in women and is capable of producing sterility if not treated early.

Graafian follicle: A mature ovarian sac that ruptures during ovulation to release a mature egg.

G-spot: A small spongelike structure lying on the front wall of the vagina behind the bladder that is responsive to sexual stimulation in some women.

Gynecology: The branch of medicine dealing with diseases of the female reproductive tract.

Health: A state of mental, physical, emotional, and spiritual well-being.

Health care provider: A person who provides health services to health care consumers.

Herpes genitalis: An infection caused by the herpes simplex II virus that is usually transmitted sexually and causes painful blisters on the skin and mucous membranes of the male and female genitals.

Homeostasis: A relatively steady state maintained by the body.

Hormone: Chemical substances, produced by ductless glands in one part of the body, that start or run the activity of an organ or a group of cells in another part of the body.

Hymen: The fold of mucous membrane, fibrous tissue, and skin that partially covers the vaginal entrance. When it is broken, small rounded elevations remain, called hymenal tags.

Hypertension: High blood pressure.

Hysterectomy: The surgical removal of the uterus.

Implantation: Embedding of the developing baby in the lining of the uterus.

Incest: Sexual relations between family members.

Induced abortion: An intentional termination of a pregnancy before an unborn child has developed enough to survive outside of the uterus.

Infertile: The inability to produce offspring.

Intrauterine device: A form of contraception consisting of a bent strip of plastic or other material that is inserted into the uterus to prevent pregnancy; does not prevent ovulation or fertilization.

In vitro fertilization: Conception occurring in laboratory apparatus.

Labia: The fleshy, liplike folds of skin at the opening of the vagina. The labia majora forms the border of the vulva. The labia minora extends from the clitoris backward on both sides of the vagina.

Labor: The series of stages during the process of childbirth through which the baby is born and the uterus returns to a normal state.

Lactation: The process of the production and secretion of milk from the breasts for the nourishment of an infant.

Let-down reflex: The ejection of breast milk from the milk glands resulting in the flow of milk from the nipple.

Levator ani: One of a pair of muscles lying at the base of the pelvis that stretches across the bottom of the pelvic cavity like a hammock as a support for the pelvic organs.

Lochia: The discharge from the uterus that flows from the vagina after a baby is born.

Luteal: Referring to the corpus luteum, its functions or its effects.

Luteinizing hormone: A hormone produced by the pituitary gland in both males and females. It stimulates the production of testosterone in men and the secretion of estrogen in women.

Male sexual dysfunction: An impaired or inadequate ability to participate in love-making, usually psychological in origin.

Mammogram: X-ray of the soft tissue of the breast used to identify various cysts or tumors.

Massage: The manipulation of the soft tissue of the body through stroking, kneading, rubbing, or tapping for the purpose of increasing circulation, improving muscle tone, and relaxation.

Mastectomy: The surgical removal of the breast.

Mastitis: Inflammation of the breast.

Masturbation: Sexual activity in which the penis or clitoris is stimulated by a means other than sexual intercourse.

Maternity cycle: The cycle that lasts from conception until six weeks after birth.

Menarche: The onset of menstruation and the beginning of the first menstrual cycle.

Menopause: The end of menstruation when the menses stop as a normal result of the decline of monthly hormonal cycles.

Menorrhea: Same as *Menstruation*.

Menses: The normal flow of blood and discarded uterine cells that takes place during menstruation.

Menstrual cycle: The cycle of hormonal changes that begins at puberty and repeats itself on a monthly basis unless interrupted by pregnancy, lactation, medication, or metabolic disorders.

Menstruation: The casting off of the lining of the nonpregnant uterus, resulting in the periodic discharge of blood and mucosal tissue through the vagina.

Metabolism: The sum of all the chemical processes that take place in the body.

Miscarriage: The loss of a baby before the twenty-eighth week of pregnancy.

Mittelschmerz: The painful sensation that occurs in one side of the lower abdomen during ovulation.

Morning-after pill: A very large dose of estrogen taken orally within twenty-four to seventy-two hours after intercourse.

Mucus: The slippery, sticky secretion released by mucous membranes and glands.

Natal: Referring to birth.

Natural family planning: Any method of family planning that does not use drugs or devices to avoid pregnancy.

Nipple: A small cylindric bump positioned just below the center of each breast and containing fourteen to twenty openings to the milk ducts.

Noninvasive: Referring to any test, treatment, or procedure that does not invade the boundaries of the body.

Obstetrics: The branch of medicine dealing with pregnancy and childbirth.

Oogenesis: The growth of female eggs or ova.

Oral contraceptive: A steroid drug taken orally to produce infertility.

Orgasm: A series of strong, pleasurable, muscular contractions within the genitals that are triggered by intense sexual excitement and cannot be controlled once initiated.

Orgasmic platform: The tightening of the lower vagina during sexual arousal.

Osteoporosis: The loss of normal bone density marked by a thinning of bone tissue and the growth of small openings in the bone.

Ovary: One of the pair of primary sexual organs in females located on each side of the lower abdomen beside the uterus.

Oviduct: See *Fallopian tube.*

Ovulation: The release of an egg, or ovum, from the ovary after the breaking of a follicle.

Ovulation method of family planning: A method of family planning that relies on the observation of the type and amount of cervical mucus secreted during the menstrual cycle as a means of predicting fertility.

Ova: Human eggs (singular: ovum).

Pap smear: A method of examining tissue cells shed by the cervix taken by collecting cells in the vagina and at the opening of the cervix.

Parasympathetic nervous system: The division of the autonomic nervous system that produces muscular relaxation and causes blood vessels to widen in the clitoris and the penis.

Peak mucus: A cloudy to clear white mucus coating the vaginal area during times of high estrogen levels at the most fertile point in the menstrual cycle.

Pelvic floor: The muscles and tissues that form the base of the pelvis.

Pelvic inflammatory disease: Inflammation of the female reproductive organs in the pelvis, often resulting in scarring, blocked fallopian tubes, and sterility.

Pelvic lifts: Conscious contractions of the pelvic floor muscles done for the purpose of improving muscle tone and sexual response. Also referred to as Kegels, after Dr. Arnold Kegel, a physician whose research proved the value of exercise to this area of the body.

Pelvic tilt: An exercise designed to strengthen the lower back and abdomen.

Pelvis: The bowl-shaped lower portion of the trunk of the body.

Penis: The male organ of urination and sexual intercourse made up of three circular masses of spongy tissue covered with skin.

Perineum: The part of the body lying between the inner thighs, with the buttocks to the rear and the sex organs to the front.

Petting: Sexual touching and fondling that does not include intercourse.

P.I.D. : See *Pelvic Inflammatory Disease.*

Pituitary gland: A small gland lying at the base of the brain. It supplies many hormones to regulate a variety of processes within the body, including growth, reproduction, and lactation.

Pornography: Obscene materials that portray the sexual degradation and humiliation of women, men, or children.

Polyp: A small, tumorlike growth that protrudes from a mucous membrane surface.

Postpartum: After childbirth.

Potent: The ability to have an erection or perform sexual intercourse.

Pregnancy: The growth and development of a new individual within a woman's uterus.

Premenstrual syndrome: A set of interrelated symptoms that recur regularly at the same phase of each menstrual cycle.

Premenstrual tension: Emotional symptoms that recur regularly at the same phase of each menstrual cycle.

Prenatal: The period before birth.

Progesterone: The hormone secreted by the corpus luteum each month to prepare the sexual organs for pregnancy.

Progestin: Any one of a group of hormones, natural or synthetic, that have progesterone-like effects on the uterus.

Progestogen: See *Progestin.*

Prolactin: The hormone responsible for milk secretion—released in response to an infant sucking at the breast.

Proliferative phase: The portion of the menstrual cycle between menstruation and ovulation.

Prostaglandins: A group of strong hormonelike fatty acids that act on certain organs. Used as a method of terminating pregnancy.

Prostate gland: A structure that surrounds the neck of the bladder and the beginning of the male urethra.

Psychosexual dysfunction: Any problem or disorder related to sexual responsiveness that is emotional in origin.

Pubic bone: One of the two bones that form the front part of the pelvis.

Rape: Sexual assault without consent.

Rectocele: The bulging of the rectum and the back wall of the vagina into the vagina occurring as the result of giving birth, advanced age, or surgery.

Rectum: The lower part of the large intestine lying above the anal canal.

Scrotum: The pouch of skin that holds the testicles.

Semen: The thick white fluid released by the male sex organs for the purpose of transporting sperm.

Seminal fluid: See *Semen*.

Seminal vesicles: The saclike glands lying behind the bladder in the male that release fluid that forms part of the semen.

Sex: A division of humans into male or female, based on many characteristics, including body parts and genetic differences.

Sexual: Of or relating to sex.

Sexual abuse: Sexual contact without consent.

Sexual dysfunction: Difficulty related to sexual expression or experience due to a physical or emotional problem.

Sexual intercourse: See *Coitus*.

Sexual identity: How a person views his or her sexuality.

Sexuality: The sum total of the physical, functional, emotional, intellectual, and spiritual traits shown through a person's identity and behavior, whether related to the reproductive organs or to procreation.

Sexual role: The expression of a person's sexual identity.

Sexually transmitted disease (STD): A contagious disease spread through intimate sexual contact.

Side effect: A reaction resulting from medical treatment or therapy.

Slough: To cast off or shed dead cells from living tissue.

Smegma: A substance secreted by glands under the foreskin and at the base of the labia minora near the glans of the clitoris.

Spasm: A sudden, unconscious tightening of a muscle.

Sperm: The male sex cell contained in semen that fertilizes the female sex cell, or ovum, in order to create a new human being.

Spermatogenesis: The process of sperm production.

Spermatic cord: A stringlike structure by which each testicle is attached to the body.

Spermicide: Any chemical substance that kills sperm cells.

Sphincter: A strong circular band of muscle that narrows a passage or closes off a natural opening in the body.

Staphylococcus aureus: A type of bacteria that produces a poison causing toxic shock syndrome.

Sterile: The condition of barrenness; the inability to produce children.

Sterilization: An act or process that renders a person incapable of reproduction.

Stress: Any factor that requires response or change on the part of an organism or an individual.

Stressor: Anything capable of causing wear and tear on the body's mental, physical, emotional, or spiritual resources.

Striae: Streaks or narrow furrows in the skin resulting from stretching. Also called stretch marks.

Sympathetic nervous system: A division of the autonomic nervous system that triggers the release of substances that speed up the heart, narrow blood vessels, and raise blood pressure.

Symptom: Something felt or noticed by an individual that can be used to detect what is going on within the body.

Sympto-thermal method of family planning: A method of family planning requiring fertility awareness—based on the ovulation and basal body temperature methods of family planning.

Syphilis: A sexually transmitted disease caused by a type of bacteria called a spirochete.

Tactile: Of or relating to the sense of touch.

Tampon: A compact pack of absorbent material designed to soak up the menstrual flow within the vagina.

Tension: The condition of feeling strained or under pressure.

Testicle: See *Testis.*

Testis: One of the pair of primary sex organs, or gonads, that produce semen and testosterone.

Testosterone: A naturally secreted hormone in both males and females that is capable of producing masculine characteristics.

Therapy: The treatment of an abnormal condition.

Toxic shock syndrome: A potentially fatal sudden disease caused by staphylococcus aureus associated with the use of tampons during menstruation.

Trimester: Period of three months; one of the three phases of pregnancy.

Tubal ligation: One of several sterilization procedures in which both fallopian tubes are sealed to prevent conception from taking place.

Tubal pregnancy: A pregnancy in which the fertilized ovum implants within the fallopian tube and cannot develop normally.

Tubercles of montgomery: Small glands that resemble pimples on the surface of the areola that release a fatty lubricative substance.

Urethra: The canal that carries urine from the bladder.

Urinary stress incontinence: The involuntary passage of urine when coughing, sneezing, or laughing—resulting from poor sphincter control of the urethra.

Urinary tract: All of the structures involved in the release and elimination of urine from the body.

Urinary tract infection (UTI): An infection of the urinary tract marked by frequency of urination, a painful burning sensation while voiding, and possibly pus in the urine.

Urogenital: Of or relating to the urinary and the reproductive systems.

Urology: The division of medicine concerned with the care of the urinary tract in men and women and of the male genital tract.

Use-effectiveness: The actual level of effectiveness of a contraceptive method.

Uterus: The thick-walled, hollow, muscular female organ of reproduction in which the fertilized ovum imbeds and an unborn child develops during pregnancy.

Vacuum aspiration: A method of abortion in which an unborn child and placenta are removed from the uterus.

Vagina: The muscular tubelike membrane that forms the passageway between the uterus and the external genitals. It receives the penis during intercourse and becomes the canal through which the baby passes during birth.

Vaginal discharge: Any discharge from the vagina.

Vaginismus: An involuntary tightening of the muscles surrounding the vagina caused by fear of painful intercourse or a pelvic examination.

Vaginitis: Inflammation and swelling of the vaginal tissues.

Vas deferens: One of a pair of tubes within the male reproductive tract through which sperm pass.

Vasectomy: A procedure that produces sterility by cutting a section out of each vas deferens.

Vasocongestion: The state in which blood vessels become too full, causing tissue to swell during sexual arousal.

Virgin: A person who has never had sexual intercourse.

Virginity: The state of being a virgin.

Virile: A term used to describe one's masculine characteristics or fertility.

Virilism: The masculinization of a female.

Voyeur: A person who receives pleasure from observing the sexual anatomy or behavior of others.

Vulva: The external female genitals, including the labia majora, labia minora, and the clitoris.

Withdrawal method: A technique of conception control in which the penis is withdrawn from the vagina prior to ejaculation. Highly unreliable since the preejaculatory fluid released through the urethra contains sperm. Also called coitus interruptus.

Woman-year: One year in the life of a fertile woman who is sexually active. Used to represent a unit of twelve months of exposure to the risk of pregnancy.

Womb: See *Uterus*

Wrongful-life action: A lawsuit brought against a physician or health facility because an unwanted child was born.

X chromosome: The sex-determining chromosome carried by all ova and approximately one-half of the sperm. Its presence as a pair produces a female child.

Y chromosome: The sex-determining chromosome carried by about one-half of all sperm, never by an egg, that produces a male child.

Yeast infection: A fungal infection resulting in itching and inflammation of the vagina—characterized by a thick white discharge and caused by the growth of *Candida albicans*.

Zygote: The developing egg between the time of fertilization and its implantation in the wall of the uterus.

BIBLIOGRAPHY

Adams, J. *Understanding and Managing Stress*. San Francisco, Calif.: University Association, 1980.

Adels, J. H., ed. *The Wisdom of the Saints*. Oxford: Oxford University Press, 1987.

Aguilar, N. *The New No-Pill, No-Risk Birth Control*. New York: Rawson, 1986.

Ahlem, L. *Living with Stress*. Ventura, Calif.: Regal Books, 1978.

Alcorn, R. *Christians in the Wake of the Sexual Revolution*. Portland, Ore.: Multnomah, 1985.

Allender, D. B. *The Wounded Heart: Hope for Adult Victims of Childhood Sexual Abuse*. Colorado Springs, Colo.: NavPress, 1990.

American Journal of Obstetrics and Gynecology. Vol. 36, No. 3, September 1970.

American Medical Association. *Health and Well-Being After 50*. New York: Random House, 1984.

American Medical Association. *Women: How to Understand Your Symptoms*. New York: Random House, 1986.

Appleton, G. *The Oxford Book of Prayer*. Oxford: Oxford University Press, 1985.

Arterburn, S. *Addicted to "Love."* Ann Arbor, Mich.: Vine, 1991.

Atrens, D. M. *Don't Diet*. New York: William Morrow, 1988.

Banyolak, J., and I. Trobisch. *Better Is Your Love Than Wine*. Downers Grove, Ill.: InterVarsity, 1972.

Bennet, J. P. *Chemical Contraception*. New York: Columbia University Press, 1974.

Benson, H. *The Relaxation Response*. New York: Avon, 1975.

Billings, E., and A. Westmore. *The Billings Method—Controlling Fertility Without Drugs or Devices*. New York: Random House, 1980.

"Birth Control Breakthrough Almost Here." *Self*, August 1989.

Bloesch, D. G. *Is the Bible Sexist? Beyond Feminism and Patriarchalism*. Wheaton, Ill.: Crossway, 1982.

Bonhoeffer, D. *Ethics*. New York: Macmillan, 1965.

———. *Life Together*, trans. John W. Doberstein. New York: Harper, 1954.

Bowen-Woodward, K. *Coping with a Negative Body Image*. New York: Rosen, 1989.

Brand, P., and P. Yancey. *Fearfully and Wonderfully Made: A Surgeon Looks at the Human & Spiritual Body*. Grand Rapids, Mich.: Zondervan, 1980.

———. *In His Image*. Grand Rapids, Mich.: Zondervan, 1984.

Brazelton, T. B. *On Becoming a Family: The Growth of Attachment*. New York: Delacorte Press/Seymour Lawrence, 1981.

Brestin, S., and D. Brestin. *Building Your House on the Lord: Marriage and Parenthood.* Wheaton, Ill.: Harold Shaw, 1980.

Bridges, J. *Transforming Grace: Living Confidently in God's Unfailing Love.* Colorado Springs, Colo.: Navpress, 1991.

Budoff, P. W. *No More Menstrual Cramps and Other Good News.* New York: G. P. Putnam's Sons, 1980.

Buechner, F. *Listening to Your Life.* San Francisco: HarperSanFrancisco, 1992.

Capon, R. F. *Bed and Board: Plain Talk About Marriage.* New York: Simon and Schuster, 1965.

Carey, B. "The Talking Cure for Stress." *Health* (November/December 1996).

Chambers, O. *Daily Thoughts for Disciples.* Grand Rapids, Mich.: Discovery House, 1994.

_____. *My Utmost for His Highest: An Updated Edition in Today's Language,* ed. James Reimann. Grand Rapids, Mich.: Discovery House, 1992.

Cloud, H., and J. Townsend. *Boundaries.* Grand Rapids, Mich.: Zondervan, 1992.

Cole, C. D. *Basic Christian Faith.* Wheaton, Ill.: Crossway, 1985.

Coleman, G. *Human Sexuality.* New York: Alba House, 1992.

Colson, Charles. *Loving God.* Grand Rapids, Mich.: Zondervan, 1983.

Cooper, K. *The Aerobics Program for Total Well-Being.* New York: M. Evans, 1982.

Crabb, L. J. *The Marriage Builder.* Grand Rapids, Mich.: Zondervan, 1982.

Crewdson, J. *By Silence Betrayed: The Sexual Abuse of Children.* New York: Harper & Row, 1988.

Dalton, K. *The Premenstrual Syndrome.* Springfield, Ill.: Charles C. Thomas, 1964.

Daria, I. "Truth in Fashion." *Glamour* (February 1993).

Delitzsch, F. *Commentary on the Song of Songs and Ecclesiastes.* Grand Rapids, Mich.: Eerdmans, n.d.

Deutsch, R. *Realities of Nutrition.* Palo Alto, Calif.: Bull Publishing, 1976.

_____. *The Key to Feminine Response in Marriage.* New York: Ballantine, 1968.

Dillow, J. *Solomon on Sex.* Nashville: Thomas Nelson, 1977.

Dobson, J. *Love Must Be Tough: New Hope for Families in Crisis.* Waco, Tex.: Word, 1983.

Douglas, J. D. *The New Bible Dictionary.* Grand Rapids, Mich.: Eerdmans, 1962.

Eheart, B. K., and S. K. Martel. *The Fourth Trimester: On Becoming a Mother.* New York: Ballantine, 1984.

Evans, D. *Beauty and the Best.* Colorado Springs, Colo.: Focus on the Family, 1993.

_____. *The Complete Book on Childbirth.* Wheaton, Ill.: Tyndale, 1986.

_____. *Heart & Home.* Wheaton, Ill.: Crossway, 1988.

_____. *Kindred Hearts: Nurturing the Bond Between Mothers and Daughters.* Colorado Springs, Colo.: Focus on the Family, 1997.

_____. *The Woman's Complete Guide to Personal Health Care.* Brentwood, Tenn.: Wolgemuth & Hyatt, 1991.

_____. *Without Moral Limits: Women, Reproduction, and the New Medical Technology.* Wheaton, Ill.: Crossway, 1987.

_____. *Women of Character: Life-Changing Examples of Godly Women.* Grand Rapids, Mich.: Zondervan, 1995.

Everly, G., and D. Girdano. *Controlling Stress and Tension.* Englewood Cliffs, N.J.: Prentice-Hall, 1979.

Finch, B. E., and H. Green. *Contraception Through the Ages.* London: Peter Owen, 1963.

Foster, R. F. *The Celebration of Discipline.* San Francisco: Harper & Row, 1978.

_____. *Money, Sex, and Power: The Challenge of the Disciplined Life.* San Francisco: Harper & Row, 1985.

Friedman, R. C. *Behavior and the Menstrual Cycle.* New York: Marcel Dekker, 1982.

Gannon, L. R. *Menstrual Disorders and Menopause: Biological, Psychological and Cultural Research.* New York: Praeger, 1985.

Garner, D., et al. "Cultural Expectation of Thinness in Women." *Psychological Reports* 47 (1980).

Getz, G. A. *Loving One Another.* Wheaton, Ill.: Victor, 1979.

Gibling, M., et al. "From Fantasy to Reality—An Interview with Malcolm Muggeridge." *Christianity Today* (April 21, 1978): 10.

Gilder, G. *Men and Marriage.* Gretna, La.: Pelican, 1986.

_____. *Sexual Suicide.* New York: Quadrangle, 1973.

God's Design for the Family, Navigator Studies, Books 1-4. Colorado Springs, Colo.: NavPress, 1980.

GynoPharma Inc. "Is an IUD the Right Birth Control for You?" Somerville, N.J.: GynoPharma Inc., 1988.

Hafen, B. *Nutrition, Food and Weight Control.* Boston: Allyn and Bacon, 1981.

Hatcher, R., et al. *Contraceptive Technology,* 16th rev. ed. New York: Irvington, 1994.

Henry, C. F. H. *Baker's Dictionary of Christian Ethics.* Grand Rapids, Mich.: Baker, 1973.

Henry, M. *Matthew Henry's Commentary.* Grand Rapids, Mich.: Regency/Zondervan, 1961.

Hilgers, T. W. *Fertility Appreciation: The Ovulation Method of Natural Family Planning.* Omaha, Neb.: Creighton University Natural Family Planning Education and Research Center, 1983.

_____. "The Intrauterine Device: Contraceptive or Abortifacient?" *Minnesota Medicine* (June 1974).

Howard, J. G. *The Trauma of Transparency.* Portland, Ore.: Multnomah, 1979.

Huggett, J. *Two into One: Relating in Christian Marriage.* Downers Grove, Ill.: InterVarsity, 1981.

Huggins, K. *The Nursing Mother's Companion.* Cambridge, Mass.: Harvard Press, 1986.

Hunt, G. *Ms. Means Myself.* Grand Rapids, Mich.: Zondervan, 1972.

Hunter, B. *What Every Mother Needs to Know.* Sisters, Ore.: Multnomah, 1993.

Hurley, J. B. *Man and Woman in Biblical Perspective.* Grand Rapids, Mich.: Zondervan, 1981.

Jelliffe, D., and E. F. P. Jelliffe. *Human Milk in the Modern World.* Oxford: Oxford University Press, 1978.

Jones, K. L., et al. *Health Science,* 5th ed. New York: Harper and Row, 1985.

Joy, D. M. *Re-bonding: Preventing and Restoring Damaged Relationships.* Waco, Tex.: Word, 1986.

Kahar, B. M. "Pharmaceutical Companies: The New Abortionists." *ALL About Issues* (February 1989).

Keyes, D. *Beyond Identity: Finding Yourself in the Character and Image of God.* Ann Arbor, Mich.: Servant, 1984.

King, L. *An Affair of the Mind.* Colorado Springs, Colo.: Focus on the Family, 1996.

Killich, R. "Ovarian Follicles During Oral Contraceptive Cycles: Their Potential for Ovulation." *Fertility and Sterility* 52 (1989): 580.

Kippley, J., and S. Kippley. *The Art of Natural Family Planning,* 3rd ed. Cincinnati: Couple-to-Couple League, 1984.

Kippley, S. *Breastfeeding and Natural Child Spacing.* New York: Penguin, 1975.

LaHaye, T., and B. LaHaye. *The Act of Marriage.* Grand Rapids, Mich.: Zondervan, 1976.

Lance, K., and M. Agardy. *Total Sexual Fitness for Women.* New York: Rawson and Wade, 1981.

Lawrence, R. *Breastfeeding—A Guide for the Medical Profession.* St. Louis: C. V. Mosby, 1980.

Lewis, C. S. *George MacDonald: An Anthology.* New York: Macmillan, 1946.

_____. *The Four Loves.* London: Fontana, 1963.

_____. *Mere Christianity.* New York: Macmillan, 1943.

Lindbergh, A. M. *Gift from the Sea.* New York: Vintage, 1978.

Llewelyn, R., ed. *The Joy of the Saints.* Springfield, Ill.: Templegate, 1989.

Macaulay, S. S. *Something Beautiful from God.* Wheaton, Ill.: Crossway, 1980.

_____. *How to Be Your Own Selfish Pig.* Colorado Springs, Colo.: David C. Cook, 1982.

McDowell, J., and P. Lewis. *Givers, Takers & Other Kinds of Lovers.* Wheaton, Ill.: Living Books/Tyndale, 1980.

McGee, R. *The Search for Significance.* Houston: Rapha, 1990.

Mason, M. *The Mystery of Marriage.* Portland, Ore.: Multnomah, 1985.

Mead, F. S., ed. *12,000 Religious Quotations.* Grand Rapids, Mich.: Baker, 1989.

The Mosby Medical Encyclopedia. New York: New American Library, 1985.

Miles, H. G. *Sexual Happiness in Marriage.* Grand Rapids, Mich.: Zondervan, 1967.

Moulton, R. G. *Lyric Idyl: Solomon's Song in the Literary Study of the Bible.* London: Isbiter, 1903.

Narramore, B. *You're Someone Special.* Grand Rapids, Mich.: Zondervan, 1978.

Neifert, M. *Dr. Mom: A Guide to Baby and Child Care.* New York: Signet, 1986.

Nelson, E. C., et al. *Medical and Health Guide for People Over 50*. Washington, D.C.: American Association of Retired Persons, 1986.

Newton, N. *Maternal Emotions: A Study of Women's Feelings About Menstruation, Pregnancy, Childbirth, Infant Care and Other Aspects of Their Femininity*. New York: Harper and Brothers (Paul B. Hoeber Medical Book Dept.), 1955.

_____. *The Family Book of Child Care*. New York: Harper and Row, 1957.

Nilssen, L. *A Child Is Born*. New York: Dell, 1978.

Nursing '85 Drug Handbook. Spring House Corporation, 1985.

Nystrom, C. *Before I Was Born*. Wheaton, Ill.: Crossway, 1984.

Ortho Pharmaceutical Corporation. *A Guide to Methods of Contraception*. Raritan, N.J.: Ortho, 1979.

Paul, B. *Health, Culture, and Community*. New York: Russell Sage, 1955.

Penner, C., and J. Penner. *The Gift of Sex*. Waco, Tex.: Word, 1981.

_____. *Restoring the Pleasure*. Waco, Tex.: Word, 1993.

Peterson, E. H. *A Long Obedience in the Same Direction: Discipleship in an Instant Society*. Downers Grove, Ill.: InterVarsity, 1980.

_____. *Earth and Altar: The Community of Prayer in a Self-Bound Society*. Downers Grove, Ill.: InterVarsity, 1985.

_____. *The Message*. Colorado Springs, Colo.: NavPres, 1993.

_____. *Praying with Jesus: A Year of Daily Prayer and Reflections on the Words and Actions of Jesus*. San Francisco: HarperSanFrancisco, 1993.

Pettis, K. W., and R. D. Hughes. "Sexual Victimization of Children: A Current Perspective." *Behavioral Disorders* (February 1985).

Powell, J. *The Secret of Staying in Love*. Allen, Tex.: Argus, 1974.

_____. *Why Am I Afraid to Love?* Allen, Tex.: Argus, 1972.

_____. *Why Am I Afraid to Tell You Who I Am?* Allen, Tex.: Argus, 1969.

Press, A. "The War Against Pornography." *Newsweek*. (March 18, 1985).

Pryor, K. *Nursing Your Baby*. New York: Pocket Books, 1973.

Rakowitz, E., and G. S. Rubin. *Living with Your New Baby*. New York: Berkley, 1980.

Raphael, D. *The Tender Gift: Breastfeeding*. New York: Schocken, 1978.

Roetzer, J. *Family Planning the Natural Way*. Old Tappan, N.J.: Revell, 1981.

Rossetti, D. G. *The House of Life: A Sonnet-Sequence by Dante Gabriel Rossetti*. Portland, Maine: Thomas B. Mosher, 1898.

Rousseau, M. and C. Gallagher. *Sex Is Holy*. Rockport, Mass.: Element, 1991.

Schaeffer, E. *Common Sense Christian Living*. Nashville, Tenn.: Thomas Nelson, 1983.

_____. *Lifelines: The Ten Commandments for Today*. Wheaton, Ill.: Crossway, 1983.

_____. *The Art of Life*. Wheaton, Ill.: Crossway, 1987.

_____. *What Is a Family?* Old Tappan, N.J.: Revell, 1975.

Schaeffer, F. *Genesis in Space and Time*. Downers Grove, Ill.: InterVarsity, 1972.

_____. *Letters of Francis A. Schaeffer*. Ed. Lane T. Dennis. Wheaton, Ill.: Crossway, 1985.

———. *The Great Evangelical Disaster*. Wheaton, Ill.: Crossway, 1984.

Schaeffer, F., and C. E. Koop. *Whatever Happened to the Human Race?* Old Tappan, N.J.: Revell, 1979.

Schrotenboer, K., and G. Subak-Sharpe. *Freedom from Menstrual Cramps*. New York: Pocket, 1981.

Seaman, B. *The Doctor's Case Against the Pill*. Garden City, N.Y.: Doubleday, 1980.

Searle Laboratories. "For the Patient: Cu-7." Chicago: Searle Laboratories, 1977.

Seid, R. P. *Never Too Thin: Why Women Are at War with Their Bodies*. New York: Prentice Hall, 1989.

Selye, H. *Stress: General Adaptation Syndrome and the Disease of Adaptation*. Montreal: ACTA, 1950.

Sheehy, G. *Menopause: The Silent Passage*. New York: Pocket, 1993.

Shettles, L., and D. Rorvik. *Rites of Life: The Scientific Evidence of Life Before Birth*. Grand Rapids, Mich.: Zondervan, 1984.

Smedes, L. *Sex for Christians*. Grand Rapids, Mich.: Eerdmans, 1976.

———. *Forgive and Forget*. New York: Harper & Row, 1984.

———. *The Art of Forgiving: When You Need to Forgive and Don't Know How*. Nashville, Tenn.: Moorings, 1996.

Sproul, R. C. *Ethics and the Christian*. Wheaton, Ill.: Tyndale, 1983.

———. *Pleasing God*. Wheaton, Ill.: Tyndale, 1988.

———. *The Holiness of God*. Wheaton, Ill.: Tyndale, 1985.

Storch, M. *How to Relieve Menstrual Cramps and Other Menstrual Problems*. New York: Workman, 1982.

Storey, D. and S. Kulkin. *Body & Soul*. Sisters, Ore.: Multnomah, 1995.

Stott, J. *Christian Counter-Culture: The Message of the Sermon on the Mount*. Downers Grove, Ill.: InterVarsity, 1978.

———. *Involvement: Social and Sexual Relationships in the Modern World*. Old Tappan, N.J.: Revell, 1984.

Teresa of Avila. *A Life of Prayer*, ed. James M. Houston. Portland, Ore: Multnomah, 1983.

Thielicke, H. *The Ethics of Sex*. Grand Rapids, Mich.: Baker, 1975.

Trobisch, I., and F. Roetzer. *An Experience of Love: Understanding Natural Family Planning*. Old Tappan, N.J.: Revell, 1982.

Trobisch, I. *The Joy of Being a Woman*. New York: Harper and Row, 1975.

Trobisch, W. *A Baby Just Now?* Downers Grove, Ill.: InterVarsity, 1978.

———. *I Married You*. New York: Harper and Row, 1971.

———. *I Loved a Girl*. London: Lutterworth, 1970.

———. *Love Yourself: Self-Acceptance and Depression*. Downers Grove, Ill.: InterVarsity, 1976.

U.S. Department of Health and Human Services. *Facts About Oral Contraceptives*. Washington, D.C.: U.S. Government Printing Office, 1984.

Wangerin, W. *As for Me and My House: Crafting Your Marriage to Last*. Nashville, Tenn.: Thomas Nelson, 1987.

Weideger, P. *Menstruation and Menopause: The Physiology and Psychology, The Myth and the Reality*. New York: Knopf, 1976.

Weschler, T. *Taking Charge of Your Fertility*. New York: HarperCollins, 1995.

Wheat, E., and G. O. Perkins. *Love Life for Every Married Couple*. Grand Rapids, Mich.: Zondervan, 1980.

Wheelis, A. *The Quest for Identity*. New York: Norton, 1958.

White, J. *Changing on the Inside*. Ann Arbor, Mich.: Vine, 1991.

_____. *Eros Redeemed*. Downers Grove, Ill.: InterVarsity, 1993.

_____. *The Fight: A Practical Handbook for Christian Living*. Downers Grove, Ill.: InterVarsity, 1976.

_____. *Flirting with the World*. Wheaton, Ill.: Harold Shaw, 1982.

White, J. and M. *Friends & Friendship: The Secrets of Drawing Closer*. Colorado Springs, Colo.: NavPress, 1982.

Wirt, S. E., ed. *Spiritual Awakening*. Wheaton, Ill.: Crossway, 1986.

Wright, H. N. *Communication: The Key to Your Marriage*. Ventura, Calif.: Regal, 1974.

_____. *Understanding the Man in Your Life*. Waco, Tex.: Word, 1987.

_____. *The Pillars of Marriage*. Ventura, Calif.: Regal, 1979.

Zatuchni, G. I., et al. *Vaginal Contraception: New Developments*. Hagerstown, Md.: Harper and Row, 1979.

$\mathcal{I}$NDEX